When That's Gone, Th...

Charlie W.

When That's Gone, That's It

Charlie W.

(Graphic content: language, drugs, violence, sex, black-magic.)

Copyright Notice: by Charlie W.
All rights reserved
When That's Gone, That's It.
ISBN:9798344970080
© 2024 by Charlie W.

Charlie W. is a pseudonym: other names, details and locations have also been changed to protect the privacy of those subjects. The moral right of the author has been asserted.

To Maureen, Chackley,
and the addicts...

One.

I'm not sure why I ran out of the room sobbing, the fifth guy in line had parroted the others, seemingly coincidentally but it was all just too much. I scuttled out of the room with my confused head in my hands, more like a frightened rabbit than the scary wolf I'd always hoped I manifested as - they each said more or less the same thing, with nine left to go; what if they said it too?

It was the last day of a five-day assertiveness course spread over a few weekends, I'd signed up hoping to get a handle on my anger, to convert it into something more manageable, and this, the closing module was simple enough. We would sit in front of each other, privately, and tell each other something honest but complimentary to help bring the course to an end. Then we'd move around the room until we had all spoken to each other.

The first guy sits down and we try to hold each other's uncomfortable gaze, 'Hi Charlie, it's been great getting to know you over the course; to be honest I didn't really like you at first, but having got to know you, I think you're a real nice guy.' erm, okay. Thank you. I offered up my own complimentary observations in return; 'pleasure' 'articulate' 'funny' sort of things; inoffensive stuff.

Next one; 'Hello Charlie, I thought you were a right cunt to start with but now, I kind of like you...etc.' Scarily similar, I think - but okay.

And again, similar, 'Bit of a prick' to 'sound-geezer.'

And again. This is getting heavy.

And again. Woah, what the fuck? Tears started forming in my eyes; the lump I swallowed felt like the size of a whole tangerine and I ran out of the room.

I didn't get to find out what the others had to say, the session carried on without me and we then had a post-mortem about why people find compliments difficult to accept largely glossing over the fact that everyone seemed to think I was a dickhead to begin with. Maybe it was the idea people didn't like me at first or, liked me eventually or, that it was a recurring theme – but something tripped my switch and I really don't like to show my emotions in public. My once heroic father's most regular boast had been that he didn't even cry at his own mother's funeral. The prick.

Two.

'Please don't hit me again officer,' I replied but he didn't write it down. They didn't have video cameras in the charging area of cop shops back then, nor cameras on mobile phones, come to think of it.

It was a mid-morning Tuesday; most people wouldn't expect to be pulled over in a legal hatchback by twelve riot squad coppers but these were doubtless bored and at the time the police almost certainly had my licence plate in their database with the owner flagged "B.O.A.C" - bit of a cunt, maybe. The fact I'd been found not-guilty for assaulting one of their own a year or so previous meant that as soon as I saw their van in my rear view mirror I knew they were gonna pull me. Also, from their perspective, stopping and searching two youngish white guys no doubt helped their racial profiling figures; by stopping us they could then go on and harass more black guys. I looked a bit twatty back then, shaved head, a pirate tattoo on my forearm, blah blah; cosmetic barbed-wire in essence but I didn't acknowledge my own fears in those days.

I didn't know Mario was carrying drugs, what happened next kinda served him right for being such a selfish dick in not sharing them earlier but these cops were TSG, Territorial Support Group, with nothing to do – a warm Tuesday morning as it was. Even if I had tempered my behaviour we were defo getting rolled; they'd invent a dodgy light or tyre or something to harass me with.

Red mist already in my eyes I leapt out of my car bounding towards their van, I was fucking outraged that they had the audacity to stop us and I'd been told all our drugs had been finished hours before. I was at their own driver's window before he opened the door but others were piling out of the van kerb side coming round to support their driver. In America I would have already been shot by this stage; mine wasn't the advised reaction to a traffic stop but our cops didn't even have Tasers back then.

'What the FUCK have you stopped me for?' I screeched.

'Sir, get away from the window,' said the driver somewhat bemused, he knew he wasn't in danger, his chums were onto me, ushering me away from the window in a second.

'Don't fucking TOUCH ME! I know my rights, what have you stopped me for?' I shouted.

'Mind your language sir, there's no need to be rude'. I was going to be locked up anyway; it's what they did, locked me up every now and then for just under the maximum 24 hour period because so far, I had a clean criminal record and that pissed them off; particularly since the one I clipped with my boot as he was loading me into a van some other night had had to take time off of work. I knew I was getting locked up, I'd already gone too far so I decided I may as well take the piss. Besides I had my street cred to maintain and I still kinda fancied Mario, he'd be bound to go off me if he knew I was really a pussy; they were twisting my wrist.

'Oh fuck off you cunt!' I said, hurting.

'Sir-'

'-WHAT HAVE YOU STOPPED ME FOR?' I demanded.

'We saw you passing something to your companion and suspect it was drugs'.

'You lying twat!' I wouldn't mind if I had, seriously I wouldn't. Had they even said they were a bit bored and wanted to wind me up I'd have respected them more.

'Sir, I won't warn you again, if you continue to swear I will arrest you under section 5 public order.' I was fairly sure this cop would tuck his Under-Armour t-shirt into his Under-Armour underpants but for now was he just a prick in a street-gang that got overtime and medals for bashing heads like mine in.

'Listen,' I said breaking into legalese around the familiar law he'd threatened me with, 'for someone to be alarmed by my words and actions there has to actually be a *fucking someone around to hear them*, but look,' I pointed at the empty street 'all there is is you cunts and us two,' none of the cops would ever really risk their pension if they thought people were watching or able to easily record it all.

'SIR, last warning on the lang-'

'-Oh shut up you enamel-coated cunt,' - I swear I used that C word so often that day and I'm sorry to subject you to it now but I trust you want a true account, I can be one too as you've probably guessed by now.

'I bet you can't even spell can you cunt-stable? I'll help you it's C.U.N-'

'RIGHT! That's it I'm arresting you for section five public order offences, you do not have to..' etc and with that, after a bit of a palaver I'm in handcuffs, my arms in my lap and somehow sat on the ground – there was too many cops there for any real effect but if you just go limp on arrest, like a sack of shit, it's a real pain for them to move you but it can't be called resisting arrest and there were enough of them to sit me on their van-floor at the back door. All bar the arresting officer got back out on the street and went to harass Mario, I'm left in the van with this one copper, I'm sat on the van floor and he starts with the repeating of my rights; not listening I weighed my options. The fundamental mistake they had made was hand-cuffing me to the front; but since I'd gone all sack of shit I guess they took the easy route. Bash! I smashed my wrists and cuffs upwards into my own eyebrow a couple of times, the metal splitting the flesh above my eye.

Blood.

'What the fuck are you doing?' screamed the surprised copper. I just knew he'd have sent Valentine's cards to himself as a single teenager. Mind you, I did put a few old cards out for myself one year. The blood slowly seeped around my eye, not tons but I could feel it run down my cheek, I had no idea how bad it looked but, as long as it didn't look good it was some kind of result. I looked at the copper, direct in one eye.

'You, you cunt,' I said calmly, 'you did that.' Other cops huddled back to the van.

'He just bashed himself in the eye,' said the confused, arresting officer to the others at the door.

'You lying fucker,' I said calmly. A couple of those out on the street were clearly amused and turned their faces away grinning. I got the feeling they weren't the biggest fan of their colleague but they were all in it together, that was never in doubt as they continued their cop stuff

'Oh sir,' said one of the others as they clambered back into the van to depart, pointing over at the council estate a few hundred yards away, 'we moved your car onto that dangerous estate just there, it's behind the garages. I think I *may have forgotten* to lock it though, hope it's safe and still there when you get out of the nick. The arresting officer has your keys look,' he said handing them over. That's what I mean about them being cunts.

At the custody desk I had complained my handcuffs were too tight.

'I'll sort the cuffs,' said one cop to my relief, whereupon he had gone behind me and made a show to loosen them but he actually tightened them up.

'Oh okay, I geddit,' I said - I was expecting a beating anyway. Later as they took me to the cell I dropped to my knees and tilted my head towards his feet, 'go on, take your best shot you cunt' I'd taunted him but nothing came of it. See, the thing is, they are cunts, but they aren't usually stupid cunts; I've been arrested loads of times but they've never actually duffed me up - so far. I would probably have duffed me up if I'd have been them to be honest, so credit where it's due.

I can't pretend anything else extraordinary happened at the police station, they fed me, had the nurse see if they could section me as she looked at my eye but, like them, I'm not that stupid. For any subsequent complaint I might make, everyone else at the station had to see a compliant, polite and law-abiding detainee. I could play their game, and besides it was fucking Tuesday, I didn't have much else to do. Friday was my day to sign-on, other than that I was free all week.

Almost the full 24 hours were up when they decided to let me out on the Wednesday morning, *'Under Investigation'*. To get released you have to stand in front of the Custody Sergeant who, oddly enough, doesn't really care if you've murdered your granny or shit on a seagull, not as long as you're there legitimately.

They ask if you have any comment to make in relation to the matter as they hand back any personal items; 'Please don't hit me again officer' I'd said cheekily. With a sigh the sergeant wrote, "No comment" in the box and pushed the form my way. Duly I signed it, I was as bored as an usher at The Mousetrap theatre by now but I wasn't entirely done with it all.

Three.

A few days later my door-buzzer rang; I had a view of the streets outside from three windows making it, coincidentally, a quite defensible flat if ever there were a zombie apocalypse but the only zombie at my door was a senior-copper with a lot of icing sugar shit on his cap. This certainly wasn't a raid and I knew then that whatever beef the cops may have had with me at that time, I might have won - for now.

After being released from the cells I had gone to retrieve my car, sure enough it had been left unlocked but mercifully it was untouched. I would later find out Mario had been arrested and cautioned for possession but on release I didn't know that, not that I would have been that bothered anyway to be honest; when the shit hits the fan it's everyone for themselves.

Back home I'd wasted no time typing up an official complaint, within three hours the letter was in the post. Something along the lines of *lack of due cause, false arrest, over zealous policing, police brutality, injury in custody, car left unlocked.* I didn't accuse the copper directly of hitting me but the line, *'the evidence will reveal I was driving unscathed and unwounded, yet on arrival at the police station I needed the attention of medical staff and my head was covered in blood'.* The mention of a quiet Tuesday morning, *twelve* police officers and overkill were in there too.

And now some police chief type was sat in my living room starting the conversation, *'about your complaint Sir,'* I have no official record of what happened on his visit, what was said or inferred, but perhaps somewhere he had to record actually turning up at my door even if only in the cop-car mileage book and my complaint would have to be registered somewhere, which is why I recorded the postage.

I knew from past experience that as long as I didn't allegedly *hit* another copper I could more or less say anything I wanted on arrest, *as opinion, not threat.* In court back then my barrister had asked that copper (from the assault case, PC Time-Off-Work), what it was about my behaviour that night that had caused *him* alarm and distress.

Late at night he and a woman copper, who was driving, had shouted over at us, 'Lads!' out of the side of my mouth I quietly told Shawn to just keep walking.

'Go away, I'm not in the mood,' I'd replied and I wasn't. Shawn and I were dating and we'd been arguing about something, we were both a little pissed. The copper had jumped out the van as his colleague was parking up.

'Lads, lads, I just want a quick word!' he said. Reasonable so far.

'Well, have a *fucking* word then,' I'd said, perhaps unreasonably but actually they had no just cause to stop us and then he came out with the lame *'we saw you passing him something'* pretext which had pissed me off so I told him to fuck off; I hate liars. And so yeah, we were arrested, Section 5 Public Order, and as he was loading me into the van he *allegedly* sustained an unfortunate minor injury. Oops.

My father had been one of those volunteer Special Constables and, at that point in my life, although dead, he still featured as an honourable man in my mind. So, believe it or not I actually had time for properly administered policing. But none at all for lying toads like this one; we hadn't passed each other any drugs, we didn't have any left to pass; we'd eaten or smoked them all.

In court the copper replied, 'When the defendant said, *well,* have a fucking word then,' in answer to the barrister's question.

The brief fired back without hesitation, 'and it was the word *'fucking'* in the reply that caused you Alarm and Distress officer. The word *fucking?*' emphasising the key words, my guy was good.

PC: 'Yes, sir.'

'...In Ha-ck-knee?' this from the Magistrate himself chirping up rhythmically like a canary.

In spite of three witnesses against us and, the two police all giving evidence he found us Not Guilty; he said they had no right to even stop us in the first place. Thank you Sir.

So when it came to the handcuffs-in-the-face arrest; I kind of knew that saying *'fucker'* or even *'cunt'* to a copper wasn't really grounds for a Section 5 Public Order conviction; the public had to be the offended party not the police. And in *my opinion,* they could be metaphorical cunts as clearly they weren't factually reproductive organs or copulating. Okay, it's not very polite of me but then neither is my being stopped by twelve cops for made-up reasons. And it's a waste of public money.

Years later when some cops from Downing Street complained loudly that an MP had sworn at them, the London Standard printed a letter from me saying that if any officers found swear words challenging then they certainly shouldn't be given access to machine guns.

So the big cheese copper with the icing sugar shit on his hat didn't have any great cards to play in my living room. If I were to pursue any complaint his role, as a manager, could be in question. He wouldn't want that and he offered me a *'solution'*; an *"Informal Resolution,"* against the arresting PC and no further action on the arrest. To me, at that point in my life, that was a result. Nowadays, I might be tempted to sue the fuckers but this kind of shit hanging over you takes its toll, it really does. I'd seemed to have had some legal case or another on the go for years; spurious minor stuff mostly but it didn't feel minor when it happened. I'd always won but that doesn't mean I always expected to or even that I should have. So, without any witnesses or anything written down, I agreed to the offer. I took icing-hat cop guy at his word and sure enough what he said would happen, happened.

I've secured three other informal resolutions against coppers so far; won nine separate court cases with not guilty verdicts; still have a clean criminal record and I have also won two other civil cases where I sued private individuals - for being wankers basically. Okay, I'm probably the biggest of them all - sometimes.

Oh yeah, I've also made four citizen's arrests so far: I'm not anti-law and order at all, just anti-fuckwit.

Four.

"We have been asked to point out that in our story last week, 'MP Attacked at Section 28 Demo' that the person making the arrest was not an undercover police officer as reported. We apologise for any inconvenience caused and are happy to issue this correction," was more or less what it said.

I'd acted quickly; Chris Smith the first openly gay MP was giving a speech at Trafalgar Square and this pissed-up vagrant-type had tried bashing him with a placard. As I was close and the MP was quite frightened, I jumped in, twisted the attacker's arm and citizen-arrested him, pushing him face down to the tarmac. Some of the outlying gays rustled up some regular cops and they took the fella away. I figured they might lock him up for a few hours to sober up as they never asked what happened or took statements or anything but I didn't give it much further thought until it made the gay press. Front page, albeit small but *"Thug Arrested by Undercover Cop"* or some such it had said. I had had to insist on a correction; I think the press clipping is in my brother's loft.

Two of the other citizen's arrests were pretty run-of-the-mill, some woman was being harassed on a tube platform by a drunk and in the other, a young guy with probable learning issues was screaming like he was gonna die when his pushbike was snatched from him by some opportunist twat. All street robbery is pretty scuzzy but regardless I would have got any kid's bike back if I was able to. It seems like this particular scuzzer had history though as he got eight years when other stuff he'd done emerged. I have to stop doing shit like that though, citizen's arrests and getting too involved, 'cos one day it could go tits up and I could easily be brown-bread. Peter Bottomley said as much when, as Home Secretary, he replied to me about another arrest; *"Whilst it was very brave of you to disarm the offender, I must urge you to avoid putting yourself in such danger in the future and alert the appropriate authorities."* Which I felt was a bit rich to be honest since I'd written to him to complain about the police's lack of support in the first fucking place.

I had been in the then infamous gay bar *'Brief Encounter'* in London's West End and witnessed some guy get rejected by his evening crush. The Brief was a great place for casual hook ups; it was way too dark and noisy to get a full picture but when the crush left and the reject followed him straight out, it had looked a bit sinister. I was probably only 10 or 20 seconds behind the reject but caught sight of him rounding the corner. I was expecting something and so my reflexes took over as I came across him threatening the younger guy with a broken glass, I grabbed the arm holding his weapon and twisted it behind his back, he dropped the glass and I lay him on his stomach and sat on him on the pavement. The guy whose good looks I had potentially saved promptly scarpered so it was just us two and a crowd of people looking on from the nearby pub. I didn't know what to do so decided to keep the offender on the floor and wait for a cop car to come near, we were near the station anyway. I could have been waiting an hour for the eternity it seemed but eventually I did flag down some cops and figured justice would be done.

A cop got out and came over, one of those unfit types who was more shirt than stab vest; he asked what the problem was, 'I was coming round this corner' I said, 'and I came across this guy here threatening another guy with a broken pint glass so I grabbed him until you arrived and there's the glass there'. The glass, all shards and edges, lay in the gutter of the road.

'Gimme a sec' I said and went over to the assembled drinkers outside the pub. 'Could someone come forward as a witness and say what they saw?' I asked. There's maybe fifteen or eighteen folk there, mixed ages etc. Nothing. Tumbleweed.

'Come on, you all saw it,' I'm pleading almost. Nothing. Silence.

'Seriously?' I was pissed now, 'No-one?' I sighed as I went back to the cops. Straining stab-vest cop addressed the potential murderer guy, now on his feet; 'Sling your hook and don't let me see you anywhere round here again tonight,' flicking his head to one side in a sort of, off you go, kind of gesture. And with that the potential killer is cleared to scoot away, I was instantly livid. Like broken red lava lamp livid.

'Are you fucking serious, why did you let hm go?' I asked incredulously.

'He's a wanker, we spoke to him earlier' the cop is climbing back in the car and closing the door as he said this.

' - all the more reason to take him in--' but before I even finished the sentence their car was rolling away. Repeating the number from his epaulettes in my mind I wrote it in the dust of a parked car until I could borrow a pen and paper. I'm clearly entertainment for the nearby pavement drinkers at the pub, the sort of people who could witness a potential maiming and then develop selective blindness as it suited them.

'You lot should be fucking ashamed of yourselves', I say loudly as I pass, mostly they pretended I didn't even exist.

So I wrote to the Home Secretary, like any self-respecting citizen might, what else could I do? *I may have even written to the*

Queen and Prime Minister, it wouldn't have been the first time but perhaps not that for that one. A senior cop contacted me and invited me in to the building that is now Scotland Yard to discuss the whole thing.

'May I just shake your hand,' he'd started as we sat down in some office, I offered my hand, 'well done,' he said as he shook it, 'but please don't ever do anything like that ever again, you could have been killed,' I smiled and went on to outline my complaint. 'You're right, he should have been detained,' said the cop, 'even if just to get him off the streets until he calmed down a bit.'

'Yeah' I agreed, 'he could have gone on to kill someone, even if he was released without charge, he needed some action against him.'

'I would propose then' says Inspector Gadget eventually 'that an *Informal Resolution* may be the way to address this. That means the officer concerned is made aware of the complaint against them, they acknowledge it; a note of it is recorded on their file and will follow them around for their entire career.' It sounded wonderful to me and I agreed readily. A letter would eventually arrive at my address confirming the nature of our discussion and outlining the steps that were being taken.

So, one way or the other I was known to the police which may go some way to explaining why when the cop van was behind me that Tuesday morning I knew I was gonna be harassed. They get on my case, I get on theirs - and so on until we all die I suppose.

But thus far having that clean criminal record, it meant that when I soon saw a role that intrigued me advertised in the paper I knew I could apply and, if I got accepted, I could take the piss out of the Old Bill on a completely different level. The idea of arriving at police stations unannounced, demanding to be admitted and inspecting them and their poxy procedures appealed to my sense of humour. I was accepted fairly quickly, trained at the actual Police College in Hendon and became a volunteer *Custody Visitor*.

The big problem with being a lay visitor though was that I always had to go with someone else to protect the integrity of the role and, one supposed, that of the police as well. Sadly, the others on the local visiting panel were like really well-meaning but old-fogie, actual clipboard-clasping types and the chance of getting one of them out at three in the morning for a night-visit with me was zero. If I was going to score points against the Old-Bill, going on a Wednesday lunchtime was never gonna highlight any great shortcomings I didn't suppose.

'Hello, we're Lay Visitors and need access to the cells for an inspection,' I would say into the cop station intercom and hold up my ID to the camera. An ID that had "Metropolitan Police" on it and was signed by some Chief Inspector cop - it was quite trippy. They didn't hesitate though to be fair, we were always buzzed in without delay. We could raise issue if a prisoner didn't have a blanket, hadn't seen a lawyer; needed food, water or say, a pencil and some paper but that was about the limit of our influence. I can't be certain any of the cops ever recognised me, there were lots of them after all, but I sure hoped they did. I wasn't a total prick at the role but I did ensure the rights of the detainees were being upheld wherever I needed to. Our intervention wasn't needed that often to be honest, no-one ever complained the cops had duffed them up but I was sure it happened, probably during the night when my volunteer colleagues were asleep.

This one time I went into the custody suite, the only place we really had access to, and I could hear a bit of commotion and readied my weapons - my pen and clipboard; if they mistreated anyone, I was going for them. Seriously! I had it bad - the chip on my shoulder where a copper's epaulettes might go.

'You're only doing this because I'm black,' said a loud voice. Bingo! I thought before I set eyes on the melee. Just what I needed, some unscripted racism on a mid-week afternoon. Fucking result!

'Yeah,' said a cop as they came into view; two big cops, and a bigger black guy with dreadlocks and handcuffs, restrained between them, 'we're only doing it 'cos you're black,' added the cop sardonically, 'Oh and this,' and from behind his leg he produced an evidence bag holding a machete as big as my entire arm.

I felt my mouth open as I lowered my clip-board. And that was that. I realised that if my own mum was ever chased by some guy with a big fuck-off machete these might be the guys to step in and stop him; I needed to get over my vendetta with the police and what, maybe grow up a bit? Well, chill a bit anyway.

Whilst that incident did accelerate thoughts of leaving the visitor panel, pretty soon I had had another arrest myself and was supposed to notify them that I had to stand down anyway. They probably still think I left 'cos *I didn't want to interfere with the police work*, or waste police time which is what I'd said instead, but I got a nice certificate of thanks anyway. Bit cunty of me I suppose but hey. I can't remember what I was arrested for that time, usual shit I suppose; Failing to Inflate the Ego of of a Police Constable.

Five.

There were six years between taking my first drug and my second, not that I didn't enjoy my first time, I did, but I also kind of knew I could end up in trouble if I went down that first road twice and I could get hooked. Because it was so utterly fucking amazing!

I'd never done an illegal drug in my life before then, or any real illegality at all I don't think. Amyl-nitrate or Poppers as they are known was as edgy as I got back then; I knew some drugs could fuck you up and I wasn't stupid. It was summer early-nineties; by and large I was already an alcoholic - though, had you asked me at the time, I might take umbrage at the very idea; I certainly didn't think I had a problem, other than just having the one mouth I mean.

I'd been stood on the pavement outside a bar called The Coleherne in Earl's Court on the off-chance of some sticky action; pubs closed Sunday afternoons back then. There was wind of people going missing occasionally, like literally disappearing from the scene overnight. AIDS was dropping folk like flies – and though we weren't to know for certain, there were whispers of a serial-killer stalking gay bars at the time.

The guy who sidled up to me was horny as fuck; his proposition terribly simple; 'I have a tab of acid in my pocket, how about we go back to yours, take it and fuck?' he'd said. To be honest I thought I'd struck really lucky but I didn't even know what *acid* was. My self-esteem being as low as it was in those days, given the bullying of my older brothers and shit, I always figured that folk were doing me a favour to shag with me. I'd go on to be a safe-sex model in later life but for now this stunning shorter guy with skin the colour of warm olive-oil wanted an answer. I knew to hesitate would be to lose him; I wasn't the only one looking to pick up.

'Sure thing,' I said and with a flick of my head in the direction of my car I ushered him, Andy, away. I don't recall any turmoil of thought along the lines of wondering what the fuck acid was as we headed home; I mean it was obviously a drug, I wasn't stupid but I would never take crack, heroin or LSD which I'd had heard of and were non-starters. I had to pretend to be sober enough to drive, make small talk whilst checking to see if he had any AIDS like bruising or symptoms and, satisfy myself that he wasn't the serial killer and likely to bash my head when it was servicing his appendage. Meanwhile, I had to create the impression I knew what I was doing, that I wasn't gonna give *him* AIDS and that I wasn't the serial killer either. In retrospect that's kind of what any serial killer would do but I didn't want him jumping out at the traffic lights either way; I'd take the risk on the acid stuff poisoning me.

We got home to my place in Brixton, took the acid and got naked. It was like the size of a quarter of a postage stamp, made of actual paper, and he tore it in half and popped it on my tongue – after he swallowed his first, obviously, I'm not *that* stupid. Talk about underwhelming, like a tiny bit of paper the size of a match-head. I wasn't expecting much to be honest. I make it sound so flippant, *"we got home, took drugs, got naked"* - but that's exactly what happened and almost as quick but like Picasso it had taken a lot of practice to make complicated processes seem easy.

'WOW! I'm fucking freezing,' I said whilst marvelling inwardly at how I'd somehow ended up in bed with this awesomely sexy guy with skin like the warm day outside but I was suddenly cold, like literally shivering; acid does that to you occasionally it seems.

'Here, have some covers,' he replies whereupon, I swear to god, he starts burying me in fucking snow. Like real, fall from the sky, fucking snow.

It's insane; I'm like, 'Stop covering me in snow,' nicely like; I don't want him to fuck off. He's, giggling, 'Here, have some more,' and he gets more snow from behind him (I didn't know at the time it was just the white duvet and pillows) and puts that snow on top of me. I laugh, we both laugh, he leans over, nibbles my ear.

'You're on drugs,' he whispers, laughing, I laugh too.

'B-b-b- but it's snowing...in the bedroom,' I add incredulously. I figure there's only one thing for it and that's to sniff some more poppers. Poppers are taken like smelling salts; they come in a tiny bottle as a liquid and you just inhale the fumes like you might smell wine or well, someone's sexy armpit I suppose, if that's your thing. He does smell nice; my senses are tingling.

I'm shocked to hear a noise from inside the tiny bottle; there sounds to be an orchestra trapped inside; I shake it slightly - strings, trumpets and kettle drums, louder with the cap off. Bizarre. This was dangerous stuff this acid, not because I felt like I was in danger but because it was all amazing. I knew that I couldn't go looking for this experience ever again, or I'd be hooked.

After Andy left I had another few hours of pacing up and down my flat looking out of the window, examining the veins in the back of my hand and occasionally grinning at memories of the snow duvet, the orchestra and the way his shoulder had started talking to me. There was no Google back then, I had no fucking idea how long the weirdness would last other than Andy said it'd wear off in a few hours. There were no giant spiders scuttling over the ceiling or anything scary like that; occasional shadows flickered about but they didn't bother me – I knew enough to know I was on drugs and that this is why people probably took them, so I relaxed into it. The carpet pattern moved, the light on the wall was playing tricks but I was much too contented by the whole encounter to be worried.

Monday I spent mostly in bed catching up fitfully on the sleep I had lost to the drugs. In retrospect I wondered if the *oh so amazing sex* may just have been a lot of me grunting and oohing and ah-ing but suffice to say, until that point, it had proved the most earth-moving, spine-tingling, body-coupling sexual experience of my entire life and I spent much of Monday trying to recall what I could about it. I understood why drugs were so addictive and that frightened me a bit. If I went looking for this experience again I knew my life might never be normal again.

Luckily, I knew nothing about how to get hold of drugs nor about the costs involved or the effects of other types; I was new to it, a day-tripper, and that Monday morning I decided I would write it off to experience, a holiday-romance sort of thing. I didn't want to be a drug addict; all I knew about them was what the media told me along the lines of mugging old-ladies for money to get syringes full of AIDS juice - I was much too stylish for that kind of life.

It had been awesome though; really genuinely awesome. Life might have been a lot simpler had I known that acid was another name for LSD and I might not have taken it. If that Sunday had ended up shyte or I had had a scary experience my life might have gone a very different route. Regardless, next morning I decided drugs were best avoided and I was happy doing what I was doing, occasionally sniffing poppers and getting totally rat-arse pissed whenever I could.

Six.

There are about five hundred more people on the average busy tube train than lived in the Lincolnshire village where I grew up - and the entire population of the nearest big town, would all fit in Wembley Stadium. It had its blessings, country life, lots of open space, minimal crime, a real sense of community but it could be as boring as fuck.

My dad, my two older brothers and I had moved there for good, from the nearby jaded town of Grimsby, when I was about eleven. Previously we'd been living in the guest-house of his irritating lady-friend, Paula; primarily a business arrangement he was though, in retrospect, clearly fucking her. I'd been born locally and when my folks split and he'd sold our house to pay our mother off, we'd moved into Paula's house for a few years and lived with her and her son Ray.

The details of my folks splitting were not something I ever gave deep thought to, a fact that proved to be to my detriment in later years, but queries at the time were met with a firm put down of, *"children shouldn't ask difficult questions."*

Ray's dad was the local butcher and he was an only child so always seemed to have the best of everything. We three kids were the poor relations in the equation and me, being the youngest, I was the poorest of them all. When I got a jumper, two other people in the house had usually worn it first. My first bike was Ray's old one but, this isn't 'boo-hoo' just the way it was; it didn't occur to me that ours was an unusual set up or that the youngest children in other families might get new stuff of their own.

Dad and his lady friend weren't drinkers; my mother and her new man Eric, a deep-sea fisherman who would become my step-dad, were controlled drinkers. They measured their drinks, usually gin and tonics, using pewter measuring cups, 'at least that way, you always know how many you've had,' one would say 'and not over do it,' the other would add.

In the village there was one pub, one shop and one return bus a week. If you could get the few miles to the main road, the buses ran every couple of hours but no-one walked anywhere. Road fatalities were common; I myself wrecked three cars before I was even out of my teens, a friend of a friend of us kids had already been killed out walking.

Norman, the old-geezer with iffy teeth who ran the village pub was a stickler for protecting his licence so underage liquor sales were totally out of the question. In my early teens he'd sell me cigars for my dad at the side door but only whilst checking furtively for onlookers. I knew he didn't like doing that but my dad had some kind of respectability in the village. Something in retrospect I see he cultivated and must have loved at the time. Very few folk called him Francis, usually using his surname and he dressed like some kind of mild-eccentric; always in a jacket, tie and with a pocket handkerchief.

Once, when my brother Sebastian and I had made some friends in the council houses our dad had suggested we might do better to befriend the garage owner's son, Colin, and not hang around with the rough lads. We were rough lads.

Colin turned out to be a prize cunt, not to me particularly, just in general. He had me occasionally drive to pick up guns he was *'collecting'* and for which I'd get a tank of fuel. It was pre-Dunblane so you weren't guaranteed jail-time if you got caught with handguns but I had some kind of need to prove myself amongst my peers, having not long passed my driving test. Obviously we didn't drop our council house friends either, the village was way too small for any eugenic bullshit anyway.

Turning up at the football pitch with a machine-gun seemed like almost a normal thing back then; naughty not insane. Guns were easy to get, or at least so it seemed, bullets though were a whole other ball game. It was some ex-war thing, the machine-gun with two handle grips like you'd see in films where Rambo types draped ammo-belts over their shoulders; except we didn't have any ammo – for that.

There were some bullets for a small handgun though one time; we would get one shot each. They blasted through the cans we were firing at and also through the wooden wall of the shed behind and into the door of the old-banger car parked inside. It took three shots to realise we'd fucked up. Colin didn't much care though; he beat the door with a hammer somehow and hid it all with some junk. He would fill up all our cars for free when his folks were out, his poor dad would end up selling the garage as he thought the underground fuel tanks had ruptured. Colin collecting machine guns wasn't that big a deal; without bullets it was just a fucking paperweight to us lot, our collective parents would have had massive aneurysms about it all though.

Allegedly from knowing some dodgy police officers due to his gun collecting Colin claimed to know about this old guy, Flash, who had moved into the village. He was, said Col, a paedophile that had been relocated to our village so he would be out of the way. The guy had a little yappy dog, and he would take it for a walk most evenings around the village block. When he came by, Colin would go, 'alright Flash, you dirty old bastard?' or similar and the innocent-looking frail old guy would ignore him and go about his dog walking business. Pub Norman would refer to the guy as Flash as well to be fair and he was well in with the beat bobby cop who occasionally patrolled the area. We other kids felt Colin could well be right and did nothing about him insulting the old guy.

One night Colin brought out a lightweight air-pistol and said he was off to shoot Flash. It wasn't a gun that would kill anyone, certainly from a distance but the idea wasn't to kill or even really wound Flash, so much as just terrorise him. No one, me neither, raised any objection.

I sometimes found myself wondering well, what if Flash wasn't a paedo? And even is he was, he had obviously served some kind of sentence. I also wondered if some of the guns Colin had access to might have fallen into iffy hands and been used for shitty endeavours. I heard that Colin lost his bottle in the end and got rid of all his guns after some raid - though fuck knows where his stuff ended up in the long run. We were surrounded by legal weapons of course, shotguns mostly, it didn't keep me awake at night.

I was apt to conclude that chances were that Flash was indeed a sex-offender and that if he had been guilty of some kind of pervy crimes than it was karma had put him in Colin's sights and his getting to taste a bit of fear was rough justice in action. One can only hope that if any of Colin's guns were to end up terrorising anyone, karma would visit him similarly.

If we had been able to score booze easily back in those adolescent village days then I shudder to think what might have happened. It could be boring but we did what we could to ease that – and things around us just normally happened. The village hall was packed with concerned residents voicing opinions when the telephone company wanted to move the phone booth - just a stone's throw away but it seemed terribly important at the time.

A family lost its father and two kids in a road accident; the village grieved – and when the brother married the widow, they gossiped. Alan was decapitated in a motorbike smash. The speed of his bike gave rise to much speculation; I had my own opinion too, we all did but his funeral was rammed.

Two couples who regularly came into the pub created a stir when the men packed their bags and moved into the other's houses across the street, swapping wives, houses and families. They were very matter of fact about it and it wasn't the kind of village where we left dead rats on folk's doorsteps – we tittered and gossiped a bit sure, but if they were cool with it, the rest of us had no choice but to be cool with it too.

But in the meantime as we kids waited to be old enough to acquire mopeds and then cars, we just hung around outside the pub eating candy bars, crisps and drinking pop. The only things old Norman would ever sell to us.

We had a village hall for birthday parties and shit like that. One night when I was just under sixteen there was some kind of party with a legal anomaly that made it possible for youths to drink cider as long as food was being served. So we got twatted for the first time ever, totally twatted, me and the other Two Musketeers, Phil the Philster and Clem, my school mates.

They were both from rich landowning families and I suspect their own folks started out suggesting they should hang with me, my father being this respectable college lecturer but that night was just the first of many pissed up escapades. Though we seemed inseparable in those early days neither would invite me to their eventual weddings. I wrote both matters off quickly at the time, we had drifted apart by then besides Clem's bird was posh as fuck. I thought she was just a stuck up witch and blamed her when I didn't get invited. Drunk one night I'd also asked Philster to wank me off which I don't suppose helped, shame he didn't really. Oh well.

Decades later round at my dealer, Kev's flat, I was bemoaning casually this resentment I still had about the weddings when he chimes up saying,'I don't blame them.'

'What you on about?' I'm aghast, but he isn't finished.

'I wouldn't invite you to my wedding either,' he adds 'you're a piss-head, you'd ruin it for everyone.'

And with that years of resentment were instantly over-written by shame. He was so right, and I had never stopped to think about it long enough for the pieces to fall into place. Luckily I was off my face on drugs at the time so I wasn't that bothered but yeah, it kinda made sense.

Kev kept a hammer at hand on his table, it's not that he wasn't scared, Kevin was always scared but he was always prepared. Telling people the way it was, or at least the way he saw it came easy to him and, as we were friends, I believed him. Shame he didn't tell me I was a fucking junkie at the time as well though, but I was a good customer of his by then after all.

Seven.

It seems odd to look back now and not know I had a problem; in the cold light of day I think I can say honestly that the worst shit that ever hit my fan was all related to alcohol; arrests aside I pissed in the bed when I stayed at my brother's, I pissed on his sofa another time when I slept downstairs; I've pissed over at least three straight guys I had been hoping to shag and had ended up in bed with *'as mates'*, nothing else happened - too pissed. I pissed in Norman's confectionery cupboard; I pissed all over Andy Jessop in his sleeping bag when a few of us went camping and, I have woken up, covered in my own piss in my own bed at least a hundred times. I was aware I got lairy now and then on spirits so kept to weak lager where I could; the problem with that was liquid volume.

Twice I have robbed hotel rooms; but only of dry mattresses. I'd once woken up wet in a hotel in Austria, cursed and gone on a stealth mission to find an unlocked door, stolen the single mattress, and taken the one I had soiled back, with its wet sheets and sort of made it look okay. Then I've gone back to my own room and slept like a baby only to wake up in total panic about what lunacy had occurred. I was though, also mildly amused that some poor fucker might have gone to bed only to find it pissed in; hopefully they'd be pissed and blame themselves. (Maybe that happened to me?) I did the exact same thing years later in Spain only 'cos I'd got away with it before, can you imagine? What a fucking head case.

The thing is, and this is nobodies fault, no-one (until dealer Kev) had ever called me out my being a problem drinker really, worried no-doubt that I would kick off, but yeah, looking back of course I was a piss-head, piss-bed, alcoholic.

The worst 24 hours of my drinking career, had no witnesses, physical victims, court-case or injuries but it fills me with shame to this day. It was in my early London days after a night of festive drinking on board a Thames party boat with colleagues from Harrod's. I'd worked there to get some Christmas spending money; we got well mashed, me and my three posh departmental chums; we were the only ones at the party in Black tie; I'd had to buy one years before for a trip away with Norman.

I'd got home to Brixton, only to realise I'd left my overcoat on the fucking barge thing and it had my keys in it. I had no idea where I'd got off the boat or how I'd even got home but I had to weigh my options out in the cold and I took a step back to think. A dinner suit in Brixton wasn't a regular look, I couldn't fuck about for too long.

It dawned on my pretty quick and, being pissed, it seemed like the most obvious and natural solution to my problem, besides I was pretty sure the flat along from mine was in fact empty. So I kicked that main-block door open and bounded up their stairs; I knew enough to know that once started I had to be totally committed. If anyone heard or saw me kick the front door in, the police could soon be on my case. I kicked open the door to the neighbouring flat and rushed straight in to what was very obviously (without seeing anyone) an inhabited flat; cooking smells, warmth, a light in what I took to be the bathroom area. Shit! I'd picked the wrong fucking door but I was committed at this stage and didn't hesitate; somehow instinct and adrenaline took over. I bust open their balcony doors from the living-room, I suspect turning the key and the handle would have worked but I didn't try it, and with that I was out and along the balcony to my similar, locked, French doors.

Without really slowing down I smashed a small-square window-light around about where I knew my door-lock was and opened it, sneaked in and closed it off to the outside world with a heart beating like a fucking express train. Total time elapsed since kicking the main door in, less than a minute. Seriously.

My broken glass had fallen mostly inward so really my place looked fine but for about an hour I lay in the dark way too scared to turn on any lights in case the doorbell rang or the police appeared or something. Slowly, as I lay there pissed and panting it dawned on me that I didn't have any other keys at home. Which meant I was effectively double-mortice locked in my very own flat. Even if the cops had rung my bell, I couldn't even unlock the fucking door! I was, to all intents and purposes, a prisoner of my own design. There was fuck all else to do, so eventually I climbed under my duvet and went to sleep. And of course, I pissed the bed.

When you're drunk and wake up wet and are still tired, sometimes it's enough to change your shreddies, flip the mattress, find a dry patch, get some towels to throw around and get some more sleep. Somehow, when your eyes next open, yes, there is a palpable sense of dread and self-recrimination, but also a bit of a plan. Waking mid-morning I was locked in my own flat though, I had committed a fairly offensive, frightening crime to get there and well, in spite of sleeping on it, I had no fucking idea what to do; and I was soggy wet.

Around noon I was able to establish by ringing around a bit that the boat was at anchor until at least 5pm that evening. Locked in my flat worried that there might be a break-in investigation going on just feet away, at least I had time to make a plan as my hands were shaking and my brow was sweating.

There was an internal window from the common-hallway into my bathroom but the owner had fitted mirrors over the bathroom side and made it into a bathroom cabinet. It was the only way out without calling for help or joining soggy bedsheets together to make a slippery rope. Over the next hour or so I dismantled it and prepared my escape, leaving it as an access back in case the ship with my keys on had sunk in the night - or more likely, someone had nicked my coat.

Later in the long day I thankfully got my coat, and keys and was able to get home and sneak in and no-one ever mentioned the incident at all; not that I really spoke to my neighbours anyway. I fitted the bathroom cabinet back and deftly touched up some scuff-marks in the common hallway as the fan heater blew the smell of stale wee around the place a bit more for added ambiance.

Eight.

'I have never been spoken to like that before in my life,' old Norman the pub landlord said angrily on account of me being rude when he had come to my cabin door to wake me up. I have no recollection of what I had said to make him that cross but I suspect it was something along the lines of; *'what did you wake me up for, you cunt?'* given his ire. He probably hadn't been called the c-word much in the pub come to think of it. Such conversations were not unusual for me but this was a side that Norman hadn't ever seen before, and I do hate being woken up unnecessarily. He was many years my senior and was paying for my expensive trip – a cruise ship to 'The Land of The Midnight Sun' over the arctic circle - I guess I should have been a bit more polite.

The thing is with a couple of drinks in me, Norman would say you got, *the best out of me*. I'd be less hung up about all my insecurities; tell jokes, laugh, dance; be the life and soul of the party so it seemed. But they were usually the only bits I could clearly remember. After a couple more drinks, as Norman now knew, I could get quite lairy.

I couldn't remember what happened but it was obviously bad for Norman to say anything at all though he was just sort of stating facts. I believed him. He was a perfect gent; his bad teeth he covered by not opening his mouth too far but in his dinner suit he had the look of a dignified foreign secretary.

On the day I had told my mother I was gay she immediately asked; 'Does that mean Norman is too then?' I was horrified.

'Seriously? I have no idea.' I didn't actually know; my best guess was that he was asexual and would probably die a virgin but I continued, 'but if he was, do you really think I'd sleep with him Mum?' Even with some cosmetic dentistry he would still be about forty years my senior and he was just like an older mate; the idea of him even having a penis was not something I'd ever thought about. Most of my friends were like genderless action figures to me, if I thought it was anything but smooth down there I'm not sure I could even sit down with some of them.

'Oh sorry son!' she had backtracked quickly but was clearly very confused and thrown by my gay revelation.

'You must have known Mum,' I implored.

'No. No, I didn't,' and it seems she hadn't. I had, it appeared, been some kind of master in not seeming gay in any kind of stereotypical way. It took the middle-brother Seb, a postman, a couple of weeks to get his head around it too; Matthew my eldest brother had fucked off to join the Army by this point; I'm not sure when he found out.

Even though Sebastian regularly called me a puff, he thought I was joking when after telling my mum I had said, 'By the way Seb, I'm gay' and he'd just brushed it off and we kind of moved on to other stuff. I didn't really give a shit not talking about it but, two weeks or so later, he had come round having been on the phone to our mum and was like, 'Is it fucking true then?' confrontationally.

'What?' I wondered.

'Mum asked if you had you told me yet; I said I thought you was joking. Is it fucking true, are you really bent?' his mouth kinda dropping open a bit, dumb-fucker looking.

'Yeah, what of it, I'm gay, big fucking deal?' I replied.

'What really?' he hesitated before adding, 'Well, I don't want any of your friends round my house.'

'WHAT?', I'm fucking seething. 'STICK YOUR HOUSE UP

YOUR ARSE YOU FUCKING cunt!' I shouted right in his face as I'm pushing out of the door 'I don't wanna come round your poxy shit-hole house again anyway, you wanker,' and I rushed out and got in my car, a red Capri, to burn a bit or rubber round the village and calm down.

And that's the sort of environment I was handling my sexuality in, all at about the time when the papers were saying on their front-pages that there was this new gay-disease and basically inferred that anyone who favoured penis over pussy would be dead by Christmas. And yet still some folk, even people making the laws, thought people like me picked out our fucking sexuality like a fashionable new tank top – fucking morons.

My anger may explain why Seb's never challenged me much on anything since, like say my drunkenness and what have you. I think I scared him then but prior to that day, I was always considered the bullying underdog; I drove round to his house twenty-minutes after our flare up ready to fight him but it was obvious he'd been crying and he actually apologised; he said he was just surprised that was all and of course my friends (he didn't say *gay* friends) could come round. I credit his wife, Jane, with the change of heart but regardless that was the last time we fully fell out. He never moaned subsequently when at his house I pissed on his furniture or was a prize drunken prick at a couple of Christmases; I had scared him; 'bout time the tables turned.

But yeah, on the ship with Norman, probably since we were in the middle of the ocean, he'd doubtless concluded that to remain annoyed with me might compromise his holiday so little else was said about our 'robust' conversation and we went on to have a memorable time. For him at least, for me much of it was a blur. But not all of it; one night I will remember for ever.

The whole trip had come about on account of me working part-time in the village pub where bachelor Norman had been the landlord for like ever. He had never been on holiday and at this time he was about sixty, going on eighty. We used to go for days out, sometimes in groups to the races or the County Show, that kind of malarkey and we'd go for dinner at local restaurants every couple of weeks or so. Some could argue that he was ostensibly grooming me but I'd reject that, I think he just liked having someone as a friend. That's certainly how I thought of him and it was handy that he usually paid for it all.

He had brought up the idea of catching some kind of mail packet-steamer thing along the coast of Norway. I said I'd go with him but steered him towards a brochure full of women in cocktail dresses and men dressed as penguins and eventually he'd decided to go for it. Norman must have been loaded 'cos he never spent any real money. Not on women, housing, cars, clothes, music, gambling, sports, boys, presents or fuck all. And the village pub had been consistently busy for his entire life and much of his father's before him. So yeah, I didn't feel like it was a big deal for him to pay for my holiday; I'd carry his bags and keep him company and besides it would probably be a chore a lot of the time. I viewed it almost like it was a charitable service, sort of thing, doing my bit for a nice old guy.

Half the village probably thought I was fucking him up the arse for pocket-money when I eventually came out but it never really bothered me to be honest. And no one ever said anything like that direct to me. I never discussed my sexuality with Norm at all, nor he with me, it just wasn't relevant.

On the ship, a big old-style liner, I had suggested we sit at a big dinner table so we would meet new people - and not bore each other shitless. The cocktail pianist, Tina, who was beautiful and elegant, was seated with us as were a local-newspaper guy, Tony, and his wife who accompanied a group from his paper. Second night in and we're all getting on fine, the wine helped *(early days)* and our dining companions are clearly curious as to the dynamic between Norman and I, knowing that we had separate cabins. Tony, the newspaper guy said that he thought he'd start telling folk that I was a Lord, travelling incognito and Norman was my personal secretary and valet. We thought little else of it, just joking about it now and then through dinner but Tony did put it around, starting with his travel-group and it seemed to stick. Telling one dowager-duchess type that I was an apprentice mechanic a few days later, she'd said, 'ha, I bet you can't tell one end of a car from the other bugger,' which oddly was sort of true, I was a hopeless mechanic; I'd wanted to be a dancer.

On the ship there was an actual prince in his late 20's from a foreign royal family with his bodyguard detail of about eight or ten guys and some women of various status. The security guys carried yellow stick things since guns were naturally forbidden. Odd but you know, who cared; they were a bit of a ship's curiosity, something we gossiped about over dinner.

"A bit theatrical really!" "Unnecessary!" "dis-concerting!" "Paranoid!"- you get the picture.

Just under a week into the trip, the gossip at dinner suddenly got a bit more gossipy though, 'Have you heard about The Prince?' asked Tony the newspaper guy. I hadn't heard anything but I was instantly all ears.

'What?' I asked, masking my real concern.

'They've all left the ship. Him, his family and all the bodyguards, everyone,' Tony said. Inside I was sort of shitting myself, I had had a happy smile on my face as we'd looked around some crusty Norwegian town but I wasn't smiling now.

Where the prince came from I could certainly be executed for what he and I had done the night before – and quite what could have happened to him and his bodyguard heaven only knew. The bodyguard had gone first, entirely consensual on my part you understand, before leaving and fetching his boss, the prince. I was as happy as a dog with two tails, pardon the pun, and certainly wasn't about to breathe a word at the table; when avocado is being served how could I possibly mention anal?

'Why?' I managed to ask Tony, my voice probably like that of a cartoon mouse.

'Well,' he says, ' it seems that because the guards couldn't carry guns, the prince didn't feel safe.'

'Really?' asked Tina the pianist, 'did something happen?'
Tony's wife makes finger air quotes, 'Just "His Royal Highness" didn't feel safe ashore without armed guards.'

I was relived, it sounded plausible and obviously not everything that happens in the world is about me but this was - but no-one could ever know the truth. Thank fuck we were back at sea already.

I knew enough about politics and religion to know that people could actually come after me if I said anything. They'd deny it anyway but I guess if it got too heavy I was disposable. I wasn't entirely certain they hadn't left someone on board to throw me over the side in the night to make any potential problems sink to the bottom of the ocean. Make no mistake, this minor royal and his bodyguard having sex with another man could have been a huge domestic incident for them, possibly an international diplomatic incident too if the UK press got hold of it. Particularly had I said I was taken advantage of even though, if there was any actual advantage taken, I suppose it was me of them.

I'd come across a lone handsome bodyguard in the hallway and, pissed as I was, grabbed my suit crotch and smiled provocatively. He'd taken the hint and beckoned me to follow him to this big cabin where he'd fucked me; my very first experience of that role. He then told me to stay where I was and disappeared momentarily. The prince then appeared and looking at my naked ass asked with an open hand gesture if he could have a go. I nodded and pushed my head into the pillow with a smile. It was over in a matter of minutes and the prince promptly disappeared. The bodyguard made wank gestures with his hand which I took to mean do you want me to wank you off before you leave? but given my own flaccid booze-filled dick I declined.

'No, nah, I'm good. I'm off ta,' and with that, about five or six minutes start to finish I fucked off and eventually found my cabin and went to sleep. Without pissing the bed but - bum virgin that I had been - with quite some smile; twice in ten minutes, bingo!

Thinking about it, they must have quickly had a crisis meeting and realising that they didn't even know my name, where my cabin was or anything else at all, leaving the ship at the very next port in the morning, probably made some kind of sense. It could have gone very tits up for everyone. Indeed,Tony's story that I was an incognito British aristocrat may well have saved my fucking life; we will never know. I never heard anything about the matter again and wouldn't tell another living soul for years. How could you, who'd even believe shit like that anyway? I've run out of petrol in a Rolls Royce and once had two art galleries in Mayfair. Most people exhibit tell-tale signs of disbelief about those facts come to think of it. But no, they weren't tied to a pay-off from the botty sex debacle.

Nine.

When I eventually managed to find some 'clean time/recovery' I heard someone say, *"if you want to know why you took drugs, stop taking them."* It seemed a bit trite at the time but looking back there's no doubt a lot of my intoxications were based around an inherent shame around my sexuality. There are still about eleven countries where gay sex is a capital crime; it's one thing feeling different but when they could literally stone you to death for a five-minute fumble, a better decision might be just getting stoned.

Back in the days of the village hall discos there was always this excruciating fifteen-minutes toward the end where the DJ would put some slow ballad shit on and the guys would dance with the girl that they most wanted to fuck; they were the only times many of those guys would ever dance at all.

I *loved* dancing, I was almost always the first guy on the dance floor. The girls all sort of danced around their handbags. Literally, they would put their bags on the floor in a pile and dance around them. Hardly any tough guys ever moved in dance wise until right near the end, unless there was obvious competition for a girl.

Clearly my being that little bit different, I would quickly get a bit tipsy and find whichever girl would tolerate me dancing with them. I didn't know how to dance in any formal sense; when I threw them around they never knew which way I was gonna chuck 'em. I didn't give a shit, I just loved letting loose with and finding some kind of vibe in the beats. And the girls loved it too. The ones who weren't obsessed with how everything looked; usually the bigger ones if I'm honest, they loved that someone asked them to dance but back then guys would never ever dance on their own; that was to come with the rave scene.

As the last fifteen minutes would start to draw near, the guys would gather at the dance floor and pounce on their 'bird' of choice when the slow stuff started. My defence mechanism to this peacock bullshit was to be as pissed as possible so as to not have to get off with a girl. I remember at some point in my youthful years thinking that there was something wrong with me as none of the girls ever really looked at me. Maybe they did but I guess I was too busy wondering if they had sexy brothers.

In mid big-school, early teens, I had started each day looking out for an older boy who had caught my eye at assemblies. To this day he doubtless doesn't even know I existed; I have no idea what his name was, what class he was in or where he lived; besides, our school catchment area was massive, easily a hundred square countryside miles. The only time I ever saw him was as he walked into the hall each morning. Mousey blonde, tall, maybe a head higher than me, slim, fit-looking and his grey jumper marked him out in a sea of largely blue sweaters. His tie knot was always huge and his pants seemed so snug, though I don't recall speculating beyond his belt loops.

I would be relieved each morning that he hadn't died in the night as I would marvel at the way he carried himself walking across the hall, I thought that if I could get a jumper like his then maybe I might look cool too. Looking back he probably also felt like an odd-one-out, being made to wear a grey sweater but he made my day every time I saw him; I don't recall ever having sexy thoughts about him but on reflection he was my first real man-crush.

In the school-holidays my step-dad Eric took me to sea with him; I'd go again a year later when he was the captain but on this, my first trip, he was the mate, second-in-command on a big trawler. Eric had six kids of his own but he was estranged from them by his seemingly bitter ex-wife so he treated me like his own son. I liked Eric and he was kind to my mother whom he always called 'The Fuhrer' in that politically incorrect way of the 70's. So yeah, I was well up for getting away from my bullying brothers, the butcher's son and his increasingly whiney mother. The ship was like the picture on the Fisherman's Friend packet and I guess there were maybe ten blokes on board as well as Eric, the skipper and me. The weather smiled on us and the entire trip was calm, sunny and beautiful - it nurtured in me a love of the sea I retain to this day.

Eric never got to learn that I was gay. Not long after she had asked me if I was sleeping with pub Norman, my mother had said we should avoid telling him for a while. When Eric croaked, unexpectedly in his late fifties, my mother apologised for him not being updated, 'It's not that he would have minded with you or anything,' she had ventured, 'it's just that on the ships they had such trouble with it all.' The it being homosexuality it seemed.

'Oh okay, I didn't know, don't worry Mum,' I had said to spare her guilt but yeah, deep-down it was just another ton of shame to process.

'Cut with the grain,' Fred, a deckhand had said, 'look, here let me show you,' he reached across the small table of the ship's eating area; with his hand he motioned north-south over my steak, 'this way look, the way the texture runs.' I'd been struggling to cut up the culinary treat I had never even tasted before.

'Oh right, yeah I see, thank you,' I said looking at Fred, not long since a man himself but I was slightly embarrassed I was so retarded at the table so I flashed him my best smile.

'That's all right smiler,' he said 'he's always fucking smiling this kid, look at him beaming,' the other guy in there, Alfie, in his fisherman's blouson looked up and smiled back.

'Ha,' Alfie said before shortly finishing his own food and raising to leave the small cramped room, 'You need anything else Smiler?' he asked as he manoeuvred out from behind the tight furniture. I smiled, my cheeks emptying a delicious mouthful of steak down my throat as I reached for my tin mug of pop - they never gave me any alcohol; I was a kid.

'Yeah,' I said lifting my mug up a bit to spare any blushes, 'you got any cunt books?' I asked unhesitatingly - I have no idea where I got the balls to repeat the line I'd overheard earlier or use the big c-word that has ever since been a firm favorite; maybe because of the reaction I got. These were cut-throat sort of men and I had never seen a fanny in my life. Or of a cock either come to think of it; well apart from in the changing rooms at school where I spent as little time as possible. The man left the mess-deck wordlessly. I looked down at my food, Fred never said a word, if they exchanged looks as Alfie left the room, I'd missed it.

He came back within a minute or so with about five porno mags, never said a word and just put them in front of me.

'Thank you,' I said and smiled again. It was hard to stop smiling but I knew Fred was watching me as I gingerly opened the pages and was confronted with my first vaginal close up. On the opposite page was a picture of a flaccid cock too, a bit of it lost behind the magazine's staple. In that small room of masculinity with Fred watching me and now also with the cook putting his head round the door and asking, 'What you got there Smiler?' I finally grasped that I was a homosexual; I also knew instantly, that no-one must ever, ever know.

'Just some cunt books,' I said being sure to direct the line of my vision to the filing-cabinet part of the lady and not the sausage bit of the gentleman. cunt books could show vaginas a plenty back then but believe it or not, in the UK, to show an erect penis in a magazine or film was actually illegal.

Years later I'd get arrested *(and acquitted)* for selling videos full of erect gay cocks in Soho but that was to come. There on the ship I couldn't be found out; nothing would have happened I'm sure and back then I didn't have the knowledge that some of the crew probably tossed each other off. I dare say I'd have been too terrified to suggest a circle-wank anyway, besides I was still many years shy of consent, set then at twenty-one between males; less for fucking girls, literally fucking girls, which makes no sense at all if you think about it. They used to allow smoking on planes back then too and had only just thought to put wheels on suitcases, it was a weird time to be coming of age but no time at all to be coming out.

I still didn't even know what wanking was or what gay men did to each other back then, I knew my dick went firmer now and then but not why or that I could use it for pleasure. My brother Seb had told me it was normal when I had enquired if his *'thing sort of got longer and like a sausage sometimes?'* and quickly fucked off somewhere else, embarrassed. So when, at the table in that room I felt myself stirring under the table I made the connection that this is what sex was. If they had had stiff cocks in the mags I guess it would have helped but I had no idea of the biology of it all. I concluded from the mags that the guy had to lie on the lady and wee in her to have sex. When I did eventually start to ejaculate and once tasted and swallowed some of my own sperm I fully expected to be shamed as a sexual deviant being the world's first ever pregnant male. Seriously, I checked my belly for quite a few weeks to see if I was carrying my own baby.

As far as sex education went, well, there was practically none at school nothing at all from dad - but my mum had once said that *a gentleman always removes his socks.*

The nearest I had come to knowing gays even existed was playground taunts and the word *"homosexual"* in the dictionary, I kid you not. The closest I'd previously got to the mention of any sex in print was a passage in the book Jaws by Peter Benchley. Something about fingering his girlfriend in a convertible car as I recall, and how it might look to the authorities were he to crash. It was hugely exciting when my brother showed me where to find the passage. My dad had hundreds of books but there was no porn ever lying around so this was a ground breaking moment for me on the ship; looking at my first fanny and feeling, well, nothing at all really. I tried to keep from staring at the penises - even when eventually sat on my own as I couldn't be sure I wasn't being watched in some reflection somehow. Knowing I was actually what it said in that dictionary, *"Homosexual; sexually attracted to one's own sex,"* was a very big deal, I now knew for sure that I wasn't normal and I would never fit in anywhere at all.

*

'Saturday Night Fever' was the number one movie in the cinemas as we had left port and when the tune, 'Staying Alive' had come over the ship's radio I had the literal thought that I couldn't wait to get back home so I could dance to it which was, I suppose, kind of super gay. Not that I wasn't enjoying the trip, I was and the gay shit wasn't that scary; I guessed it just had to be managed somehow.

Eric was as good as gold on that trip, he made sure I was fed, rested and was shown whatever I was interested in learning. The only real thing I didn't like was the way they gutted the fish almost straight away and while they were mostly still alive.

The net would be hauled up on deck and hung over these like fenced-off areas and opened into them. Some fish would flap their way into gullies where good-luck and gravity would flush some of them back into the sea. Quite what those fish thought had just happened to them beggars belief. No doubt they would go to undersea cocktail parties and talk of alien abduction but secretly I willed lots of them back to safety. Unceremoniously the men would start slicing into those left behind with sharp knives, gills to bumhole, ripping them open out and tossing their guts overboard like a little kid might throw a tennis ball backwards.

When the net was pulled aboard the birds around would all start a feeding frenzy. I saw gannets for the first time, the most elegant and graceful things I'd ever seen, they could dive down at like a million-miles an hour and go really deep for their fish gut treats. If it wasn't all so barbaric it would be almost poetic but it was still a sight for sore teenage eyes.

The most common complaint I hear from drug users when they get clean and sober is that they felt as if they didn't fit in – though to be fair I don't think that feeling is exclusive to drug users or alcoholics. I daresay most everyone harbours the notion about themselves but certainly on that ship that particular little malaise started to take root, particularly in the company of the cook, who I'd sort of liked for a while.

One day this cook, Matt, a nice, tidy, mid-twenties guy who wanted to work on ocean liners, suddenly started chucking bin-bags of rubbish overboard, like eight or ten of them for fuck's sake and with a grin, 'biggest dustbin in the world Smiler,' he'd said but I was quietly aghast. The birds bobbing around were delighted; they would pick at the slowly-sinking bags with their beaks to feast on bits of leftover steak, potato-peel and what-have-you but the fucking pollution confused me. Nothing could eat the tin cans, bottles and plastic bags after all; I was upset but I didn't want to go all gay on them, I had to be extra careful from now on.

Suddenly though the cook grabs a long boat-hook, leans over the deck rail and bashes a seagull right in the skull, killing it instantly; 'Take that you bastard!' he shouted as he aimed the now bloody hook at another bird as they all shot to the sky in a wild cacophony of birdy insults. I went inside, the guy was clearly a moron and I just didn't get it at all, why would he do that?

And I couldn't bring myself to gut the poor fish either; I did one or two to show some kind of willing but I was glad to be getting in the way and holding up the line to be honest.

'No! The OTHER end,' sort of shit they shouted as they tried to get me to slice the fishes bumholes open. My wrinkled nose told them all they needed to know and I was soon assigned to ice-detail, packing the gutted fish corpses down in the hold. Sometimes that feeling of 'not fitting in' is pretty fucking accurate but I still sort of enjoyed all the other bits at sea; just a shame my step-dad wasn't a captain in the Royal fucking Yacht Squadron huh?

Ten.

It was about six years after my first acid trip that I took my second ever drug, ecstasy. I was more or less living in California, dipping in and out on tourist visas.

I'd met Ivan online in the London gay chat room of the early AOL, a like stone-age version of Facebook and he was coming over from the US to *'go to the ballet'*. Did I want to meet? Why the fuck not, I figured, so we did.

I didn't fancy him but we clicked straight away and he was great fun. He was wearing this woollen poncho cape thing and we went to an iffy gay bar, he would spin around in this fucking ballet twirl and the poncho would circle out like Marilyn Monroe's skirt; it was hilarious and the more I laughed the more he did it - but I was a bit tipsy I guess. 'Sweetie Darling!' he would say with a Russian(ish) accent, 'you should come and live in California'.

Over the next few days, in which we didn't kiss or fuck and I didn't even see the inside of his alleged four-star hotel room, I would learn he was an ex-Bolshoi ballet dancer; had a Jaguar XJS, a Maserati and he supposedly lived in a house built around a rock he had turned into a fountain. Oh and he had another house some place called Santa Barbara and he would say; 'Just come sweetie darling, you will love it. If not just come back to this, er, love-er-ly climate,' it was cold out.

So yeah I went. Not straight away, it took a few weeks to get my shit together to get out there for a fortnight and check it all out. I had a return ticket in case his stories were all bullshit, which I suspected they probably were - so if he actually lived in a shitty studio-apartment and I had to suck him off to sleep on his floor, I was mentally equipped to do so.

But he met me off the plane in a nice Jag with some fancy number plate; I felt bad for ever having had doubts. Within the hour we had parked at the beach at Santa Monica and were seated at tables in the actual sand ordering appetisers for lunch. I didn't fuck about; 'Wow, this is amazing, I *am* gonna come and live here,' I said, I'd decided.

'Really sweetie? You should,' Ivan said; we had a great lunch and drove up into the hills to some posh looking neighbourhood called Pacific Palisades.

As we pulled into the forecourt Ivan opened the garage door remotely and as it lifted up I spotted the fountain boulder and a silver Maserati Bi-Turbo, albeit under a thin layer of dust. Fucking hell, I thought as I went into the house, maybe I would have to suck him off anyway and have him fall in love with me. Not that I was actually that sort of person, but I had the thought process. It was probably as easy to build around the massive rock thing as move it I thought; it was like elephant-sized but it might benefit from a bit of lighting re-design. Maybe Ivan would pay me to do that for him some time, I thought.

The back of the house was like a film-set with secluded views over the mountains; large sliding-doors led out to a terrace, pool, jacuzzi and barbecue pit. It was fucking awesome. The pool wasn't even pool shaped, it didn't have a single right-angle and the hot-tub was built discreetly into one end.

He must have been Rudolph-Fucking-Nureyev himself or something huge to afford all this, it was astounding. And then his dog appeared, a British Bulldog called Yuki whose breathing in the hot sun sounded like a blocked toilet; the picture was complete. I was going to be very happy here.

'Oh hello,' said a woman's voice not far behind the dog, 'I'm

Nancy, how nice to finally meet you' as a hand extended towards me which, while confused, I politely shook. Not having the remotest clue who she was I ad-libbed and brought the musical My Fair Lady to mind; the fuck-off sized diamond on her finger suggested this wasn't the maid.

'How do you do?' I said like Elisa Doolittle meeting the actual fucking Queen before following up; 'How kind of you to let me stay' not knowing quite what was going on.

'Not at all, you're so welcome,' said Nancy, *'any friend of Ivan's is a friend of mine.'* Which meant, as far as I could tell, that we were BOTH guests, me AND Ivan, and he *was* a bullshitter after all. Quite who might need the sexual favours for my emergency accommodation was now a total mystery but she was obviously the loaded one.

I never did ask what their deal was and never fully found out, it was all very cryptic-crossword. I was brought up not to ask difficult questions after all and it was their business not mine but it defo wasn't his house and cars and shit. I'd find out more over time but for now I got through on my wits and charm. I had nice hair, some decent clothes and I could hold my own conversationally. Oh and my watch, a Cartier Pasha, *(smoke and mirrors)* was worth as much as a new Mini so really I think I had a similar kind of allure as Ivan did but he was a bullshitting fucker really; birds-of-feather as the saying goes.

Ivan and I had had fun in the UK and now on his turf we had fun again. Somehow I was able to regulate my drinking to the point that neither he nor Nancy saw me as a liability and before long they were both encouraging me to come and stay more permanently; I could make my base at her place where I could have my own room; at least for a few weeks until I got established.

In those first two weeks; we'd go out to restaurants, usually the three of us. I would pay my way obviously, Nancy would take her turn but when it was Ivan's he would just flick his hand out horizontally towards Nancy like he was feeding birds from his palm, barely even glancing in her direction. She would gather her handbag in front of her and pull out a bundle of notes. Ivan would peel off a few, place them on the saucer without much care at all other than with a, *'thank you sweetie darling,'* and hand the rest back. Quite whose money it was I never asked but it's not like he was sat there in swim-trunks, he had pockets in his pants, his hand just never went into them.

After dinner I would fold myself into the back seat of the Jag, the Maserati needed repairs apparently, and we would head home – and they would retire to their own respective rooms and me to mine. He didn't try to screw me and I'm pretty certain he wasn't required to screw her. It was an odd arrangement but really, none of my business, I was good at staying out of other people's business - unless it started interfering with mine.

I decided to roll the dice and fully move out there. The fact that I was potentially going to be illegal was a question laughingly brushed aside with *'we will find you nice girl to marry sweetie darling,'* that kind of thing, but we all knew that was never going to happen.

In London I sold almost everything I owned and drew cash on the limited collection of credit sources I had and within a few weeks I had accumulated six or eight months budget. Not a fortune but enough to establish myself. I would buy a plane ticket with a three month return date, ostensibly to renew my tourist visa but also as another escape clause should it all prove harder than I thought.

It was all made easier by my life in London going through an insufferably irritating period due mostly to my being emotionally terrorised by my old flat-mate Nigel; his shrink had told me he was in love with me which I thought was just rude, we were supposed to be mates. The fact I'd similarly crushed on unavailable guys before never entered into it; years later I'd be badly on the other side of this sort of equation but back then, suffice to say, running away to the U.S. was a timely opportunity and, whilst no doubt worried, my parents were separately quite supportive. It was though extraordinary that none of us ever considered the necessity of health insurance at the time; I was lucky health wise and didn't even scratch myself when, pissed as a rat, I wrecked Ivan's Jeep one night.

Ivan, and Nancy had picked me up at LAX and I established a remote mailing/office address and telephone answering service the first day; I got a social security number, it didn't mean I could legally work, it was just an official ID. From there I was able to open a bank account and within two weeks I had bought a car and found a place to live on Hollywood Boulevard. Sounds glam but I called it The Roach Motel, it was kind of a borderline shit-hole but it had caught my eye out driving. Set in a square around a pool my 'bachelor-unit' had its own kitchen area and shower room and wasn't actually riddled with roaches. In calling it The Roach Motel in my self-effacing way it avoided inspection by Nancy and Ivan, neither of whom ever came in, though we stayed in regular touch.

I'd spotted an art gallery I liked the look of, selling reproductions of familiar paintings on the edge of Beverly Hills, put a letter through the letterbox offering to work for commission only and, before I moved out from Nancy's place, I had a job too.

'WOW,' Nancy exclaimed, 'just under two weeks and you've got a car, an apartment AND a job. Way to go Charles, you Brits.' The art gallery guy had left a message on my service and following a quick interview he took me out for lunch. I think he was must have been bored on his own all day really and having someone else to talk to must have been appealing in itself. Especially with no retainer to pay. Outside it was hot as fuck though, my British suits were way too thick for the climate I thought as we ate pasta at some al fresco place.

I liked the guy's chutzpah; he had a replica Ferrari 250, lived in the grounds of some famous movie-mansion, albeit in the pool-house, had changed his Italian name to something terribly English and what's more was selling fake oil-paintings to rich Americans who, very often, would fool their richer friends that they owned originals. What's not to love I thought? Over lunch he said that were I any good he could get me a green-card, not to worry, and we would both make a lot of money.

I lasted two weeks, sold seven paintings for a decent wedge each and the phoney twat never paid me a fucking cent. He started bitching one day when I hadn't asked for the contact details of some obvious time-waster, this in spite of me shifting more of his dodgy paintings than he'd sold in a month. I told him I wasn't new to selling but I think to be honest I'd embarrassed him by being quite so at ease with his clientele. When he said I could leave if I didn't like doing it his way, I did.

In subsequent arguments about my commission he threatened to call immigration. There was fuck all I could do to get my money; even kicking up a medium fuss could have had me arrested and the police over there had guns. I knew when I was screwed; the annoying part though was not the commission, it was losing two weeks when I could have been doing something else. One reason I had got out of Nancy's so quick was that a week's rent at The Roach Motel was less than the cost of a dinner out for three. There was method in the madness; living on my own, no-one need know when I got down to beans on toast.

At this stage I was vaguely manageable and I've never, to this day, pissed a bed in America but my party off switch could be a bit temperamental even when I was *'watching my money'* and now and then I'd forget I wasn't in Britain. One night I told some guy to fuck right off and he was completely un-phased by it in a way I had never experienced before. I concluded he must be carrying a gun. Like I say, it was easy to forget where I was, they all spoke English after all.

Out with Ivan one night in his Jeep I had missed my booze-stop and got a bit too pissed. Nancy and I never really got to the bottom of the deal with Ivan's other house or where the Jeep came from, the two of us suspecting that he had a Sugar Mummy or Daddy there as well. At this point she was comfortable telling me she didn't think he'd actually ever been in the Bolshoi and had done some very limited, early-internet research. I was reasonably non-committal about it all, I mean, it's not like my own life would bear much investigation either.

Anyway, Ivan had jumped out of the Jeep to get some cigarettes and I thought it would be funny if the truck would have disappeared when he came back. Oh, how we would laugh, I undid the parking brake and giggled to myself as the truck stared to roll back out of sight; oops, slap-bang into a fucking tree! The tailgate window shattered, a branch ripped the headlining and the bumper curved itself around the tree. Ivan hadn't seen a thing, I saw the look of mystery spread across his face, his head moved so his vision could take in the slope and slowly he saw his half-wrecked truck. To his credit, he wasn't outwardly seething, though I suspect he must have been.

'So, sweetie darling,' he said after I tried explaining, stopped apologising and offered to cover the damage, 'I think the best we can do is go dancing,' and with that he starts the truck, shoves it in gear forward; the branch screeched and pulled out more of the roof-lining out as it freed itself from the car.

We got drinks, danced and for a while at least forgot the wreck of the car. That's why we made such good friends really; neither of us ever got hung up on details.

Even subsequently we never fell-out about the car, it obviously wasn't his and I never handed over any money in spite of asking several times only to be brushed off. I think Ivan just blagged it with the sugar-person on my behalf. I felt we were kindred spirits as far as other people's money went but it was at the big beach-house of another friend in Ventura Beach that I would take that next drug. Ecstasy.

We went to his friend, Sara's house some weekends. Really she just was house-siting and it was sort of an informal-church thing, they called it a Ministry anyway but it was a popular house and there were always people visiting. 'Come Charles, I'll show you to your room,' she'd said first time. It was a dream place, it had an orangery and its own fucking ballroom I shit you not. Mind you, the ballroom was full of donated surplus clothing to be sent to poor kids in South America but that's a whole other story; as was them saying they prayed for me now and then. Maybe I should have been a Vicar I thought, it was all fucking free living as far as I could see. The man of the house, Sara's husband ended up being a skank in the end, I guess that could easily have been my route too.

Some jocks who Sara's step-daughters knew, one day were *'going for some "Easy's" Charles, did you and Ivan want in on the deal?'* Ivan shrugged his shoulders at me in that, 'if you're in, I'm in' kind of way and with that the jocks hit the road to score some Ecstasy.

On their return people soon peeled-off to their own regions of the house and Ivan and I, ecstasy virgins, popped our pills and sat waiting for something to happen, without any other company, any music or TV. The next thing I really remember is coming round on the sofa with him sucking on my mostly limp dick.

I wasn't outraged, in fact I didn't even object, I just propped myself up on my elbows and looked on as he became aware I was watching him whereupon he stopped, saying, 'I don't think that's a great idea no?' with no great shame or anything. He might have been trying to sew on a button really for all the thrill either of us got and the next day we would both skirt the elephant in the room - that he'd effectively sexually assaulted me. But I didn't really give a shit to be honest, not beyond a mild disappointment with him and humankind, that shit had all been normalised for me by then.

When you're a young gay guy you never really know who your friends are; more so if you don't look like you've been hit by a falling anvil or something. Almost all older gay guys will want to fuck you; many younger guys too; women will befriend you because you probably won't try and fuck them and so you'll wonder if that even counts as friendship at all. Other women will worry in case you, 'bum their boyfriends,' and the boyfriends will joke about that too. But some will genuinely come on to you, 'curious,' they might describe themselves as but I used to say *'I need my men very gay.'* The last thing I needed was some guy staving my head in with a rock thirty seconds after ejaculating because he couldn't handle being thought of as an arse bandit; shit like that happens all the time in the wider world.

On reflection I could perhaps have been more sore with Ivan for crossing that line, especially as I'd left London to get away from unrequited love but to be honest, by this point in my life it had happened so many times that it was no longer news. If anything I was surprised Ivan hadn't done it earlier but blaming the drugs was a handy get out clause and besides, I had wrecked his car; quid pro fucking quo huh.

Eleven.

One of my earliest memories, before she left home, was of my mum calling me into the kitchen from our scruffy yard outside, the Cliff Richard song, *'Congratulations'* was on the radio and for a few happy seconds she and I danced to the tune and shared a moment of pure joy. Another time she called me into the kitchen to put some rubbish into her newly acquired plastic swing-top bin, the height of domestic tech back then. I marvelled at the back and forth motion of the lid through the summer air, the lid was a light blue colour, the bin itself dark-blue. To this day I think of those moments as special and the only real recollection I have of any joy in my infancy; Cliff Richard and a fucking dustbin lid.

I also recall a less joyful trip to the dentist. I don't remember the actual treatment but I do remember waiting at the bus stop with a scarf around my mouth and some random old guy quizzing my mother about why I looked so sad. Maybe I was whimpering, and resultantly she drew me protectively near and told the man I had toothache and I looked up at her and I knew she loved me and would keep me safe.

Not that long afterwards she left home.

My folks never argued in front of us kids, if they had the parting might have been more understandable. 'Your mother is going away on a little holiday,' my father said as they sat each side of the kitchen table. On it was a red and white plastic tablecloth, a tear-shaped burgundy vinegar bottle, a chunky stainless salt and pepper set and assorted other domestic bric-a-brac. Above it on the high ceiling there was a clothes drying mechanism that came down on a rope when it was too miserable to dry stuff out in the Grimsby air.

My mother beckoned to me and drew me close, planting a kiss on my neck as I struggled to avoid it, 'Could I borrow your little green radio?' she asked. I had a transistor radio at the time, this was the hi-tech of its day and about the only thing apart from necessities that was actually mine, but sure she could borrow it. I just didn't understand why she seemed so sad; holidays were meant to be fun. I wasn't even old enough to formulate relevant questions and without any great ceremony she soon went and my impressionable little mind was left to figure out what was actually happening entirely on its own; eventually it would seem she wasn't coming back - and neither was my radio.

The conclusion I came to over time, my father being such a tight wad, and Eric the fishing skipper being a four-day millionaire whenever he appeared, was that mum had wanted a better life. It wasn't a conclusion I shared with others much but little in my life contradicted that idea and no-one ever discussed the details much again. It was always there, you know a periphery thing; the elephant locked outside of the room but an elephant none-the-less. By the time she died I genuinely thought I had loved my mother as much as any child could; albeit a child who had been effectively abandoned by their mother - indeed the elephant had always been there just shitting footballs on the lawn.

My father croaked first and I was chosen to give the eulogy, my mother attended the funeral, listening to me speak in glowing terms of him being my best friend, of manning the lifeboats of divorce and steering them calmly through choppy waters.

Mum didn't comment much other than to say it was a lovely funeral service and that I had done well. If ever there was an opportunity to tell me that the guy who did such a sterling job manning the divorce lifeboats was the same guy who had sunk the fucking ship in the first place, it was missed. But yeah, his funeral probably wasn't the right time or place; was there ever a right time and place for conversations like that?

On reflection over recent years I've concluded that she had somehow wanted us to respect our father and to protect us. It may have been that as I grew into adulthood any opportunity to address the issue calmly was missed. When I did eventually find out the truth it broke my heart and fucked with my head to the point of genuine insanity. The thought I had backed the wrong horse and could have loved my mother more; that she had possibly been slapped about and that she left home to save her own skin at the hands of my dick of a father, haunts me to this day.

I had practically built my entire persona around the foundation of being able to get over my mother leaving at age six and, nothing anyone could do to me would be as hard as that time. A time when being hit or duffed up was a daily thing; by my brothers at home and other kids at school. As an adult nothing anyone could threaten me with would be any more scary than what I'd already dealt with as a child; emotionally I mean.

So when that foundation was washed away overnight, suddenly my personality seemed in danger of total collapse, I went a little bit bonkers. It was like all the values, thoughts and ideas in my head were whisked up with a food mixer in some kind of experiment to see how much confusion one person could actually handle.

Getting help seemed paramount, fucking essential. Now and then I'd left my flat in Hackney hoping some pedestrian would bump into me so I could beat them up and just vent. I had never known anger like it, I was a boiling rage. I took street drugs to try and calm down.

At one point I sat in my car singing nursery rhymes to myself to stop me getting out and killing someone, anyone; voices in my head were telling me to do it.

'Go on, be a man. Get out; take the steering-lock and bash that guy's head in!' insisted the voice in my head as a pedestrian walked by; and it wasn't even my voice; this was a whole new head-fuck.

'Frere Jacques! Frere Jacques!' my real voice countered in the car.

'Kill the cunt!' the inner voice commanded, the insides of my head was like a twisted horror movie.

'Doremez-Vous!' I said louder 'Doremez-vous!' louder still, I was literally shaking, almost crying with fear. I knew this could actually fucking happen but I also knew obeying was wrong, very wrong; the torment inside my head was absolute. 'He's got kids,' I told myself out loud.

'You're fucking useless. If you kill him everyone will know your name!' said the other voice in my head, as clear as the radio

'Sonnez es Matines! Sonnez les matines!' I said in my real out loud voice - it was touch and go it really was but such is the nature of psychosis. Some part of my brain, the bit attached to my actual voice had decided to recite a French nursery rhyme but the other thoughts in my brain just couldn't be stopped by what remained of any of my rationale; it showed that there was very complex chemistry at play.

'Ding dang dong!' I said loudly.

'Do it Charlie, bash them!' in my head.

'Ding dang dong!' and then I started the rhyme again, I was really frightened.

I have to admit; I'd been 'experimenting' with my brain-chemistry, self-medicating as they call it. I'd been snorting ketamine and had smoked some skunk but that was everyday stuff, at a level of which I kind of needed just to do the washing up at this stage. But in some kind of misguided attempt to develop my incredible brain I had also necked some selenium supplements as well; something I had no previous experience of at all. I'd ordered them off of the internet having researched brain-power enhancement as I was coming to terms with the fact I was undoubtedly a world level genius and was curious about telepathy. Which if you think about it, kind of worked, it's just a shame my very first contact was with some kind of phantom serial killer. Oh, I also thought *I was very possibly part alien.* My doctor up to this point had been no help at all with my heightened mental fragility and just promised a referral to mental health services at some point.

With my inner psychological turmoil and actual chemical meddling it all made for a perfect storm. Never again would I dismiss the nature of psychosis as being something imagined or trivial – losing control of your own thoughts is terrifying; not being able to control, influence, argue with or shut up a different voice that's talking in your head is utterly fucking bizarre. In the car I'd thought I was never coming back even though I knew I was on drugs, I thought it was more to do with my mental health. I was so terrified I went to see the doctor the very next morning on an emergency appointment.

'But Charles,' he said patronisingly, he was a student doctor, 'I have sent the referral letter,' he continued, 'they will be in touch'.

This guy had 'mistakenly' asked how long I'd had my (non-existent) cancer diagnosis once. Although I caused a fuss writing in, I decided it was a student doctor thing; like how many times can they mention cancer in a day or something. Twat.

'I don't think you understand Doctor,' I replied, 'what if someone was worried they could kill people or like Jeffery Dahmer himself had come to ask for help and you hadn't acted on what he'd said, well, then where would you be?' He phoned me later the same afternoon and I was in front of a shrink for assessment the following day.

At the time I was pretty convinced I was being stalked by the global elite as, to a certain extent, I was honestly beginning to feel I had probably been put on the earth to prevent it from being destroyed as the Mayan Calender suggested, so I had to keep my wits about me. I never mentioned that bit to the Doctors though as I could never be certain who was on whose payroll. In fact I didn't explain about the stranger's voice in full either, I wanted help but I couldn't afford to be locked up. I had the world to protect.

When I eventually stopped taking drugs and was attending recovery groups, (something I never thought I would do) one of the phrases that stuck out, and there are fucking hundreds of them, was; *"we thought we could control mind-altering chemicals"* which was bit of a wake up call. I'd never thought about it before then really, but yeah, I was well into mind-changing chemicals – what a wanker I was to think that once altered I would know how to control mine.

When it was altered though I did have a tendency to fill it full of anything that served to validate my crazy ideas; it's like one side of my brain manufactured bullshit and the other side bought it. Ideas exacerbated by chemicals but who can say which ideas were chicken and which chemicals were the eggs. What I know now though, is that as I took less street drugs my mental health improved proportionately, but I had to find that out in the future. Back then I didn't believe the doctors, if they weren't gonna give me anything to calm my mind I would have to buy it on the streets.

Thanks to the internet when I thought I could have been fathered by aliens, my earth father being such a fake and all, I started looking looking around for the UFO my alien papa's spunk arrived on and, sure enough, someone had spotted something in the sky around the right time and place and reported it. Off my face it all made perfect sense and I did actually think that my paternal DNA must have been alien - and I'm still not totally convinced, years after I last used a drug, that I was entirely mistaken. I mean come on, the world didn't fucking end with the Mayan Calender after all did it?

So, yeah world, you're welcome!

Twelve.

I wish, as a child, someone had told me the point of education but from my perspective school was just somewhere my father warehoused us three boys, though at least I got proper food there. Had someone said in the early days that the teachers didn't have all the answers; that I could go on to learn stuff that actually interested me instead of shit like algebra I might have come out of my school days with better results. Exams seemed about memory to me and since my memory was shit for things that didn't interest me I knew I was screwed in the long run. In my final year I was awarded the school prize for mathematics, which was cool but it happened before the exam results arrived. Mine were bad, less than average but I was pleased the maths teacher could see my brilliance; I loved physics and it was the only subject I scored top marks in but that teacher was engaging and kind, it always helped.

At technical college where I went on to do my apprenticeship studies as a mechanic I would sail through a lot of the theory, it being basically physics on wheels, but I'd struggle with the practical. It was a tiered study thing over four years, the first three of which I aced with distinctions. For the final year's exams for membership to a professional institute I got the best marks in the country they'd said in a phone call arranging another prize giving - only to ring back a week later to say there had been *'a terrible mistake; you did very well in the theory subjects but it seems you weren't able to secure a practical credit?'* someone had said down the line.

'What does that mean?' I asked.

'You failed your practical. But you can resit it again next year.'

Screw that I thought, in much the same way I'd thought of parenthood when some girl I occasionally fucked had said she might be pregnant. She wasn't it turns out but while I reassured her I would be there for her no matter what, I was already wondering if the abortion section would actually be under A in the phone book. There was no way I was staying another year at that shit-hole garage.

I'd put the phone down to the guy from the motor institute and had to go tell my dad the prize giving was off, it was all a bollocks. He'd probably already told his colleagues we were off to the swanky hotel for chicken in a basket and an award ceremony but now it was all cancelled. But it was largely his fault; he'd got me the job I didn't want in an industry I didn't like for some wanker bosses I couldn't stand. I wanted to be a dancer.

It might have helped if I'd actually ever mentioned that to someone I suppose, but I'd never said a fucking word about it. Ever. It just seemed well, too gay come to think of it.

At career counselling, us kids had gone before a panel to chose our subjects for the last three years of schooling. It was like a thirty second farce. 'Why do you want to do drama?' one of the three had asked.

'I want to be an actor.' There I said it, I was so proud of myself, okay it wasn't a dancer but it was in the right direction.

'No, you should do French not drama; develop your vocal skills, that might help you more if you still feel that way when you grow up,' said the headmaster.

'erm, okay,' I struggled, 'bu--'

'--thank you. We have a lot of people to see.' And that was that.

The only other thing that was to interest me a bit later, after I had been to sea with my stepdad twice, was a career on ships; though more luxury-liners than trawlers and I really did love being at sea.

Amazingly, a space came up for our school, shithole that it was, for one pupil to go on a two-week, old-fashioned sailing-ship experience cruise. I was beside myself with excitement, I knew it would be life-changing to get some proper sailing instruction. I'd been on my first sea trip with Eric and the other kids at my school were more interested in tractors, guns and cow-shit, I got the boy's nomination.

They'd had to put it out to the girls as well, and there was only one place. Diane Hodder, who last I heard was printing photographs on tea mugs, was up against me, and it all came down to a coin toss. The same tutor who'd made me take French, a subject I hated and was totally shit at, flicked the coin. I lost.

I took it on the chin ostensibly and Diane went on to have a great time but I couldn't bare to hear too much about it; I was fucking crushed, it was so unfair. Eric was disappointed for me and said I could go to sea again with him in the same holidays, he was the skipper now, it was a great consolation prize. Or at least, it should have been.

*

My first time at sea with Eric, he was second-in-command, and well, you could see why he'd make skipper. Diligent, safe and hard working - but in charge, as the boss, he was a fucking tyrant. Not to me exactly, but to the crew.

Six miles out on this trip, technically international waters, Eric unlocked the 'Bond Locker', the store for duty-free liquor and, I think in an effort to bond with me, proceeded to try and drink the fucking lot.

The crew were given their allowances of course, and I was forbidden from having any, strict instructions from 'The Fuhrer'. But less than a day out at sea I knew he was going to be a total nightmare. And there was no way back.

I had never seen him, nor anyone, actually pissed before. My mother would openly discourage him from drinking too much at home and she wouldn't allow any whiskey at all in the house. Quite what happened when us kids weren't around I have no idea but on the ship he was a total twat and I soon understood the whiskey ban at home, that turned him from a twat into a right cunt, and a nasty one at that. Though to be fair not really to me.

Small in stature, late-developer that I was, I knew him unsheathing his fish-knife on day two and ordering the ship's mate Bill, up to the bridge with a nasty tirade through the window; 'Bill! Get up here now,' was setting up to be a bit challenging. 'What did you fucking call me?' he screamed at Bill as the door opened, Bill looked at me.

'You're scaring the boy,' said Bill calmly, the door was open but he stayed outside of the threshold.

'WHAT. DID. YOU. CALL. ME?' screamed my stepfather; the knife at his side all too evident.

'Nothing, I didn't call you anything, Now pull yourself together, you're scaring the boy.'

'WHAT! I'll fucking kill you if you say it to my face,' Eric's got a vein on his temple looking fit to burst.

Bill crossed the threshold, they have high steps to keep water out, his hand unlocking some press stud thing on the gutting-knife sheathed on his own belt.

'Stop it!' I screamed in my loudest pre-pubescent shriek and I rushed into the gap between them arms outstretched like crucified Jesus; not touching either of them but symbolically keeping them apart.

Bill turned on his heel and left, his boots clanking heavily.

'Fucken Prick,' says Eric as he went to his cabin; the helmsman had never said a word.

Some kind of uneasy truce developed on the ship for the next day or so as we steamed north to the deep water beyond the Orkney Islands; whoever was on watch would come up and do it fairly silently. Like everyone knew the guy in charge was a fucking psycho. He was slurring into the ship's radio to nearby friendly ships a lot of the time and I would spend as much time away from the bridge as I could. But going through some distant islands I was up there as he manoeuvred the ship through what seemed like a gap not much bigger than the ship. He was pissed and would doubtless have gone to jail had anything happened but he did make it look like a magical illusion, I don't know how we got through unscathed or even if we were allowed to go that way; maybe it was a just short cut to the fishing grounds, but the rocks had sure looked close. Given he'd already more or less threatened to kill the mate, no one said a word; they just let him get on with it. He could easily have killed us all. You'd think someone would mention it.

'There!' he said the following afternoon, thumping his hand down on the chart for my benefit; in his head he was no doubt bonding with his favourite step-son, 'That's where the fucking fish are!' he banged his pissed-up finger on the map again for effect.

In spite of a shit education and a lack of any navigation training, I kind of knew enough to suspect that a red skull and crossbones symbol on the chart probably didn't mean fish but that's where his finger stabbed.

'And I'm going to catch the bastards,' he added, 'that's where we're going,' and he barks some instruction like, 'ten degrees port,' or some such nautical cobblers to the man of the watch.

Luckily, weather wise it was dead calm, like the previous trip, a *'mill-pond'* he called it in a telegram back home. My mum sent back a reply 'caught any whales yet?' which no doubt cost like a million pounds to send in those days but while it was nice to get, it just made me long to be home.

The thing about ocean water is you have no real idea what lies beneath it. The net went in, we trawled around, instructions got shouted out and people followed their slurred orders. It was kind of embarrassing but nothing bad happened.

The net got hauled along behind the ship by massive metal cables, 'warps' as thick as a baby's wrist, held open by big door-wing things that acted against the current to open the mouth of the net. You'd stop the ship, start the winch, the cables closed the net and you'd haul the whole lot out of the water; easy peasy lemon squeasy. The doors would clank on the side of the ship then a crane would bring the net on board for the fish to be processed. A lot of fish and everyone is happy; the less fish, the less happy since the less everyone earns - and for the exact same amount of time at sea.

As we stopped moving to haul the net, the massive winch started winding the heavy steel warps in line by line onto the drum like a giant cotton bobbin; suddenly there's a warning screamed out; 'STOP WINDING! CABLE! CLEAR!. WATCH OUT CABLE!' and as one the men all twisted their backs towards the water in a rehearsed industrial ballet move. The end of the heavy cable slammed against the bulkhead wall with a crash, like the towel of a giant bully in the locker room. The winch stopped turning and a severed cable flaps to a halt on the deck like a dead rattlesnake. There are no doors, no floats, no net, no fish. Nothing. Just a severed cable; he's lost all the fucking fishing gear! Every bit of it - seemed I was right about the skull and crossbones thing, but I didn't think I should mention it..

'FUCK, FUCK, FUCK, FUCK, FUCKITY FUCK!' shouts Eric - but what else could he say, the fucking idiot. I felt I shouldn't really leave the bridge and go below as I was worried that the men might blame me somehow; that it was my fault. Another place not to fit in.

'Eric, come on Cap'n! You can't keep drinking like this,' I said when I could later, tentatively reaching out to hug him, which wasn't something we ever did.

'Yes,' he sort of shouts, 'that's it, hug me son!' it wasn't a pervy thing, we had finally bonded. His breath was like petrol.

They carried spare fishing nets and gear, clearly this happened now and then but perhaps worried about what the 'The Fuhrer' might say he did actually stop excessive drinking and we went on to catch tons of fish. Like tons. Thank fuck; it was a near record trip. His bosses just ate the gear loss and he didn't get fired since no-one grassed him up and I never mentioned a word to my mother. Eric never spoke of it again other than to say, in front of my mum, 'the lad gives good advice, we caught a lot of fish' and that was that. My suspicion was that he probably didn't remember the skull and crossbones bit and I wasn't likely to ever remind him.

You'd think that might put me off both the sea and alcohol really but it didn't, not a bit. The tall-ships experience I lost on the toss of a coin would have been more value career wise but in terms of educating a kid, the two trips with my stepdad taught me more about the real world than anything I picked up at school.

I had a real sense that I would like to try a career at sea; my father was a tutor in marine electronics and communications and had once also been a seafarer. Whilst I had found my voice at sea though and helped diffuse the knife fight I was still somewhat wary of my dad.

He was talking to my brother Seb one evening, oddly trying to talk him out of studying architecture at university, mostly I suspect because it would cost money. I wasn't following the conversation until it suddenly turned to me, 'I mean look at your brother' my dad said meaning me, I was all ears suddenly, 'he doesn't want a career at sea do you?' he asked. I could feel my face warming as it no doubt flushed up. Passive aggression was a real skill of his, we had never ever had a conversation where this had come up before and I suspect it was a tangential dig at my step-father.

'Well erm...' I was a bit flustered but managed to add, 'yes, I think I might.'

'Oh really?' he asked a little surprised that I had contradicted him. 'Oh, I didn't know that,' he said. But he wouldn't know because we never really spoke beyond common courtesies. I'm still a teenager back then but we would eventually become friends, I think in part because of his adeptness at passive aggression. As a kid, from toddler to school leaver, all I ever got was the impression that us *'kids'* were a pain in the arse and we were lucky he didn't sell us into slavery or abandon us; the sacrifices he'd made we were remained of often. So when I matured it seemed like I should make friends with him at least and we'd go to the pub together and shit; I felt it was the least I could do for all his great sacrifices.

The evening he'd asked me about the sea career though he'd come back into the kitchen as I was drying the dishes from the evening's burger and chips, Cinderella as I was then. 'I don't think the

Merchant Navy is a good idea,' he said, 'it's a contracting industry and going all containerised now,' and to a certain extent he was right, freight shipping was mostly containerised but the rest proved to be a bollocks in time, there's never been as many cruise liners. 'You should think about satellites,' he said as headed back to his cigars and newspapers, 'there's a *future in space* if you study hard enough,' and with that the conversation was over.

Perhaps in his mind, changing the engine oil of cars was a natural first-step on the way to the clean rooms of satellite construction as he got me an apprenticeship I didn't really want at the garage where he bought his vehicles. I think hoping I would at least mend his cars for him but it was dire, they taught me fuck all, like practically nothing except how to change oil, tyres and exhaust systems but it did allow me to go to technical college once a week which was an escape from the drudgery. To this day I can picture how a rear axle differential works in theory and I could even work out the maximum speed they could go round certain corners at one point - but it was all irrelevant to life. I wasn't even shown how to light an acetylene torch in four fucking years. But I didn't really want to do any of that dirty shit either so perhaps I have a part to play; I made my self useful selling petrol and polishing new cars. All around me were folk, mostly guys, fascinated by engines, football and titties on the calender; it was just another place I didn't feel I belonged. I can't even imagine how tortured life might be had I mentioned I really wanted to be a dancer.

I was really thick when it came to practical motor technology. At the Motor Show we were all being shown around some swanky new motor and this guy is like; 'and it has an onboard *computer* to regulate....' some bollocksy thing, fuel consumption I think but I was blown away by how they had hidden a fucking great computer system as I couldn't see a monitor, mouse or keyboard anywhere. And me the potential satellite genius? I had a lot to learn. I do consider those four years to have been the most wasteful of my entire life, even though it was to be my longest ever stretch of uninterrupted employment by other people.

Thirteen.

When we could actually get some occasional tins of beer, us village youths just got a bit tipsy; that's all there really was to do. Gina's mum let her have a room in the house where she had an informal youth club thing but the minute we were all allowed in the pubs, that was history.

I smashed three cars up before getting my actual licence. The first was when we were about thirteen, Clem and I got hold of this old banger car, a Ford Escort and his grandad let us drive it along the farm road. We did loads of times but Clem got out for a piss and, driving on my own for the first time, I rolled it over twice at about 15 miles an hour. I genuinely wasn't trying to show off but kind of panicked and went off the road. I thought I would die, in fact I walked out of the broken front windscreen like a ghost, astonished to be relatively unscathed.

'I'm alive!' I said to my chum and he got a phrase he would take the piss out of me with for the rest of our school time together. I had one tiny cut on my hand. But I daren't tell my dad what happened as I thought he'd be furious; he never even knew we had a car. I stayed in my room all night shaking and nursing what I now understand to be shock.

Another time Philster had passed his test and was sat beside me as I drove on learner-plates to the pub with Clem and two local girls in the back, Tina and Tracey - I think he was fingering them to be honest. They were all eighteen, me seventeen, still the youngest which was why I didn't yet have a full licence and why I'd been bullied so badly in school. After a couple of pints of shandy I'd screeched round one corner in a small village to see some old duffer drop his walking-stick on the crossing and run, literally run, out of the way. We all thought it was hysterical, we'd fucking cured him after all. We were kids, but it's no excuse. Sorry feller.

An hour later after another pub stop Clem had told me to slow down on one country bend that was a, 'bit iffy, go easy, it's reverse camber,' which I naturally took to mean, speed up. Narrowly missing a car coming our way we went in the opposite hedgerow a foot down or so and I creased the whole side of the motor, which although a banger to begin with, a red Viva, now wouldn't start; I was a shit mechanic - I had no clue what was wrong.

I quickly went to see if the other car was okay around the dodgy bend but they hadn't stopped, probably because they thought it was their fault and I think it kind of was. We pushed my car home, it took a good couple of hours but that part of the countryside is flat and with four pushing it was little more than just painfully boring. There were no mobile-phones and indeed, no non-adults to even call that could or even would help I didn't suppose. I would have to get the car and myself home so it made sense to insist we pushed it as we walked. But outside my house was a fucking cop car, no cop in it, which meant they were indoors with my Dad. My friends scarpered but the big mystery was why the police were there, we hadn't called them, and how did they find me?

The other car hadn't fucked off at all, it had skidded off the road and into the bottom of a ditch and was being recovered as we talked. The people were okay thank fuck, but I needed to give a statement. They had noted my number as we pushed the car away. This was my first ever personal interaction with the fuzz and to his credit my dad was good. He insisted I was a minor at seventeen and he had to be present for the interview. A bonus no doubt from his time as a volunteer Special Constable; my mother had jokingly said he just liked the uniform.

I answered all the questions – but the cop asked for names I wouldn't give, I said just friends, and he didn't actually breathalyse me. I might have passed anyway given the long push home but then he said, 'So tonight an offence has occurred which it is my duty to report to the Chief Constable who will decide if a summons needs to be issued. Do you understand?'

'Erm, yes,' I replied. The cop starts forming a 'Y' on the page.

'No,' chimes in my father, 'that is not his answer, his answer is, *'now that has been pointed out to me,'* and the cop scrubs out the Y and writes exactly what my dad had said. And that was another really significant part of my education. It clearly mattered what one said to the cops. The right words mattered. It was huge revelation to me, especially when I never heard another thing about the crash. Not from the cops, the other party, insurance companies or anything. And I attribute all of that to the right choice of words and well, there were no big computers in those days I suppose.

By this time I had shot up vertically and become one of the *'three strapping lads'* as my dad had taken to calling us and I already suspected he was a bit scared of me. He'd had this hurtful technique of a short-sharp flat-handed slap to the head if we got caught doing kid-mischief but in my mid-teens I'd broken some door glass and he went in for the head-slap. I stopped and looked at him, 'NO!' I said and he hesitated and didn't do it. From that point I guess I was top dog, I just didn't realise it at the time but I was never about to take him on. His years of manipulative language had me feeling grateful for his every breath. When I came to learn about him perhaps slapping my mother and abusing her verbally I found it hard to compute; but then he'd done it to us and we were just children. He may have manifested as a learned gent to the rest of the village but the truth was little cloudier - in spite of his tie and pocket fucking handkerchief.

To this day I have two really differing reactions to people trying to hit my head but Carl Gibbons may be as much to do with it as my father. If anyone does it, like goes to tap or slap me on the head, in fun or in anger, I go kind of berserk. Carl Gibbons was my brother's spectacle wearing mate who pinned my shoulders down with his knees and threatened, whilst slapping my face, to kill me with a punch between the eyes.

'Go on then, do it,' I'd said and well, he didn't, obviously. But if someone slapped my face a bit, as part of what one might call, 'slap and tickle,' then I'd find it very sexy. Eventually I made some kind of connection between my tendency to make passes at guys who wore glasses and this bullying in my life; crazily when I was getting bullied I suppose I felt I was at least getting some kind of attention.

On swimming trips with my two brothers and the butcher's son my party trick was to jump into the deep end of the pool when I couldn't even swim. I wanted to a part of the group, albeit by default, not splashing around in the shallow end while they were doing big-boys stuff. The thing is they kind of liked it too; it made them into heroes for saving me and they would all laugh about it for months. There's no doubt that without their interventions I could have drowned. I remember doing it in a pool at Butlins holiday camp and there were windows under the water so folk passing by could see the swimmers from a cafe. I doubt they're allowed now on account of pervs and phone cameras but then, as I sunk to the bottom, people were all pointing at me. Then they'd see me being scooped up by the butcher's son and me treading on my brother's head to try and get out of the pool. Great fun.

I suspect I might have been diagnosed with some kind of attention disorder had anyone bothered to worry about me back then but I think it was just a simple case of not getting any attention, rather than wanting more than any other child.

As a toddler I'd blown the house electrics once when I tried to stop the bullying from my brother Matthew; *'I'm going to burn you,'* I'd said as I grabbed the steel fire poker and put it in the electric fire. There was a bang and the room went dark, my father came rushing in. Luckily his first reaction was to bollock me, had he shown any loving concern I might have done it every wet Wednesday. Apparently, had I not been wearing slippers the current would have earthed through me and I would have almost certainly died; had I killed Matthew that day though, I think I would have been a much happier kid.

The third car I smashed up before passing my test was green; a colour that Eric said was unlucky; seafarers are notoriously superstitious and well, there it was, I had my proof. My car, a shit Chrysler Alpine went in the ditch because it was unlucky and I swore off ever driving another green one again. Clearly it was cursed.

Years later I was able to realise the colour probably had less to do with it going in the ditch than the fact I was three-quarters pissed. At the time Seb had passed it on his way to work next morning and had stopped to ensure I wasn't still in it. Opening the door he said, a beer-bottle had rolled out. I still never thought my drinking was unreasonable or a problem; I thought that hangovers, car wrecks and wet beds were just the price one paid for having a good time.

Another night, parking up at my dad's house, after being at the pub, I had raced past, done a screeching hand-break turn fifty or so yards away, bombed up, skidded to a halt, locked the car and gone to bed. At breakfast time my dad came and faffed about getting his coffee, I could tell he was preparing to say something. Then just as he was about to leave the kitchen with his drink he paused, 'If you ever drive home in that state again, I shall simply call the police,' and he left the room. I didn't query it, for he was right but that's the only time he ever mentioned my drinking directly.

The problem was, I suppose, that I had grown to be bigger than anyone else in my family, not fat, just big, hands like shovels, like my granddad apparently. And I was angry; angry that my mother had left, angry that my school had been crap, angry that people had bullied me, angry that my job was shit, angry that I was gay and angry that I couldn't be gay. Whilst I kept a lid on it most of the time, now and then the lid would blow off. And no-one knew what to do with me 'cos I could switch on them lightning fast; that I could now be frightening in my own right, well that was a buzz all of it's own. I don't feel I ever became a bully myself, some may disagree but my conscience is clear, well fairly clear anyway.

I do though wonder what might have happened had it been suggested to me when sober that drink was not my friend, that I was bad-drunk but if there were mentions of it, and I remember only two, they were theatrical in nature.

Once on my way into the village pub door early evening I had passed one of the wife-swap women in the hallway and made a polite point of letting her through. *'Oh thank you' she said; 'I don't think I've ever seen you sober before Charlie.'* Clearly it resonated with me for me to be able to remember it now, but later that night I did get pissed again.

Another time, years later at a thing called Gay London Professionals, which we informally referred to as Queers with Careers or Fruits In Suits, my friend Nigel and I would go along and pretend we were rich industrialists or some such shit. This guy though, having tried talking to me proper, says theatrically, *'Oh it's so sweet, you're a lush, I thought they had all died,'* and walked away amused. Nigel was a lush too; I was in good company really, depending on your point of view.

Fourteen.

Finding out the truth about my parents was the most traumatic experience of my life.

Coulda! Woulda! Shoulda! Could have loved my mum more. Would have loved to have challenged my father about being violent towards her. Should have asked more questions while I had the chance.

But this was the fountainhead of the anger which had me seething in my car that night, singing nursery rhymes to myself lest I hurt a random stranger.

A while after my mum had died I'd emailed the daughter of her chum who had married a GI and moved to the USA. The slow reply was very basic but I felt they had agonised about just what to reveal; the daughter wrote; *'Yes, your grandfather had advised your mum to leave your father for her own well-being as far as my mom knows.'*

At this point I pretty much knew that was in the post. During floods up north I figured an aunt could have been flooded and I knew my mum would have wanted me to offer help. Although she was entirely safe and dry, we did communicate for a while. She wouldn't commit to soiling my father's reputation directly but between the lines I got a feeling for my mother being the innocent party. I concluded that my mum wanted her children's relationship with their father to be kept intact. *'The kid's must never find out,'* I suspect was all it might have taken; but what else weren't they telling me; don't tell Charlie that's not his real dad maybe? Had dad kept us because I was his alien science project? Indeed thinking I was a sort of *Rosemary's Baby*; the off-spring of aliens and probably brought to life to save the world wasn't that big a leap; not whilst hallucinating anyway.

It actually grew to feel very real; a conspiracy that started to consume me and I genuinely thought mysterious dark forces were trying to kill or silence me quite often. When you can no longer even trust in the basics, the absurd can seem like a legitimate hiding place.

The evidence I had found for my being an alien though was utterly compelling but if you imagine some of it was grey wool and some of it was knitting needles I was able to knit enough fog to block out the sun.

My older brothers were both born into a castle in the Lake District, they have it on their birth certificates; I was born in a maternity home in Grimsby, a tired joke of the north and my parents had moved into a council house from this big castle in it's own grounds in one of the most beautiful areas in the country. It was one of my life's great puzzles; 'why were they born in a castle, a real fucking castle, and me into a council house in Grimsby'?

That Sebastian and Matthew were four and five years older than me would suggest that I was either a mistake or a, *'let's have another kid to save our marriage'* baby. It's entirely probable that I was conceived in the castle, the mathematics add up but by the time I was ready to figure it all out anyone with definitive answers was dead. To complicate the figures I was an early delivery, by as much as six weeks. I may well have been my parent's Christmas Day fuck but I popped out mid-August. In some ways it's galling to think I could have been the oldest in my school classes; to this day I am rarely late for appointments, once bitten twice shy.

Dad was a tutor at the castle as it was a training college and his speciality was marine communications; ship-to-shore radios, radar, depth-sounders and shit like that. On the lake he and the students could potter about in boats with their electronics. Giving that up and heading to Grimsby sounded utterly insane. That the castle was cold, damp and had rats were just facts that might get in the way of my hypothesis.

And certainly the idea that aliens could inseminate women on earth solved a few technical problems in my mind. Sperm, which could freeze for years, would much more easily make it through the depths of space and the Van Allen Belt than actual beings. Surely our alien overlords were behind the real space race and had been inseminating earthlings for centuries, the missing link as it were. That I might not have existed at all were contraception pills or abortion more available was another minor detail I refused to allow to cloud my assumptions.

As I saw it, my dad was working away in the castle on marine communications and it seems, was pretty much on top of his game and well, if there were unusual radio signals that needed some kind of boffin to interpret, one could pretty much expect him to isolate and interpret them.

Sure enough, in the ufology archives is an actual photograph of four UFO's that were in the north of England in just about the right sort of time frame. Time to allow for communication with the earthlings and time to find a host for some alien jizz; just over nine or so months before I was born; well a year, but close enough.

It was obvious the aliens had come down, landed in on or around the Lake District and my father had helped interpret their messages and they'd needed to find a host for some ET spunk. He had talked my mother into being the host, the new not-quite-Virgin-

Mother, for a new saviour destined to save the world. What other evidence could I find to support my glaringly obvious, theory; I was clearly the Second Coming of Christ!

Psychologists will readily tell us about a thing called confirmation bias, that someone with a conspiracy theory will go looking for any evidence to support that idea, largely discounting anything that might go contrary to it. Exploring hypotheses, however, is how the police solve crimes I'd tell myself, and of course if I was the spawn of Space Satan as it were, it stood to reason that my mother refused to have me baptised. So I wasn't Christened, highly unusual in those days.

Today, in sobriety, its easy to see that people might think me a bit bonkers. But that is largely the point here, I did go a bit chicken oriental. I had had the shock of my life; the hero father who had died my best friend proved, in realty, to have been no hero at all and was in fact revealed as a bit of a wife-beating twat. The mother who I thought had left my brothers and I to go to some swanky-lifestyle hadn't been living it up at all, but had been thrown out on her own in a, 'you'll get the house and the kids over my dead body,' kind of way and well, nothing made any sense to me any more. I felt utterly betrayed and finding some kind of fucked up explanation I could control, helped me come to terms with the sense of bereft anxiety that had started to consume me. Drugs helped of course, ostensibly I also had control over them, self-medicating they call it, but I didn't think for a second they might make things worse.

That there could be sensible explanations for stuff never concerned me. I don't think I wanted the mundane truth to be honest, there had to be a better explanation than just well, just life.

In the sixties for example, dad being offered a brand new council house to go and teach at a new technical college would have been a boring consideration for my sozzled brain. That the castle could have rats running in the wall cavities and be freezing cold in winter didn't hamper the picture perfect view of eternal sunshine I felt they were giving up. Getting away from the scene of the insemination crime on the instruction of the aliens was a much better plot; that they could be just fallible humans was so fucking pedestrian.

But it also seems entirely probable my father had fucked the 'aunt' who was supposed to have been my god-mother and that she had had to, 'return to Rhodesia for personal reasons,' passed me by at the time. I was here to save the world and what, with the end of the Mayan calendar on the horizon, I didn't have much time. And with each passing day, I went further and further down that rabbit hole.

Fifteen.

Drugs can be like a visit to the fairground, they promise all the excitement and fun of the fair; the waltzer, the roller-coaster and the dodgems all rolled into one! In the end though, it's like being trapped on a shitty ghost-train that you simply can't get off even if you wanted to. And that's in spite of people reaching out to snatch your hand as you go round again, again and again.

Nobody ever wants to be trapped on the ride; no-one really wants to be a drug addict; genuinely happy people don't take drugs, why would they? Societies biggest misconception about narcotic abuse is that drugs are the problem. Drugs are not the problem, drugs are the symptom of a problem; they provide a synthetic state the brain registers as happiness. Even when the user is slumped in a shop doorway covered in their own shit with abscesses the size of saucers on their legs, they think they are the lucky ones.

With me being in some sort of denial about my sexuality in my teens, alcohol had provided the social lubricant I needed to navigate my adolescence. A period that whilst a challenging time for most humans, I found excruciating. I knew that people had sex, that I wanted sex but I also knew that I didn't come across anyone of my kind with whom sex might be possible; I spent the entire period from having my actual bollocks drop until I had passed twenty-one longing for sex with a man and not even having the remotest clue as to how to go about getting it. Lucky really; if internet dating had been around at the same time as early AIDS, I'd almost certainly have died but lucky is the last thing I felt back then.

Drinking was pretty much all there was for the young adult me to do and it did help me handle friendships with some guys who I felt would instantly dump me as a friend if they knew the truth. Whilst perhaps innocent fun times to them, I would be tearing myself apart wondering if and when I should breach the subject of my fancying them. Falling head over heels in lust for unavailable guys time and time again; coping with that crippling sense of difference and loneliness in the only way I knew how; exhibiting increasingly toxic-masculinity amplified by necking all forms of liquor.

Looking back, I think the biggest tragedy was that I never gave myself the opportunity to see what I was like as an adult once I actually was one. For many decades there was hardly a day when intoxicants couldn't have be found at quantity in my bloodstream. So, in substance abstinence programs any talk of 'recovery' would just seem alien to me. There was no sober adult state I could ever recover too, it would all be discovery, if it happened at all.

Boarding a massive ferry to come back from a quick boozy trip to Denmark in the winter for example, me and other village locals all lined up a bit tipsy to have our passports checked, when an officer from the ship came along the line and picked me out.

'Here he is,' he shouted back over his shoulder, 'You! Follow me,' commandingly to me, no niceties at all as he marched towards the gangplank of the ship. I looked at the others, shrugged and sheepishly followed; I'd been bollocked enough in my life to sense there was one coming. But I didn't know what for. It could be nothing, or anything - and I had to get home; easy Tiger.

I was ushered up the gangplank to the bloke checking passports, he checked mine, looked at my face and handed it back - the officer's hand darted out and took the passport.

'I am holding onto this Sir. If we have any trouble with you, there is any damage caused or any complaints about you or your party and I will hand you, and your passport over to the police when we dock,' he wasn't kidding this guy but I had no real idea what any complaint against me was. I vaguely remembered chucking a Christmas tree overboard and a tray full of champagne glasses. Hypocrite moi? Littering the ocean. Shame on me.

'Do I make myself clear?' he asked.

'But, you can't do that, it's my passport,' I said at the same sort of volume as one might expect of a kid's talking doll. I was taken completely unawares and had no stock of bravado to call upon; I sincerely doubted anyone from the staff really knew about the tree or the glasses; some passengers had probably grassed me up.

'What is all this about?' I asked, my voice finding a little bit more strength.

'It's not something we are prepared to negotiate Sir. If you want passage on this vessel, those are the terms, or you can fetch your luggage and find another way home. We leave in forty minutes.'

'What the fuc-'

' --I AM deadly serious sir, please make your decision now,' he said looking at his watch. And with that I was bound to reign it in a bit. Fun with consequences. I still didn't think I had a drinking problem.

Six months previously a manager from a works training college had phoned my boss at the garage I worked at and suggested he consider my dismissal; I stood at his desk like a squaddie at some kind of court martial, he went on to describe over the phone how I had filled the lift with furniture at the hotel and sent it down to the lobby, before grossly insulting the hotel owner, an apparently 'charming lady with whom they had enjoyed the most perfect of business relationships.' I thought it was funny and imagined my boss laughing at the other end. He wasn't. At break on the course the other guys filled me in on some of the missing details, I'd said that she, 'ought to get Rentokil to chase the wasp out of your fanny,' that while some of what I did was funny, I had, 'probably gone a bit far,' they thought, boring fuckers.

I didn't get fired but when I got back my boss told me to,'take that fucking grin off your face or you can leave right away,' I wish I had got fired to be honest, it was a shit job and any real on-the-job training was practically non-existent. But I didn't know in those early days that you could actually tell bosses to fuck off and walk out; I thought my main job was to keep my job and even a shit one as a grease monkey, was something to value. I apologised and said it wouldn't happen again. It didn't because they never trusted me enough to send me away again. I can see, looking back, that it was all about me feeling I had to prove my masculinity to whomever cared to be taking notes. How could I be fucking gay after all, if I was such a geezer?

Oh yeah, on that trip I'd gone and bought my first ever gay porno mag; there was only about eight shitty black and white pictures in the whole thing and it cost like five hours wages. You couldn't open it before buying it, the exciting looking cover was covered in cellophane. It was very disappointing; I hid it under the spare wheel of my car and chucked it away before I went home.

I didn't like football, I couldn't play football, I didn't really understand, or want to understand, football. But when I didn't make the selection for the village squad I was pissed enough to start my own fucking team. I got sponsorship for the kit from Norman at the pub so our team looked quite fabulous. And I got to see a couple of guys I liked run around in shorts while I managed the whole team from the touch line. Stats were recorded in the local press and showed that we were possibly the worst team in living history being regularly thrashed by ten, twelve or fifteen goals. The thing is, I didn't really give a shit about results, genuinely hardly at all. It was all about taking part, being included and connected to other human beings and for 90 minutes each weekend I would shout from the white lines, pretending I was a part of the actual sporting world. Afterwards we'd go get pissed at Norman's pub; the team just wanted a run around and a piss up after; they knew we were never gonna win anything; there wasn't exactly a surplus of decent players in the area.

I didn't fancy women, didn't know how to talk to them and I certainly didn't understand their plumbing, or want to understand it, no offence, just not for me. After a couple of tries with girlfriends had led nowhere other than frustration it did though seem entirely sensible to try get on a straight romance show called *Blind Date* when their audition carousel came to town.

I'd had some limited gay experiences by this time and was no longer in any doubt about my preferences but there I was mid-twenties still feeling an overwhelming need to somehow prove my masculinity. In applying to be on the show though I set off a chain of events that led to me moving to London, looking at some potential jail-time and it got someone else, indirectly, some very real jail-time.

The researcher for the show was as camp as a row of pink tents; so much so that when he phoned our house to confirm my booking and my father answered the phone he, my father, exhibited the only thing close to homophobia I ever saw from him. He didn't know it was the TV guy calling and must have thought it was some kind of gay-poof breaking all kinds of protocols to call me at home.

'Why does he have to talk like a bloody girl?' my dad had said as I went back in the room - and he hardly ever swore. Phones were always in the hallway in those days; very few homes had more than one receiver.

'I've been asked to go and try out for the show dad. That was the fella from Blind Date, I've been selected for the proper auditions!' I said excitedly.

'Oh, he was from the TV was he?' asked my dad, a lil' bit thrown that he'd got it so wrong. 'How does he get a job like that with a voice like his?' honestly, I couldn't make this shit up. I was buzzing, I was gonna be on the telly. With Cilla Fucking Black. I was gonna be famous. Maybe.

There were only four terrestrial TV stations back then. If you were on prime time TV a lot of people were going to be tuning in. Just quite how many was not something a guy from a tiny village could easily compute but I'd been about a bit by then. I'd lived a while in Germany, spent some time selling timeshare in Tenerife and had my first working spell in the USA, selling second hand flash cars near Palm Beach, (where I'd run out of petrol in the Rolls Royce). And yeah, I knew I liked cock but once I started the audition process nothing ever gave me pause to roll back on the idea. In those days there was no Twitter or Facebook to be outed as homo on and anyway, I wouldn't have really cared at that point if they did. The TV show was the star catapult of its day and I even figured being photographed going into a gay bar or something could be a career opportunity; in fact it even occurred to me to set it up. Such a scandal would have made the front of the rabid homophobic national press back then; the auditions were already front page news in the local press back home, it really was that small a town. No gay bars to even be photographed going into up there, gays though did have other ways of meeting each other.

Sixteen.

I had discovered the practice they called *cottaging*, frequenting public lavatories to meet sexual partners, quite by accident. There was a weekly gay night in a regular bar in the distant cathedral city of Lincoln. I had lingered outside maybe six weeks in a row, too scared to go in, this being a few years before the TV audition at the very start of my gay career.

I would park up and try to spot people going to the gay bar; the papers were full of AIDS stories; the gay bar in Grimsby had been burnt down, there was barely any gay porn anywhere. The age of consent was unequal and, I genuinely didn't know a single other gay person at all at the time. The only other gay people I had ever seen up until then were in a holiday brochure showing, 'a cosmopolitan gay bar in Mykonos'. I used to look at it longingly and often used it, and my mother's mail order catalogue, to fantasise; well, wank really. The thing was, the gays all looked fairly normal in the holiday brochure but if I couldn't find the courage to go into the gay bar in Lincoln, how would I ever get it together to go to one in fucking Greece?

I'd lost my male on male touch virginity, not my bumhole virginity (that was to the bodyguard and foreign prince on the ship later) to a cute young guy about the same age as me in Canada; even there I had sat scared in a rental car outside the gay bars I'd researched, but in the daytime I had seen this guy in the street (he looked rather like my brother's bullying mate, Carl) and sort of followed him knowingly. The fumble was all over embarrassingly quickly, in spite of us both walking miles out of the way in this bizarre gay courting ritual I now know to be called *cruising* but I was happy that I had found something I pretty much wanted to do for the rest of my life.

But I was still terribly hung up about it. My father would say years later, '*you were never the same when you came back from Canada,*' and he was right. But learning physically that I was actually gay wasn't the only education of the trip; my first overseas trip solo. I had quickly spent way too much of my budget on my first night's hotel so I called another small hotel advertised in the phone book. I walked in confidently in spite of also spunking way too much dosh on a cab to get there, 'Oh hello, I have a reservation,' I said to the guy behind the counter whose skin had the colour of old chewing-gum. I went to the room, satisfied myself it was bearable, reminding myself it was cheap and, it being around lunchtime, went off to explore Toronto and find some cheap food and something to drink; I didn't get wasted but I was certainly a bit tipsy when I got back.

There was a connecting-door to the next room and, though I had a bolt on my side, it seemed that one of the neighbouring voices could burst through and attack me at any second. There were two of them at least and for a while after I climbed into bed I lay there terrified they would realise I could hear them and come and stab me. Like happens in the movies.

The sound effects were quite unlike any I had heard before; some guy clearing his throat then spitting; a grunt of borderline-disgust, the sound of a hand slapping flesh and a female affirming encouragement. It was terribly confusing I couldn't tell if she hated it or loved it and I nearly shat myself in fear, pulling the bed covers up over my mouth almost too frightened to breathe. Clearly they were having some sort of sex; the noises she made suggested she agreed with being slapped a bit but not at all of being spat on. I wasn't even sure that that's what I was hearing, the idea of grown adults doing that so close I could hear them was freaky and scary. I was morbidly fascinated but way too frightened to move, *'if you do that again, I'm done,'* the woman's voice says. Surely if they knew I could hear they would want to kill me just to spare their embarrassment, it was kinda gross.

The sound of spitting again. A slap, squeal, bang and footsteps. This was it, they were definitely coming to stab me. The woman's voice had had enough; *'I'm serious, I'm fucking leaving!'* she said and like a break in the fog where the blue sky peeps through, it all suddenly made sense. She was a prostitute, he was a punter and this was the sort of hotel clients might book for a night but leave after an hour to return to their families. No wonder the man at the desk had smirked a bit. The sex-worker left and his TV sprang to life, annoying though it was, it was a relief as it covered the sound of my breathing and I knew for a fact I couldn't stay there another freaking night. Which is when I found the hotel I lost my gay fumble virginity in.

*

Back near the gay bar in Lincoln where I lingered there was a telephone kiosk behind a toilet block. It never even occurred to me to go in the toilet but, and this is the truth, I thought it might be an idea to leave a note, like a lonely heart ad, in the fucking telephone box. So I did, saying if you want to meet a young guy for sex, same time next week, to leave an X in the dirt of the phone box window. And when I went back two days later, just to see and there was an actual X on the stained window I was very, very excited. This was as near to a fucking Tinder app as it got back then.

The guy that I met at the phone box the following Saturday was okay; no great stunner but I'd have fucked with his grandfather's corpse by that stage to be honest and he did promise to take me into the gay pub the week after. But not before he asked why I didn't just go into *the cottage* to hook up and had left a note to meet, exciting though that was? I thought the cottage might be a fast food place or something, 'What's the cottage?' I asked.

'You know the toilets near the phone box,' he answered solving the mystery why some people did seem to go in there rather often. I can be dumb as a rock sometimes.

*

By the time Blind Date came along I had progressed from my first tentative steps in the gay pub to Nottingham's once-a-month gay super-club and also found the joys of furtive masturbation and hasty penis touching in various isolated toilet blocks. Like the buzz some might get from sky-diving, they were adrenaline charged liaisons but really they were the only fucking liaisons possible. Meanwhile I also fucked with the two guys from the bar I found the most attractive and another six or seven that I found the least offensive. But yeah, the velvet gloves were off. I was out. Well, half-out yeah, just. And obviously going on a straight TV dating show *made perfect sense*; what could possibly go wrong?

The night of the TV show recording was the first ever night I'd stayed over in London and I got fucked by a Royal Marine up against a tree in St James's Park. He might have embroidered pillows for all I knew but, to me, he was a Royal Marine as he'd put his hand over my mouth to quell any sound I made – like soldiers killing people in the forest in the movies do. It was the most exciting moment of my life up until that point and I knew then and there that I would move to London. And he didn't kill me obviously but I think the old scaredy-cat Charlie probably did die in that park. The show would be broadcast a couple of months later apparently.

It had never occurred to me to live in London before. It was the sort of place you visited for the day and maybe you went to an afternoon theatre show and for a posh tea after, or dinner as they called it there. I'd done exactly that a few times but we always went home on the last train. No-one could afford to live in fucking cities I had proved that on my trip to Toronto. That common people actually lived there and could get fucked in the park by soldiers was too much of a trip to ignore.

I was unemployed at the time of the show recording as having discovered sex, like man sex, I had lost all interest in a career. I figured that when I couldn't get laid any more I would pick that particular thread of my life up again. And when Cilla, the host of the dating show had said, 'you haven't gorra job at the moment have you pet?' I'd replied, 'No Cilla, I'm waiting for something suitably glamorous to come along.'

I moved to London between the recording and it going out a couple of months later, finding a room in Leytonstone via the gay press on the trip; gay bars no longer scared me and finding in London they had free gay newspapers with classified ads was a bonus.
The subject of a deposit had come up with my potential new landlord – who had a shop and a family he had told me. The room wasn't brilliant but it was a foothold in the city, I was up for moving down as soon as possible.

'But if you don't have the deposit, we can work something out?' he'd said as a question looking down at his middle-aged groin. He was wearing light brown pants but where his legs rubbed together near his balls there were little brown fabric bobbles, like bits of poop stuck on arse hairs; it was a very unattractive proposition.

'No, I have the money, I'll bring you cash when I come down,' I said quickly and this marked progress, not just sucking any old scabber off - my self-esteem was improving but still a work in progress.

Having a wife and kids obviously didn't stop him taking advantage of young gay guys but I had to ask anyway? 'Why do you advertise in the gay papers?' I enquired when the awkwardness had passed; he didn't actually touch me or anything by the way, his cash query was the limit of it.

'Oh they are much better tenants,' he replied, 'they don't steal electricity, don't leave a mess and usually pay on time' the bit he left out was *'and I get some of them to suck my cock in lieu of rent'* but from my perspective he was otherwise always a nice guy, I ended up helping him fix some windows in his shop and he was always polite; he taught me to rescue my ailing rubber plant with a drink of milk. Not a euphemism.

On my first trawler trip when Eric my stepdad had been mate I'm pretty sure his boss, the skipper, had had a wank behind my young self while he 'warmed his hands' in my waistband as he ostensibly explained the charts to me at the table. I didn't know at the time what was going on but, as an adult looking back, 'yeah, you stand there and let me warm my hand, yes, you just stand there and point out the big ships,' was a bit fucking suss. He had never touched my willy though either, Eric would have killed him I think; I'm pretty sure he was scared of Eric.

And my baby-sitter Gillian had got me to strip and show her my privates in a ritual that seemed extraordinarily cool to my seven year-old self and she had shown me her girly area; I guess she was maybe fifteen. It wasn't sexual to me whatsoever, just really naughty and I never ever told a soul. Again there was no touching involved either way but I've often wondered since why people are so fucking pervy and lame.

Before the dating show aired I had moved down to the attic room in Leytonstone. I had a white Nissan panel van and parking in the streets wasn't an issue back then so it was a pretty straightforward move and this was five or six years before I would move to California to hang with Ivan. I soon settled into life in outer London. It was fucking miles out of London as far as I was concerned since by the time I finished in the bars the only option was a slow night bus home and I would usually fall asleep 'cos I was pissed. One of the night-bus drivers got so fed up with the palaver of finding me asleep at the bus station that he would stop the bus at my stop and come and wake me up; he said it was easier that way. And still my intoxications seemed of little relevance; I didn't think I had a problem

But in the meantime Blind Date was to air and I was pretty sure I could arrange to get some publicity, perhaps notoriety, after it aired. I was hungry for money and fame and well, all the stars we aligning.

The night the show went out though any thoughts of fame went right out of the window. I was riding the tube into town later and people were noticeably pointing, smiling and laughing; not maliciously, just out of recognition. Like LOTS of people, like what seemed like the whole fricking carriage; the next day too. It was busy and people were picking up on the vibe from each other; with only four TV channels it seemed like everyone knew who I was and wanted to catch my eye. It was fucking excruciating. If this was fame they could keep it. I knew instantly why famous people wear sunglasses; catch anyone's eye and they'd want a piece of you, it was dreadful. There was no way I was putting my cunning fame plan into action; had smartphones been around I'd probably have been trending on socials before I even got into town but it would all die down pretty soon, I was fairly sure of that.

Seventeen.

'The police have been on the phone and need to speak with you,' my Dad said, very business like and matter of fact, it was about a week after the TV show had aired, 'they said an allegation of a very serious nature has been made against you?' Holy fuck!

'Like what?' I asked, shocked - but the nature of my then quiet life meant it could really be only one particular avenue of misdeed if it was genuine; *cottaging*. It's the only thing I had ever done so far that was iffy. I hadn't even done that first tab of acid at this stage and I didn't shop-lift; it had to be something to do with the bogs. But the allegation was of a, *'very serious nature,'* I was racking my brains for memories and I certainly hadn't raped anyone; I had no real skeletons in my closet but what if they had CCTV of my knob sliding through a glory hole?

'Don't worry Dad, I haven't done anything wrong,' I said convincingly, 'I'll call the fella tomorrow and sort it out, probably just someone seeing me on telly wanted to get in the papers or something I'm sure,' we ended the call. He had a good habit of not asking difficult questions or going too ape-shit when dealing with me as an adult but the only way to calm my anxiety was to have a bottle of wine. I'd filled a new wine rack when I'd moved in in some kind of vain attempt to seem sophisticated should visitors call. I went to the shop and got some wine, I was keeping magazines in the always empty wine rack.

Shaking, I called the detective the next day, turns out the, *'very serious nature,'* was indeed about cottaging. 'A complaint has been made against you of gross indecency,' he started, 'having assaulted the complainant in the Market Street toilets you made your escape in a white Nissan van, licence plate..blah blah blah!' my head was spinning, like, what the actual; *escape?* It could have been any one of many toilet fumbles but I'd never run away. It had never occurred to me that the adrenaline buzz of police apprehension could follow you home from cottaging but this buzz made me nauseous and not at all horny.

The policeman continued down the phone finishing his next line with that sort of upward inflection that would create a question, 'And he is only seventeen?' a pause. The words cut like a knife. 'Which would make him a minor and unable to consent,' he paused again, almost a question. Trial by telephone.

The age of male-consent then was twenty-one, not that one ever asked for ID if someone stuck their cock through the partition wall. I didn't know who he meant. I had observed a few cocks through the wall of the toilet and well, any favours were usually reciprocated but you couldn't even see their faces if their junk blocked the hole, much less check their passports for a fucking date of birth. The toilet block was in a car park; people would sit in their vehicles waiting to see who went in rather than hang around waving their cocks at passers by taking a piss. It wasn't as offensive to the general public as it sounds, none of us were stupid or careless. Well, usually.

Prior to this I'd actually been dating a seventeen year old guy from the Lincoln gay bar for few weeks and he was still at fucking school, albeit in the Upper-Sixth Form just prior to going to uni but he and his mum made me very welcome at weekends and she'd had him cook me mussels as *'the way to a man's heart is through his stomach'*. I'd stayed over a couple of times and took breakfast with him and his mum. No one in that equation thought anything was wrong but than with the law, one I was peripherally involved in changing years later but Douglas, the guy I was seeing then, had even given me a Monopoly 'Get Out Of Jail Free' card to carry in my wallet as a joke. Now with a cop on the phone and a technically underage witness making allegations it was possible I might even need it and I sure wasn't laughing any more.

'Do you have anything to say to that allegation?' the copper asked down the line; it went through my mind to apologise and own up to cottaging or something but I didn't; I remembered the lesson my dad had given me in finding the right words for the police.

'Well, I'll be happy to try and help with your enquiries but I have absolutely no idea what you are talking about,' I'd said and I kind of didn't.

'Can you come in and make a statement?' asked the cop, two-hundred miles away.

'No, I live in London now but you can come here and I'll give you one, not that I'll have much comment to make.' I said my mind racing.

'Okay, we'll be in touch' replied the cop. But he never actually was, and for another two years I never heard another thing about it. That's not to say I didn't think about it; it went round and round my head for weeks and months afterwards, the anxiety it induced numbed by drinking; it could have been anyone. I imagined myself in an identity parade of penises having to stick my knob through a police curtain so some stranger could point at it.

The story my head had told me had happened back then still seems entirely plausible today; Blind Date comes on the telly and the young guy concerned would be watching it with his folks; he would say something like; *'I don't know what he's doing on there, he's gay!'* 'What, how do you know that?' his mum would ask, her hand going to her mouth.

'Yes, how do you know that?' the father would inquire, more pointedly leaning forward in his chair.

'Because, I'm gay! I sucked his cock in the market toilets,' before jumping out of his chair, running upstairs and slamming his door.

'You come down here this instant,' the father would holler up in his toxic-masculine way and eventually the mother would go, perch on his bed and coax some kind of story out of him, probably modifying the bit where he stuck his own cock through the toilet wall. The father would then have called the police.

Two years later, visiting my own family back up north, a local updated me on the gay scandal that had rocked the gay community. The toilet teenager had kept a diary full of details of his sexual dalliances; loose-descriptions, dates, AND lots of car-numbers and his folks had called the police when they had found his list after my TV appearance. They had then got three convictions with one guy even going to fucking prison for six months on the back of it all. It's worth adding here that offences back then that are now legal, consensual stuff, were all pardoned by the law changes earlier this century, Alan Turing providing the impetus. But that doesn't negate that lives were ruined just 'cos I went on the telly. Had he been a girl, no one would have given a shit; weird huh? Mind you I'm not sure how they'd do oral through a wall but you know what I mean.

Just a few more things to unpack when I came to look at reasons for my drinking or taking drugs.

A few years after my experiment with TV fame and having moved from Leytonstone through the Brixton, lost-keys-flat, I was living in Mayfair where laughingly, I also had two small art galleries. One should have been called *Smoke* and the other *Mirrors* but there I was anyway and I was watching a Gay Pride March pass by with a few pissed up friends having hosted a *'Mayfair Pride Party – admission by Champagne only'* at mine and Nigel's flat. The galleries didn't last long, they were boring as fuck anyway but there on Piccadilly outside our flat some familiar camp guy points at me and heads my way, pushing through the crowd of thronging marchers.

'YOU!?' he says, 'Are you ---?' his hand was gesticulating around at the crowd and the look of incredulity suggested he meant, 'are you gay?' I was wearing a t-shirt with Barbara Cartland on it at the time, surrounded by queers. It was only the fricking researcher guy from Blind Date, the one whose gay voice my Dad had objected to over the phone.

In a couple of minutes, before he rushed off to rejoin his friends in bewildered surprise, he vomited out that the police had called the TV show after I had been on, asking for my details, making *vague sexual allegations*, he'd said.

*Not without a warran*t he'd replied (bless him) but they couldn't really say what it was about though they had asked if he thought I was gay. Not on your life he'd said, and yet there I was on a fucking gay pride march. Would you Adam & Eve it? I guess that's why the cops didn't follow up on me and my name and fame didn't get dragged into the cottaging arrests.

It was a funny fucking time I tell you. Funny peculiar, not funny ha ha. Very roller-coaster.

Eighteen.

Dad had died when I was in California doing the Ivan thing and I'd had to return to the UK after only a year in the US but it had got tiring being borderline-illegal anyway so I was soon able to re-establish myself back in London, helped by a modest inheritance, whereupon I soon discovered clubbing.

Ecstasy was all over the news and the driving force behind the rave movement; slowly rave was venturing into legal spaces having been driven off of farms and warehouses by draconian new laws. I soon made some new London pals and discovered why the new party drugs were so popular - dance. Prior to this time I'd just thought of nightclubs as places to pick up guys and have sex in the toilets, so to go and not give a fuck about fucking, to just dance for dancing's sake, and to be able to dance without a partner was a whole new world and that careless joy I had felt as a child effervesced into something quite wonderful.

Each week we would leave the club in Clerkenwell claiming we'd had the best night of our lives. And it seemed to be true, they were awesome times; with just a pill and by filling a water bottle in the toilets anyone could have an awesome, cheapish night out, get a bit wasted, dance like a twat and not, oh joy of joys, piss the bed.

Juan, one of the group I hung out with at the time, used to take two spare shirts to the club with him he'd get so sweaty from dancing and he summed up what we all perhaps wondered about now and then, 'If I'm careful,' he said, 'I can do this for the rest of my fucking life,' he meant drugs and dancing of course. It was the early days of ecstasy though and they were a bit pricey and snide; yeah you could have an awesome wonderful night but you'd pay for it over the next few days with an iffy comedown. The highs though at this stage were well worth the lows.

There was always a queue to get into the club; a queue to hang up coats, one for the bog, another for the bar and then three, literally the longest of them all; one for ecstasy, one for cocaine and one for acid - they may as well have had checkouts and a loyalty scheme, it was as subtle as barbed wire at a nursery.

One of the drug dealers Big Neil, used to turn up at the club in a beautiful classic Jaguar E-type, park it on a yellow line outside and swig Dom Perignon champagne from the bottle. I last saw him across the visitors room in Pentonville as I visited an unconnected friend but it was easy to think the good times would never end. He'd waved across the room at the prison.

Acid at the time was a third of the price of ecstasy and one tab would last me from 10pm 'til 6am in the morning; the entire club night so it seemed like a no-brainer to me. Thanks to having Dad's legacy money I wasn't bothering with work again but I wasn't stupid either, I needed to pace my spending to get the most out of it, 'if I was careful, I could do this for my entire life.' As long as I necked the acid about 10pm it would just about have worn off enough to drive home by kick out time. I did get home once in the morning only to notice I'd driven the entire way with the boot hatchback open but at least I wasn't pissed or even full of bed-wetting liquids either, so it was largely win win.

Up north after my father's funeral I had gone for a haircut in some random salon and well, she fucked it up really. I just said she should shave the lot off and, after checking I really wanted that, she did.

That simple action sort of changed my life; I'd never had a skinhead before and it did give me a rather thuggish brutal look. As I left the shop in a mild-mannered part of Lincoln, a woman with a kid in a buggy noticeably crossed the street. Markedly so, to avoid me. It was a nice feeling oddly enough. Back in London on the club scene my new credentials proved helpful.

It must have looked like I was tough and knew what I was doing but I was all smoke and mirrors. Because I hate queuing I would chat the staff up to avoid having to do the stand in line thing. Within a few weeks I didn't have to queue much any more. One bouncer Martin would wave me in and eventually used to roll me coke-spliffs to smoke the minute I arrived; all FOC. The blond coat-check girl Bez would put me on her guest list, helpful in case Martin was away; the drug minders would wave me round the back to get served from the dealers without having to queue; the DJ's would gift me mix-tapes, and the cleaner would give me lil' packets of stuff he'd find around the place all because I was nice to them and would ask how they were. I invited the cleaner to a house party once the kudos of which kept me in found drugs for months. Because of the 'tough' way I looked, and that I seemed to know everybody, people were adding two plus two and coming up with five; I seemed to know people; I'd just come back from LA and, seemingly I had a bit of money, (dad's) well, that all suggested I was some kind of player. Naturally I did nothing to dampen their imagination; I didn't ever tell anyone anything tough guy or lie but sometimes it's what you don't say that fuels their curiosity. In fact often when they asked what I was up to nowadays I'd just say, 'nothing much,' or my favourite,'same old shit,' and let their heads fill in the blanks. So well, it was only a matter of time until someone wanted to recruit me into the drug business; one of the peripheral dealers who went to the club on his nights off, he did house to house deliveries and wanted to meet up.

A moustachioed Freddy Mercury type, Pete talked a good game, there was nothing he wasn't going to do money-wise but the way he was so open with me so quickly suggested his days might be numbered. Before he died in police custody a couple of years later I agreed I would act as his driver; I wasn't touching the drugs though, the bags they were in or any of the money, those were my conditions of employment, no fingerprints. Thus I could see a get out clause if the shit hit the fan, I would be an illegal cab driver at worst; though it might have meant a bit of paperwork there was no way I would get into that much trouble, if I was careful.

'DDD! Daily Drug Delivery,' is how Pete would answer the phone with a giggle and to be fair it was kind of easy money for him and me; well, until he died. Waiting outside while he dropped off coke to the rich fuckers of Shepherd's Bush was easy enough. Five nights a week meant I could earn as much as a road digger for mostly listening to music for three hours a night and I'd always get a bonus of something green to smoke. It was risqué fun to be honest but one night I had to drive him so he could pick up what looked like a bin-bag of fucking pills; I didn't ask. I wasn't happy but I was already committed by then. Another night he went and literally dug up some grass patch near Barnet to find some marijuana he'd buried. My cab driver defence wouldn't hold up to much scrutiny those times I didn't suppose.

So what had started out as largely a blag became some kind of reality; with the driving I was actually involved in the drug business I supposed. I'd arrange after-parties at various peoples flats and houses and Pete would serve up drugs and give me commission, mostly in drugs - fun times. But then ketamine arrived.

When Pete turned up at a chill-out at my place with this new letter of the alphabet, K, in white powder form we were all intrigued. And it wasn't illegal; at least not in the class A or B sense. But it was fucking expensive, like two and half times the cost of coke in those days. Bear in mind, most people hadn't even heard of it yet so Pete would put out pin-head sized bumps to get potential customers interested, but it was like fucking rocket fuel even in those tiny portions.

I loved it, fucking loved it! It gave me a trip not unlike that of acid but one that was over within about a half-hour, certainly within the hour which was so much more manageable. The first time, a tiny bump was more than enough for anyone. Some squaddie guy punched my wall and started hyper ventilating; 'You. Could. Start. Fucking. Wars. With. This. Shit!' he exclaimed before someone shook their keys at him like a kiddies-rattle and he calmed him down a bit. A match-head sized bump did that. Pete wasn't the only dealer with it at first but I took much my income from him in that white powder. The idea it wasn't yet illegal, in fact perhaps the first of the legal highs, just added to the dubious notion that everything would be fine, and it soon got cheaper. A quarter the price of coke eventually.

Stopped alone on some random occasion and searched by the police I was once arrested when they found my ketamine since they thought it was cocaine. I told them they were wasting their time but they had never even heard of ketamine at that point. I spent another night in the cells but not before they had tried strip searching me; so I milked it, 'So which one of you homophobic cunts wants to shine a torch up my shitty gay arse then?' I'd asked before bending double and spreading my arse cheeks. None of them came near me, they just told me to put my clothes back on. In my sock was a few grams of hashish they hadn't seen so I was smug buzzing. I knew I couldn't get done for the K and had swerved an actual possession offence with my ass theatre. When I went back to the station on bail the cop behind the desk said there would be no further action as the drugs hadn't tested for illegal substances. 'Yeah, I tried to tell 'em that,' I said cheekily, 'So where's my drugs then? Can I have 'em back?' I asked.

'Well erm, they'll still be at the lab I suppose,' says the cop thinking I'm serious. At this point I'm heading to the door but paused.

'Okay, well can you have someone bike them round please?' and with that I'm gone. Obviously they didn't bike them round but it was a fun moment.

Driving Pete around, I was always legal, even a light out was a no-go for me. I'd heard so many tales of people moving buckets of drugs with no insurance and they would end up in jail wondering what went wrong; I wasn't yet on police radar but I was getting a bit paranoid anyway. I was always running through scenarios of how I would say I was just the driver and then imagining Pete dropping me in it on interview so he could get off with a caution.

When he went away for a bank holiday, Pete left me in charge and I was to take over his round 'just for the weekend' answering the phone, dropping shit off, collecting money. As he left I realised how naive and stupid I was being and this was getting me deeper into dealing by stealth. Although in my head I was just an unlicensed cabbie I figured if ever the cops wanted to make a case against me they could. Pete leaving his stash at my place was actually all the excuse I needed. I hid it in a roof cavity but I could fucking smell the speed as I watched cop shows on telly, fully expecting the windows to come in with Swat teams and the SAS any second. Maybe I shouldn't have started eating my way through the sheet of acid so quickly, it sure didn't help.

I didn't answer his stupid drug phone, I didn't touch or deliver any of his fucking drugs or even unwrap or look at them. Well, apart from the acid; I ate 54 tabs over the whole long weekend but I didn't touch his powders as I knew I'd sort of have to pay for what I took. Acid being comparatively cheap it should have been a low cost weekend indoors; I'd have probably had a better experience taking just six tabs over three days, but as they say in drug recovery circles, *'one is too many, a thousand never enough,'* I even struggle to sleep if there's chocolate in the house - never mind acid.

I decided that weekend, in spite of my acid haze, that I had to knock the delivery driving on the head. It was all very well to earn the cost of a couple of grams but if I had eight years jail time under the passenger seat it wasn't really easy money. And clearly I couldn't allow myself to be used as a storage locker; I'd fucking eat everything and paranoia is hardly lessened by consuming more acid. I spent hours without much sleep watching Cops on TV. Talk about a masochist; I didn't know if the sirens were on my telly or in my street, if the cops were talking into a camera or directly to me. But I did kind of like it, I kind of knew what I was doing, as much as anyone on 54 tabs of acid might, and I sort of knew I needed to shock myself out of the situation I had gotten myself into.

When Pete came back, I gave him some of the money I owed and told him to fuck off, that he had a cheek asking me to do his fucking dealing for him and leaving drugs at my place. He did fuck off. I think he must have seen I was borderline psychotic by this point; it probably made little sense to argue with me, I suspect my eyes looked like black saucers.

The official story about him dying in custody some time later was that he'd got busted and, to stop his stash from being found, he'd eaten it in the back of the van, overdosed and died. It was about the time a copper's daughter had recently died from a dodgy pill and, whilst unprovable, we all speculated that were we bent coppers, we'd probably have force fed him his drugs in the back of the police van too.

After the driving job I went to do security at a *straight brothel* in Cricklewood. It was reasonable money for minimal effort but again I'd never really stopped to think it through either; I guess I liked people to see me as some kind of gangster; it certainly beat being a petrol pump attendant for a living.

It was also borderline legal/justifiable at the brothel in that prostitution isn't illegal per se and as long as there was only one working girl at the house, the maid (receptionist, usually an old ex-sex worker) and security (me), we were just the girl's subcontractors. However, there was some wannabe gangster behind it all; after we had both been paid, half the money left went to the house and half to the girl. Which sounds unfair but the house and working girl would regularly clear ten or more times what I got each day.

I was hired because they knew I wouldn't want to screw any of the girls and was laughingly seen as some kind of tough guy by now. The girls didn't appear to have been trafficked or anything; these were very sophisticated attractive women who knew how to make quick money. They left with thick wads of cash every day and that's why they came back, pure and simple. All I had to do was look at the CCTV to check who was coming up the drive and listen to make sure all was going okay. The girls didn't interest me but some of the guy customers who turned up I would have bent over for for free; it amazed me that fit young guys were having to pay for fanny sex. But it was easier for them than the peacock shit at the clubs I suppose. The thing about gay guys being promiscuous is largely bullshit by the way, it's just that both parties are men.

Work there meant I could sit watching the real TV with one eye, the CCTV with the other and smoke spliff all night long before dropping the girl and maid at the station and the house dosh off at the wannabe gangster's place who, by the way, never once invited me past the hallway.

At the brothel the doorbell would ring and the maid would show guys, most often just middle-aged, obviously-married men, into the sitting-room where she would go back to her TV or Word-search and they would wait nervously. I would watch the punters arrive and wait from hidden cameras but there were no cameras in the bedroom; whatever massage happened was private.

Sounds of sex; bed springs squeaking, the headboard banging, the mattress pounding as vocal sex affirming noises would permeate the house. Then a silent pause. Then footsteps, a tap-running, a toilet-flushing, a door-closing, feet on the stairs, the front-door would open and close. A figure would disappear into the distance on my CCTV screen and then after a few minutes and another toilet flush I'd hear the maid say to the next nervous client, *'You can go up now,'* and the sequence would start again. Sometimes there would be two guys waiting. I just didn't get that at all, it was pretty repugnant; sloppy seconds and all.

The money was always handed over before the men went up and brought through to me. The maid and I would speak loudly so the punters knew there was someone else in the house and in the few months I did the work, there was only one minor incident.

There'd been some raised voices, a door slammed and my name was called by the girl. I went to the bottom of the stairs and this bearded guy, naked but for a light blue turban and a condom the same colour on his drooping cock stared down as if he'd seen a ghost and stopped his shouting.

'What is it?' I asked up the stairs.

'He wants to take off condom, I said no,' said the girl from the bedroom.

'Get your clothes on and fuck off mate, you know the rules!' I said firmly up the stairs.

'Who do you think you're talking to?' he says, trying to sound assertive in spite of his nakedness, turban and and limp blue dick.

'You, you cunt!' I say raising my voice but staying at the foot of the stairs. 'Now look, you made me raise my voice in front of the ladies. C'mon, don't piss me off,' I added calmly.

'You don't know who I am, I can have men here in no time!' he said reaching hastily for his clothes which the girl has thrown from the room before slamming the door.

'Well, I'm here 'til eleven tonight mate,' thinking, yeah, don't bullshit a bullshitter but he does soon fuck off without any more posturing and the next guy eventually goes up for his turn without a word. It's a weird fucking world.

Sat back in the kitchen watching the CCTV I realised just how easy it could all go wrong. I'd already reconciled that fact that security wise I was all fur coat and no-knickers. There is no way if anyone wanted our takings that I would even remotely try to stop them. Actually they could have it all if they pressed the bell and just asked for it as far as I was concerned though nobody knew that; to this day they all probably think I was quite tough. Like I would risk a hair on my head for some cunt who didn't even invite me beyond his vestibule.

I am a bit of a coward at the end of the day, I could barely even deal with the fact I was gay without being inebriated and here I was manifesting as some fucking tough guy security guard. What a joke! I knocked it on the head a week or so after turban guy. They were held up at gunpoint three weeks later.

Nineteen.

I had some brilliant ideas on drugs. A lot of people claim that their drug of choice 'unlocks their creativity.' No matter how brilliant the idea though, most of them go nowhere when the drugs wear off because people just forget and have written nothing legible down.

Filling up my car with petrol one evening on my way back from scoring some K, and consequently a lil' wasted on it, I looked at a fire extinguisher on a trolley and had a Eureka Moment good enough to change the world. It was fairly simple; generic rechargeable batteries for electric cars. Drivers would be able to drive into fuel stations and, like buying Calor Gas for a caravan, could swap an empty battery for a fully charged one. People could pull in and attendants would open the bonnet and like a F1 pit stop, swap their batteries.

In the time it took me to pay for my fossil fuel I imagined there being streets named after me, perhaps even a bank holiday. Single handedly it would cure humankind of its dependence on oil. Electricity could be generated by fitting gearboxes on the top of heavy pontoons in tidal range estuaries, itself another brilliant idea. While I got my change, stood alongside a glass fridge I wondered why they didn't run seawater through massive greenhouses to irrigate the desert with the evaporated run off. I loved ketamine though I shouldn't really have been driving on it.

I played around with the idea for a while but a couple of days later, I knew I had neither the drive nor any funding to make it happen; besides I had to save my brilliant mind for the next great idea – like raised mezzanine lanes for bicycles; something that sort of actually happened - I had no choice really, I had to gift the generic battery idea to the nation.

I wrote a letter to the Prime Minister and a load of other parties who could make it happen; motor manufacturers, professional bodies of engineering and electronics, even the motor institute that I had failed the final exams for. Thinking it would make a for a good scene in the film they would no doubt make of my life I then decided to deliver the letter to Downing Street personally so put on a suit and tie and snorted some more ketamine. They wouldn't let me in looking like a twat I didn't suppose but I didn't actually expect to get shown in for tea and cakes, I just wanted to make sure my letter got some attention and sent on to the right people. I imagined telling the tale about the letter on the forthcoming TV chat shows I'd no doubt have to go on.

When you've been taking K for a while your bladder starts to weaken and you need to piss a lot; like 30 or 40 times a day when it gets bad. And it does get bad, no one is immune if they cane it so suffice to say when I got to the gates of Downing Street I needed a piss and figured I'd best have one in case they did show me in for tea and cakes to talk about my knighthood; I had my suit on at least.

'Hello Officer,' I said at the gate to this cop done up like a commando and carrying a big fuck-off machine gun. He seemed slightly aggrieved that he had to even talk to a pleb like me much less move to the gate, 'I need to see the Prime Minister,' I said, the cock of his head suggested he might have a right one here.

'What for?' he asks.

'I have an idea of national importance that will cure our

dependence on oil.'

'Oh really?' he asks, 'and what is this great idea?'

'I'm sorry Officer I can't tell you, this just needs to go to the science boffins so they can make it happen,' I say coolly adding, 'no offence,' as I suspect he's just taken some. I wondered if this was a good policing gig or if guarding VIP's was where they sent all the cunt cops to punish them. I guessed the latter.

'And who else knows about this great idea?' asks the cop, 'who else have you told?' - I had actually placed the idea on a fairly obscure website that not many people used simply to date stamp it so I could prove my conception. The cop's question showed me I was right to think ahead like that. Clearly I was an inch away from being *'disappeared'* so MI5 could take the fucking credit and stop the Russians getting it.

'The Intellectual Property rights have been logged online,' I said; it sounded like the right thing to say but clearly the cop was only a junior cog, he would have to take advice he'd said.

'I'll tell you what officer,' I said 'I need to go for a wee, you speak to your OIC and I'll come back in about fifteen minutes and we can work out how we shall proceed' OIC, meant Officer in Charge, it always helped to drop in a bit of lingo with these sorts; he needed to see he wasn't dealing with just any old twat.

'I have the idea right here in my pocket; I shall see you shortly,' I said and with that I went to find the nearest toilet opposite the massive Ferris wheel thing; I was half expecting to be jumped by the real James Bondy types and have the letter stolen but nothing happened - apart from me weeing out less than a thimble full of piss.

In the bog I saw I had the tell-tale hint of a Polo Mint around my right nostril; an occupational hazard of snorting lots of ketamine but I figured it was unlikely the cop would have seen it. I went back to the urinal and tried to squeeze out some more urine but my bladder wasn't having it. As I got back to Downing Street I soon felt the urge to pee again.

The cop came straight back over; 'You're not getting in to see the Prime Minister,' he said but I suspected he might like to see me try. I could imagine him as a waiter and if anyone ever complained actually trying the food only to say, 'it seems fine,' to him. I wasn't expecting to get let in after all but I did think it would make for an amusing anecdote in the magazine interviews where I would soon be featured.

'No matter Officer, then would you see he gets this please?' and with what I hoped was a flourish, pulled the envelope from my jacket and handed it through the gate.

'And how should they contact you?' he asked.

'It's all in there Officer, it's all in there' I said decorously then like a twat added, 'remember tonight Officer for you too are now a part of history.'

Why he didn't just flip the gun safety catch off and cut me in half with a hail of bullets I just don't know but that's exactly what I said.

I went home and posted the other thirty or so letters to various industrialists; the vacuum cleaner guy, the wind-up-radio fella and institutions and such like; the idea was out now; like a genie it had to be released for the magic to happen. Obviously it would take a week or two even but soon enough the phone would start ringing – and I presumed never stop.

But that isn't what happened at all.

Nothing happened, the phone didn't ring, no letters arrived, well just one; from the then Prince Charles. No one else wrote even to say I was a moron and to fuck off. That was the oddest thing of all, why didn't they even say thanks but no thanks? I didn't get it.

I was certain the security services were into my computer after my Downing Street visit. There were little barely discernible clues, like it needed to update itself twice in two days and it seemed slower; more clunky. I'm not computer illiterate, I was VERY suspicious, the drugs probably didn't help, but what do you do?

I created a new file and named it 'Dear Spooks' leaving it centre-screen on my desktop: 'I know you're here which is a little rude. I will happily answer any questions you have if you leave them here. My browsing history will clearly show you the site where the concept is lodged. Feel free to have a look around, if I knew what you were looking for I could tell you where to find it. My porn is all in the file labelled Porn; my conscience is clear; there's nothing illegal, the directory has been copied' it said. The directory hadn't been copied, I didn't even know what that meant but it sounded like I did.

Next morning when I logged on I was certain the Dear Spooks folder had moved but I suppose I was getting a bit paranoid. For sure the drugs had a lot to answer for in that department. As each day went on and the mail didn't bring news of my knighthood I was also getting a bit depressed. Prince Charles's flunky hadn't really understood that letter and I was pro-forma replied; patently by the tone of the reply Charles was not even made aware of my idea, that wasn't always to be the case but I didn't copy The Queen in on this one; it wasn't really her department but the royals always replied; it was shame government ministers didn't have such good manners.

'Her Majesty' said one reply on her behalf, one of many, 'was participially interested to learn of your idea for Neighbour Day' which was my idea for a new Bank Holiday where the notion was for neighbours to interact over barbecues, jerk-chicken, prawn vol-auvents or whatever and barriers would be broken down and social cohesion might occur. Towns and counties could do it, Yorkshire and Lincolnshire for example, nations too; Scotland and England and eventually North and South Korea and so on. It was a blinding idea. *'But I must tell you,'* the letter continued, *'Her Majesty has no constitutional authority to involve herself with such matters and I must say you did the right thing in writing directly to the Prime Minister'* whose aides had just sent another wank-off pro-forma reply.

The lack of any response about the car thing was getting depressing, Christmas was starting to rear its ugly head and the whole 'where was I going for the festive holidays' question was becoming a thing. Sat alone one night at my computer an advertising image of a cruise-ship came onto my feed. Just imagine I thought, high, that ship is crossing an ocean right now full of sophisticated people sipping glamorous cocktails and here am I stuck in fucking Hackney; I should go on another cruise.

In another of those, this is the best idea ever, kind of ways I thought that if I were on a ship, miles away from the K-dealer, I could cure myself of my K-addiction. Simple. Cheaper than fucking rehab too I should coco.

The next morning when I opened my eyes I did so with a knot in my stomach; oh no, did I really? Yeah, juggling credit cards, I had booked a ninety day round-the-fucking-world cruise! It wasn't the first time I'd bought stuff on the internet but this was bonkers. Short of feigning my own death though I couldn't see there was an easy way out of it and to be fair it was about a third of the cost of a 90 day rehab - besides I'd need to be drug free if I was gonna be famous. I decided if the payments were processed I'd try and get on the fucking boat, besides, what could possibly go wrong?

Twenty.

To board the ship I needed some vaccinations and the paperwork proving as such. I didn't really believe I was going on the cruise, I felt at some point the phone would go and a voice would tell me there had been a terrible mistake with my booking but I made the appointment to see the practice nurse anyway. Nothing had yet come of my brilliant idea so I figured they would fly someone out to reach the ship if I needed to sign patent releases or film an interview or something. Or maybe they would send a spy to throw me over the side so government scientists could take all the credit. I also thought it'd be a quite a good way to top myself; take a look at the world before slipping into oblivion, jumping and let my nieces claim the insurance money. Insurance was compulsory for boarding, more expense but I was fairly sure that by the time I got back I'd somehow be on the way to being a zillionaire and able to pay my credit-cards off. Or no living Charlie - no credit card bill.

It had been a particularly challenging year or so. Shawn, the ex with whom I maintained a hectic friendship had thankfully lost his job as a new-teacher which took some of the pressure off. *'I can't teach on K,'* he'd said one night in front of a few of us.

'What, you actually tried?' I'd asked and from that point there was a conflict within me every day I knew he was supposed looking after young kids. Luckily he got cautioned for possession one night and lost his job; sorry Shawn, I was glad. He was also wasting away in front of my eyes; working like crazy to fully qualify so his father would finally be proud of him – and he was as thin as a rake and I figured, almost certainly on heroin. I wasn't - just ketamine more or less.

Turns out he was on the skag and also he had AIDS. Like actual AIDS, this at a time when only about ten people a year were getting it in the UK thanks to game-changing drugs.

He'd had a brown patch thing in his mouth growing away and wouldn't see the doctor. I took a photo and showed it to the pharmacist; 'He needs to see a doctor. And soon!' is all they would say. I shoved him in the car and took him to emergency dental the same night. After tests they said it was Kaposi's Sarcoma – something that did used to kill HIV patients but they could now treat. He was okay within about two weeks but it taken a couple of months to get him to the clinic.

I was also processing the information about my mother being cheated out of my love, my civil-partnership was falling apart, some knob was texting me regular death-threats, and another ex, Dennis, and his new twat-boyfriend were being real cunts too. Regardless of all the rights and wrongs it was a really challenging time; so I took more drugs. The cruise ship had seemed like the best crazy idea I'd had for a long time, but first the jabs.

The vaccination nurse had the tourniquet and the needle all set but she'd have to go get the vaccines from a secure cabinet. Of course in my overly active imagination that meant she could be fetching the RFID injectable chip so they could track me where ever I went in the world. I'd spent enough time on the internet with my conspiracy theories to know that it was just a matter of time before we all had one so I was wondering if the injection would hurt when I saw she had left my notes open on the screen and I sneaked a look.

'We have been contacted by the FTAC... please contact patient to arrange assessment--' it said under my name.
The nurse's return made me avert my gaze quickly like when a partner

comes back in the room when you've been reading their phone or something, I imagine!

'Sorry about that, here it is,' she had a lil' bottle of poisoney looking stuff and shaking it starts to fill the needle. I knew I had seen something unusual on her screen and I know I probably wasn't supposed to have seen it but what did acronym FTAC even mean I wondered? I tried to mentally tattoo the initials on to the inner workings of my fragmented mind. No mean feat when seconds before I was expecting to be poisoned to death or have a microchip injected and there's the sharp scratch and, well, it wasn't poison, obviously, not instant anyway.

At home I entered the initials straight into Google and well, I then I had something to really be paranoid about, fuck!

'The Fixated Threat Assessment Centre (FTAC) is a joint police/mental health unit set up in October 2006 by the Home Office, the Department of Health and Metropolitan Police Service to assess and manage the risk to politicians, members of the British Royal Family, and other public figures from obsessive individuals.' Oh great! So that was one reason for a lack of reply, they thought I wanted to either shoot or suck off the Prime Minster rather than gift my generic battery idea to the nation. Terrific.

But then I *had* written to Queen Elizabeth a few times previously, and Charles, oh and even a supportive letter to Camilla too at the time she was being vilified; and Tony Blair of course, oh and Cherie Blair and oh fuck, yeah William and Harry too. I went to the concert the boys did for Diana; actually only 'cos I got tickets hoping to make a quick profit and then couldn't fucking sell them. It was mostly crap to be honest but I did like bits of it, so wrote and told them they should be very proud of themselves; I'm such a creep. I'd sort of lost a mother too but what I did like and supported was that they had done it; they hadn't just talked about it, they had arranged it, booked it and pulled that off. Kind of easier when you have a fucking crown on your bonce but that wasn't their fault. The reply sent on the Princes's behalf said thanks, they were touched by my letter. Fuck; I must've looked like a total fucking suck-up nut-job to the FTAC. And there was me just trying to save the world from using oil.

I figured no one really looked at the content of my battery letter to the PM, just the method of its delivery. And they thought I was mad!

Oh and telling my doctor he could be dealing with a Jeffrey Dahmer type serial killer not long previously probably didn't help this situation much. Talk about shooting yourself in the foot; I could be locked up by fucking tea-time.

I mean, I was slightly unhinged I'll give 'em that but I do know this much; if I was a doctor and a patient came to me and said something along the line of maybe being a serial killer and the cops had written to see if he was a danger to the PM or Queen I think I might suggest a home visit to make sure there weren't corpses in barrels of acid in the nut-job's house. No-one ever checked.

Twenty-one.

I used Ketamine on the train to join the ship but didn't actually board with any drugs; it all made sense really, even though we were actually calling into some iffy countries narcotic wise I was too much of a coward to try and smuggle drugs or get involved in the international trade. Okay sure, you could be in a helicopter and own a speedboat one day but that same afternoon you could be banged up and bartering blow jobs for left over peas and that was no way to live; I don't really like peas.

Besides I was sort of done with drugs all together now or would be after the cruise and clean of this ketamine shit I could get on with my life. Ninety days at sea would see me right I felt sure of it; most rehabs were either a month or six weeks, with this I'd be well sorted, save money and see the world. Winning!

Every morning when I woke up at home a mantra would sound in my brain like an early morning alarm call for ketamine; 'you know you're gonna get some, so you may as well just get on with it!' Every. Single. Fucking. Day. And for a number of years; it was tiresome but in a way almost an old friend, and it was sort of a full-time job. I had been vaguely coming to terms with the idea that I might be a drug user for the rest of my life if I didn't deal with it; the cruise trip was a brilliant idea, quite why I hadn't done it before I didn't know.

By the time I boarded the ship I was pissing thirty or more times a day, my short-term memory was fucked to the point I was pretty certain I had early onset Alzheimer's, I was prone to bursts of volcanic anger and the inside of my right nostril felt like I'd be inhaling scouring powder. A perfect dining companion. Okay, I was processing my parents deceits; my civil-partnership disintegrating and the eBay business I'd started was boring me to death, but it was the health aspects, the bladder, memory and nose thing that scared me the most; the rest I could work out. This was it, I would get clean and in three months everything would be, well, fine I guessed.

Shortly after the ship set off, after the novelty of sail-away has passed it was dinner time; etiquette wise you don't wear dinner suits first night out but I was presentable and smart. One doesn't get a second chance to make a good first impression and after all, some of the people in the best cabins would have paid a fucking fortune for their trip. I was down near the propellers - and the poo-poo processing units I supposed - but I did have a small porthole window.

I had to sit with people I'd never met before and hold my own without them getting any hint of the nasty person I could occasionally be but of course I had no drugs so it would all get easier as my body and mind detoxed itself. Getting angry with other adults was no way for a sophisticated world traveller like myself to behave.

The lady next to me had a beautiful big sapphire ring. I'd selected a table of ten again so as to meet new people, like I had on the trip with pub Norman. We were all singles, or Solo's as the ship called us; it is a great way to meet people, the same table each night.

'And to drink Sir?' the waiter asked as he finished taking my order. I'd been on ships before I knew how it worked, of course I'd have some wine. As long as I didn't overdo it I'd be fine, besides I was in sophisticated company, I could hold my own, the nutjobs and users I'd left in Hackney.

The first couple of nights on the ship were getting to know you dinners really and there's no doubt that as a social lubricant a glass of red wine does go well with red meats. And then we'd make our way to the piano bar, my swanky new friends and I. I knew I'd be fine, I'd been heard to say in the loony bin that *'my biggest problem is I'm surrounded by cunts'* and now, there I was in the ship's elegant dining rooms and cocktail lounges, with my cultured peer group. The person I ended up closest to, Pamela, Pam, I remained friends with for many years, she was an OAP, in her eighties but she had a infectious smile and was great fun; she drove around on one of those disability scooters; I called it her electric chair, she loved that. But she also went to bed quite early so missed most of my shenanigans.

From the cocktail lounge we would go down to the disco, I say us; there'd be five or six from the table, me usually the youngest but it soon became clear that the staff wanted us to fuck off to bed as soon as possible, they would turn the volume down and start upturning chairs onto tables in that sort of passive aggressive go to fucking bed kind of way; I wasn't impressed.

'Listen, don't start clearing up while we're still dancing' I said discreetly adding, 'don't make us uncomfortable, we've paid tens of thousands of pounds to be here, how dare you?' and a bit louder later, 'can you fetch your supervisor please?' You can guess the rest, I was cool though – ish.

In the first few days the routine of me getting merry at dinner, tipsy over cocktails and challenging in the disco became well established. Usually everyone else was tipsy by disco time too so my fellow passengers were quite forgiving and agreed it was insulting to be tidied up around but they would never think to complain I didn't suppose.

This 'Cruise Director' guy all in his white uniform with gold braid shit on it comes over one lunchtime; 'Oh Sir Charles,' he says all smarmy like 'the Captain would like to meet with you this afternoon,' and he gives me this note with like some room details on it and a time.

'Oh,' says Pamela, the old dear in the electric chair, 'you've been selected for the Captain's table Charles, how exciting,' and she meant it too, bless her. But as you know this wasn't the first time I'd been drinking on a ship; previously I'd had my passport confiscated on that ferry crossing the North Sea, I kind of knew what this appointment was likely to be about. I laughed as the gold braid on ice-cream outfit disappeared.

'Oh, I doubt it Pamela, He might ask me to walk the plank though,' and she threw back her head and laughed. It was good to have allies and the others, like her, were patently loaded - only really seeing 'merry Charles' through their own tipsy eyes; maybe they thought I was sound as they'd be on the dance floor having fun while I was bollocking the staff.

I went to the meeting with the Capitan radiating a strong an air of, *yeah don't you dare fuck with me* as I could; self-assured, (apparently) and polite. And prepared to apologise if I need to. Like posh kids from Eton always do when they smash stuff up. Our meeting was in like a lil' office thing near the Bridge, I knocked and ice-cream suit guy lets me in and goes behind a desk with the other two. The Captain and someone who is introduced as the Passenger Relations Director; all three in formal ice-cream jackets sat, like magistrates actually. 'Sit down,' one of them suggests.

'Oh, sorry, erm this looks rather like a court martial from here?' I say injecting what I feel is the right amount of surprise and humour into my voice as I sit down. 'Have I done something wrong? Do I need a lawyer or a witness?' Big smile; radiating innocence.

'This is a calm-ship,' says the captain without preamble, his Scandinavian lilt reassuringly calm, 'We run a calm-ship, we have no trouble. It is a warm-ship, a friendly-ship. I hope you understand.'

'Message received and understood Captain,' and I actually

fucking salute; I probably looked like Benny Hill or some other clown. 'You will have no trouble from me Sir'.

He silently jutted his head forward imperceptibly, as if to say he needs a bit more and says nothing, pause.

'Oh erm, you will have no *more* trouble from me Captain,' I say. He smiles, it's enough, ownership of my part in adding the word 'more,' he rises and shakes my hand, thanks me for coming and I ready to leave; time elapsed, a minute and a half max. Truth is I don't want putting off the ship at all but certainly not the first week out, I simply couldn't bear the shame of being sent home that early. No, if I was really gonna fuck up, I should try and hold it together until I'm at least half way round I thought. One of the ice cream suits writes some shit onto a clipboard form. It probably says 'bollocking given,' but in actual fact, as far as bollockings went, it was maybe the most civilised of my life.

That evening at dinner scooter-Pam wants to hear about the Captain's meeting and there's an air of expectation from the others too; there's no point in lying; 'Well, I took issue with them trying to shoo us off to bed early Pamela, I felt that as we'd paid so much money to be on here if we wanted to stay up dancing, we should be allowed to do so.' It's at this point that I realised how crap the meeting had been, I hadn't had a chance to make any representations at all about my side of the equation. 'You should come dancing with us tonight Pamela, early bed doesn't suit you,' I said in a flash of inspiration. And she did, she came to the disco with us in her electric-chair thing and I got them to play the conga and gathered a line up behind her and she led a conga line of over thirty people having the time of her life. And they kept the disco going all the time we were there, coming over to say they were turning it down at one point, they hoped we understood. And we did. I was over the moon actually but tried not to be too smug. Or too pissed.

I knew my card was marked.

At one point the cruise-director comes in and seeing so many people having fun is mildly amused. The thing was, I knew there was a lot of money in our disco entourage and they'd hesitated to chuck me off when they had the chance. I kind of felt pretty secure really; as long as I could moderate myself.

*

It wasn't always a disaster when I drank, otherwise I probably wouldn't have carried on quite as long as I did but I suppose what entertained me and my friends might have horrified others caught in the wake – I didn't ever pause long enough to think about that, more intoxicants the band-aid for any shame.

One time when a pal from Jonathan's bar, a city-type called Richard and I had decided to go to Boulogne for the weekend; I had dressed in a wide-boy pin-striped gangster suit, black shirt, a white straight-tie and black and white brogues with a black trilby hat; I carried a vintage suitcase which was oddly heavy but looked great. We'd drunk a bottle of duty-free vodka before even boarding the hovercraft, named after Princess Anne. On the way out we'd jokingly tired to lift the massive hover skirt to get a glimpse of her panties. On board a mother asked Richard to mind his language, he threw a banknote at her and told her to buy her kid a dummy. Lady, wherever you are now, I'm sorry for my part in that trip, we were obnoxious - more was to come.

My periphery brain was wondering what it might be like to ride a full circuit on a luggage carousel as we waited for our cases in France. Soon Richard was in hysterics as I rode it through the plastic weather curtain things into the operational side of the hoverport only to be apprehended by some cop type with a machine-gun. I got pulled back into the hoverport and Richard was still laughing, my assertion that I was looking for Customs wasn't holding water but luckily Machine Gun Sam was amused by our laughter; 'Are you wearing this for a bet?' he asks, meaning my Al Capone look. That's the look I was going for anyway, 1920's gangster.

'How dare you!' I said indignantly, 'I was a very fashionable man once' and Richard finds this hysterical too, we are both very merry it has to be said. I quickly add, 'Yes for a bet, he' I point at laughing Richard 'now owes me one thousand, million pounds!' they both laugh, Richard more so, and with that I get away with it. Another off the bucket list.

*

Back on the cruise liner my stock price was obviously enhanced by the company I kept and the staff developed a weary, yet polite tolerance for me. They didn't need to know I was there entirely on the back of credit cards. And like I really gave a fuck how rich anyone else was, their farts would never smell like mine.

Linda, my red-haired disco dancing companion, ten-years my senior but still one of the youngsters on the ship (average age like a hundred probably) was distraught one day; 'Charles, watch this' she said, 'they're bullying me. Watch Lord and Lady Snot wrinkle their noses when they come by,' we were outside on deck and they were being snooty about her smoking, albeit she was in the designated area. Lady Snot always wore her big pearl necklace and he strolled round the deck alongside her like her poodle. She defo did wrinkle her nose and he feigned a fucking cough but they really were passive aggressively bullying Linda - even though she wasn't breaking any rules.

By the next time they came round we had rearranged ourselves so I was on the outside, I had a roll-up cigarette in hand and I inhaled deeply as they came close, exhaling pointedly as they drew level. Her nose wrinkled again but they knew better than to cause more fuss. Next time round they kept a broader berth which they could have done in the first place, we were in the smoking bit for fuck's sake. Years later I would see them selling burgers from a van at a Sunday market in South London; it's good money obviously and she still had her pearls on, but they must have stunk of burgers and chip fat when they got home – words like glasshouses and stones sprung to mind.

Twenty-two.

Boats, ships and watercraft have played significant parts in my life ever since my first trip to sea with my step-dad. Since getting clean and sober I've qualified as a narrow-boat skipper, able to take groups of up to twelve people on inland waterways and I volunteered at a boat club to do just that. I still had a clean criminal record after all, even though the check took an awfully long time to come through.

I also qualified to drive speed-boats without even leaving central London but in another effort to leave drug taking behind me, before this and my world cruise, I'd decided to buy a boat with some money my mum left me, a small, twenty-year old cabin-cruiser, like the sort of thing a family of three might hire for a holiday on the Norfolk Broads.

I reckoned that the expenses I would incur in fuelling, insuring and mooring it would be more than covered by what I would save on drug spending. The deal I had done with myself was I couldn't do both; it all made perfect sense besides Chackley, my then civil-partner, liked boats too, we'd been on two boating-holidays, one on Loch Ness and one on the Broads. Chacks was ten years my junior, Turkish and Muslim, therefore he didn't drink, smoke or use any drugs. But no, that didn't work either, and it was a motivating factor for me dating and marrying him. Someone who didn't do drugs, surely that would make me stop - but I had some ketamine delivered the day of our ceremony, just to celebrate you know. His own motivation was dodging the draft for the Turkish army but to be fair we did like each other, or at least the idea of each other; we're still great friends.

I'd secured a mooring near Harlow though the boat I bought was in fucking Swindon – so about three weeks cruising away from

Harlow. Cool, Chacks would crew, it'd be like a lovely holiday. As we were climbing aboard to be waved away by the old owner, he checked again what he'd heard, 'You're going where?' he asked 'Harlow?'

'Yeah,' I said nonchalantly and then in those famous last words; 'how hard can it be?' Well, quite hard let's say.

We soon settled in and the River Thames got wider as we progressed but it was quite slow, albeit, lovely. We were starting out almost as far up the River Thames as it's possible to navigate a boat. The first night was lovely we found a pub and had a nice dinner and an early night. This was it, I knew this would work, I was quite happy, so was Chacks. Happy people don't need drugs; why would they?

Next day after an early start we were in a refreshingly wide bit of water at last so I decided to try a quick turn to make sure I could handle the boat and get out of trouble should I need to.

'Hold tight!' I hollered to Chacks up front and swung the wheel hard to starboard rather like I'd once seen my stepfather do up in the Orkney Islands. I pulled the lever to ram the engine from hard forward to fast reverse in one deft move. It's gonna be almost poetic I'm thinking, a water ballet of sorts when there's an almighty, expensive-sounding clunk! The engine raced and simultaneously we lost both power and steering. The second day.

It was a fucking disaster.

The boat had an outdrive, like the leg of an outboard motor but linking the propeller from the inboard engine, or at least it did have an outdrive; now it was like a dog's leg that'd been run over by a truck; a thin sheen of pretty grease spreading on the water. Thankfully there was no-one else around to see the disaster unfold 'cos I'm sure I looked a total dick, Chacks knew better than to say much at this point.

'FUCK!' I screamed. The two things psychologists often attribute to causing anxiety are a fear of being overwhelmed and a fear of abandonment. They were both on the cards; I was a ship without a rudder, physically and metaphorically but at least we weren't heading for a fucking waterfall. Yet.

I managed to work out that under minimal power we could hopefully limp to a boatyard where I would try and get help. I must have been a dick towards Chacks but I don't recall being nasty though it was pretty obvious we weren't going anywhere in the boat for a while. Some of my angst must surely have leaked his way since within ten minutes of tying up he'd quietly packed his bag and was heading home. 'Okay, good luck, I'll see you at home,' he said and fucked off, not being nasty, just pragmatic I suppose.

'But aren't you going to stay and help?' I asked slightly incredulously. He was though definitely leaving.

'It is your dream pet, your dream,' he said and with that he was gone but I think my relationship with him died right there. There was no big fight as I recall but I should ask him how it was for him sometime I suppose.

Our first Valentine's together I had bought him a piece of a meteorite online, for him being out of this world; an ancient silver coin, for him being priceless and I'd had written him a love poem for him being my one true love. He bought me a document shredder. The writing had long been on the wall really.

The boat had to come out of the water on a massive crane, a part ordered and waited for and fitted but thank fuck I'd insured it before starting out, but only really 'cos I needed insurance to get into the London canal system otherwise I really doubt I would have bothered. My actual out of pocket was about the cost of a decent dinner for two. And I had learned the hard way that I should wait for the propeller to stop turning one way before I asked it to go the other. Basic physics really.

Chacks suggested I should I ask Shawn, my ex, to crew the rest of the way as he wasn't working and would appreciate a holiday. I must have been a bit of a cunt to Chacks, he is actually pretty easy going usually but it was obvious he didn't want to get back on the boat. But yeah, fuck you too I thought though I didn't say too much in case Shawn didn't come and help. One thing no-one tells you about boat ownership is you need crew and wrangling volunteers is always a challenge; not a problem one has as just a cruise ship passenger.

Thankfully Shawn agreed to come and help, he was an actual piss head but I could usually manage him; this was the Shawn who'd lost his job as a teacher for possession of ketamine. He also had two old convictions for shoplifting but the school had overlooked those to hire him, they were struggling to find good male-role-model teachers. They still are.

I'd bought a couple of new metal windlass things to open the canal locks; Shawn dropped one unused in the river at the very first lock we came too. One has to keep one's cool of course, I could probably move the boat on my own but it'd be easier with help. What the hell, it was no-big deal, just a lost tool, but it was like I'd asked a circus clown to thread a needle with sausages sometimes.

The ignition key broke off so it was a real pain to stop and start the engine as I was supposed to in the locks – I had to do sad emoji face to the lock-keepers and ask for their understanding; I'm not great at asking for favours.

Shawn wasn't brilliant on the ropes, I wasn't brilliant on the wheel, we nudged other boats in the locks. I had to shut some moaning old fogie down in one of the locks telling him to shut the fuck up and that he was a boring cunt; he did but he looked like he'd swallowed a wasp. Boating is normally quite relaxed and tranquil.

Entry to the canal system for me and three other craft was

delayed a half hour because my boat-licence still hadn't been processed which pissed everyone off as we entered a ladder-lock system, a series of seven or eight locks that take hours to go through. As we went through the first it started to piss-down; like savagely, sideways-rain piss-down. We were moving through with the other boats I'd already annoyed but once under way we were committed to see the entire transit through regardless of the weather. At one point so much water was coming down the hill of locks that the current pulled the ropes from our hands and the boat did it's own ballet pirouette; some twat from another boat said loudly he 'had never seen a farce quite like it.'

It was really quite stressful, away from the locks a rogue wave caused me to slip and wind myself; never having been winded before I fully thought I was dying, however, I soon recovered and just as I thought it was gonna be pretty much plain sailing we passed some kind of weird camp site. There was an armed guard with a machine gun just stood there looking at us, all official like but he could have been just some weirdo who liked wanking with guns; I wasn't about to ask.

A few hundred yards on there was this 'phut' and a sort of whining sound and looking out over the back of the boat there was smoke and a sudden film of black oil on the water's surface. I genuinely thought the geezer with the gun had shot through the hull of the boat into the engine. I knocked the throttle back to tickover and called Shawn to grab the wheel while I opened up the hatches to take a look at the engine. It didn't look good, hot oily water was leaking into the lower bilges; oh this was fucking unbearable! We limped on for a short while out of sight of the guard and until I could find a place to moor up. This was gonna be another delay but quite how long or expensive I didn't know until the engine cooled down a bit and I was able to fully investigate.

An oil line had burst, the sustained pressure and long running times had just been too much for an old engine that the previous owner had probably just used to watch porn in. Really, I needed an engineer. Then it dawned on me, I was actually supposed to be one; I had been an apprentice fucking mechanic for four years but had no real clue what to do. I was so fucking angry, and sad. I very nearly burst into tears, I was like, 'oh for fuck's sake, I can't take any-more,' and to be honest if someone had offered me 50% of what I had paid, I would have sold the boat there and then.

We had no choice other than to secure the boat and leave it so I could try and source a new part; but looking round we were now in one of the less salubrious parts of the canal system, literally the wrong side of the bridge. I fully expected the boat to be vandalised, burgled or sunk which is, I think, why you sometimes see abandoned boats, no doubt it all gets a bit too much and people just give up. We headed home discreetly drinking a calming can of cider each on the train; thankfully we were near enough to London to get on the tube at least.

The internet told me that the only replacement part was in Japan and at least four weeks away; I had taken the faulty one off and carried it with me. Getting one fabricated was a possible solution; had I been trained properly I should at least know who to call to get one made; if I had the tools and resources I should in fact have been able to make one. It was only a fucking pipe with some bends in it and some threaded nipple things on after all. Hardly rocket science. Well, actually it sort of was, high pressure lubricant channels and shit being commonplace on rockets. From a garage I was directed to a wholesaler, to another garage and then eventually to some kid on an industrial estate who had actually been shown how to weld; he took the blown line and braised a new section and joint into it and he didn't even charge me. I gave him a tip and told him I could have kissed him. I could have too but I'm not sure whether that was hero worship or some whole other wank fantasy from my own mechanic days.

Three days after the oil-line blew Shawn and I cast off and, feeling nothing more could stop us, we set off buzzing that we might actually pull it off and get to Harlow, eventually. Although we were very obviously in greater London the the boat was a little island of solitude; it did feel nice to be close to civilisation having spent a while in the quiet river before the engine disaster. 'Do you think anyone could have broken in the night before and messed with the engine Shawn?' I had asked at one point, whereupon I'd suggested the security services might have interfered with the engine.

'You ain't James Bond luvvy,' he'd replied, but it did seem a bit odd; the guy with the gun, the 'phut' as the line blew. It could have been a small explosive device. I felt I was maybe being tested by some unknown force to see where my breaking point was, or maybe my alien overlords had decreed that I never be allowed to succeed, that I must be foiled at every turn but the dark thoughts weren't overpowering, I was getting clean from ketamine, my plan was working after all.

As we tied up early evening Shawn looked at me and asked what time it was and where we were, I could almost see the wheels in his head turning round. I had done getting on for four whole weeks without ketamine, even when I went home during repairs I had held it together. After all, these boating expenses were the very things quitting drugs was supposed to be paying for. I knew what he was thinking, his smile said it all, 'NO. Shawn, don't even think about it.' I said determinedly; he smiled wider. I should be a fucking mind reader.

'It's only an hour away on the tube, you could be back by ten,' he said, he didn't even mention drugs, he didn't have to.

'No! No Shawn, no fucking way; I'm stopping all that shit to pay for the boat,' I'm half-heartedly cross but then he gives me puppy dog eyes.

So yeah, twenty minutes later I'm on the way back to town to score some K.

A psychologist would spot the flaw in my semantics, 'I'm stopping,' is not the same as, 'I stopped,' besides we'd had a rough few days, we needed a treat and to be fair Shawn had been a diamond, very helpful and supportive, it was as much to treat him as anything, I wouldn't be taking much.

We'd moored near some bridge covered in graffiti about a ten minute walk to the station, not far from Wembley stadium and easy enough to find my way back I reckoned, though it would be much darker obviously. I looked around to get my bearings as the boats would all look the same in the dark.

I called the dealer, grabbed the tube, scored, nipped home to check the mail and was soon ready to head back to the boat; Chacks was indoors but doing his own stuff, he was civil but far from impressed with my pending relapse; it was obvious what I was doing but I didn't take drugs when I got there so as not to piss him off too much. I called Shawn to say I was just leaving, I was quite excited to be honest, I hadn't done K for ages but yeah, it was mainly for him.

'Okay, I'm off Chacks, great to see you, I'll buzz you in the next few days,' I kiss him on the forehead and go to leave but the K lure was strong, I nipped in the bathroom to have a grasshopper line for the journey.

A grasshopper line is when someone puts out such a small amount it wouldn't even make a small insect high. Yeah, well I'm not actually a grasshopper so I put out a lil' bit more than maybe I should, waved goodbye to Chacks, rushed out and jumped on a bus to

Liverpool Street, maybe ten or twelve stops away.

I was holding onto one of the yellow bus support rails when I fell into a K-hole. K-holing is something that happens when you take too much ketamine; it's called a hole because it can be like being sucked into a deep dark cave and once in, only time will release you. Occasionally you can ride them out mentally but you'll hardly ever remember you're on drugs so it's a real head fuck; they can seem like never ending fright fests as your companions turn into demons and you think you have been, and will be, stuck in the darkness of the hole for all time.

A packed evening city bus wouldn't be a great place to plan one. I looked around as the other passengers morphed into Jelly Tots with faces. I genuinely thought I had died and been reincarnated as a jelly-tot and that was why we were all crushed up together in this bright tubular package and I would be like this forever now - unless some kid shook us out of the tube and ate and digested us when the next stage of my metamorphism from human life would happen. You don't think all this at the time though, you can't really rationalise at all, it just is - and it feels like it was always like this but now at last you finally see the truth. I don't recommend it, k-holing it isn't actually fun at all; it's very disturbing. I thought I was a pebble on the beach once and was trying to get my fuzzy head around being there for another billion years; those aren't relaxing thoughts.

On the bus an automated voice announced some bus stop and it must have nudged my consciousness slightly; oh fuck I'm on a bus, what am I doing on a bus? I look out and the bus is going over the River Thames and the water glistens below. Ah - I recall something about a boat, a repair, is one of these people Shawn? What the fuck is going on I wonder?

'Where am I?' I ask the nearest Jelly Tot – if Jelly Tots were estate agents sort of thing.

The guy is bemused. He talks loud and slow, like I might be his waiter at a foreign Jelly Tot sales conference; 'You are on a bus on London Bridge,' he says and little bits of my jigsaw memory reassemble themselves. Oh yeah; Shawn, the boat, fuck yeah, I'm on K, thank fuck I'm gonna be all right. I have to get back to the boat, I struggle off the bus and head back to the water but it seems a bit odd, not like what I'm expecting. I'm on a bridge, on the river, so is the fucking boat, but I can't see it anywhere; I haven't grasped it's miles away.

'Shawn!' I yell, 'Shawn, where are you, can you hear me?'
I look over the bridge down at the water, it's a long way down, a fucking long way; not like I committed to memory at all. Something doesn't add up here, 'Excuse me mate,' I ask a passing pedestrian,

'Which way is the stadium?'

'Which Stadium *mate*?' he asks, I don't think he wants to be mates.

'Wembley,' I say thinking he might be a bit simple.

'It's about ten miles that way,' he says pointing northwards. Now I'm really fucking confused.

'Well how the fuck did I get here?' I ask the guy.

'Dunno mate, maybe a wormhole or a hot air balloon...' he adds as he walks on. Dumb fuck, the only logical explanation would be a wormhole, I've never even been in a hot air balloon – I just need to find the portal. It's a funny fucking world sometimes.

Eventually I got back to the boat, just; on the last train that night! It was touch and go. And well, I didn't stop taking ketamine at all after that. I just carried on. Eventually I would sell the boat and snort that too but before then I went on this fucking round the world cruise as another brilliant solution.

*

Yes, on the world-cruise ship I didn't take any drugs at all for ninety days - but I was pissed most nights, though when I got back I felt I had my actual drug addiction sorted. I was definitely over sniffing ketamine. When I got home I'd had a vague reply about my generic battery idea sent on behalf the Prime Minister, it was on Department of Health headed paper I kid you not.

Shawn popped round the day after I got home. We went and scored some K within about half-an-hour.

Twenty-three.

One of the big problems with getting off of drugs or alcohol is that you have to want to stop. Whatever the catalyst motivation may be, family, friends, health, or even just self development – or being sick and tired of being sick and tired, there has to be a want that trumps the need. I kind of always knew that at some point I would perhaps need to knock it all on the head but it was beginning to dawn on me that my assertion, 'I can stop anytime I like,' was pure bollocks. Quite how anyone did it was a mystery, in fact I wasn't sure I'd come across anyone who had ever stopped drugs or alcohol. But then I wouldn't; I hung out with users not losers. Quite frankly if you didn't take drugs, I really didn't want to know you anyway, I liked edgy people and what could be more edgy than breaking the law in such a cavalier fashion as taking drugs? And I could sure live without any puritanical judgements.

At one point I thought it might well be time to ask for some help with the K thing as I was pissing so often and my nose really hurt. I had no idea what they did at those drug help places, a little part of me thought they might admit me to a ward, handcuff me to a bed and not let me leave until I was cured. Which I suppose is one reason I'd never actually been before, I didn't *want* to actually stop taking drugs, I just wanted a better relationship with them. I was worried they might wave some magic wand or something and I'd lose all interest in partying and become a bible bashing dullard. Oh well, maybe it was time; but if in the process I could just find a better way to take drugs or find a substance like K that didn't make me piss a million times a day, life would certainly be better.

Far from the Golden Hour addicts might hope for when they press the help bell, my first sixty minutes at the drug-help place was a study in frustration and form filling. The worker on point and thus assigned to me, Dee, had orange hair and hand tattoos, in fairness I felt that was a good start, she was edgy, I was edgy. And then the form filling started; mundane questions; did I spit a lot, was I vegetarian for fuck's sake, did I puke up a lot? I think the point at which all hope left my body was when she asked me, literally; 'do you have a history of suicide?' I stared at her in disbelief.

'Er no,' was all I could say without being rude. It was a bank-holiday weekend ahead, this was Friday afternoon; I decided maybe she was distracted by the thought of a break. She never asked if I pissed the bed.

There were more forms but at least no sign of handcuffs or an exorcist. I mentioned being nearly a week off of K, needing a bit of guidance to power through; in truth I was maybe two days off of K, 'And I'm surrounded by fucking crack-heads and smack-heads' I said, not remotely trying to be controversial. I was only addicted to K then but the snidey drugs were all around me.

'We don't use language like that,' says Dee like she's talking to an infant.

'What *fucking*,' or, 'crack and smack heads'?' I ask surprised.

'All of the above,' she says.

'Sorry? Erm...Oh sorry, but that's how I speak, I always F and blind and am surrounded by those sorts of folk.'

'Well, we may as well start as we mean to go on,' she says; I'm starting to wish I'd just gone straight home.

'I have to be honest,' I say defensively, 'I am paying you a compliment when I speak like that; I swear in front of all my male friends and to temper my language with you, just because you're a woman, would be sexist and patronising.' It would for sure but I suspected she'd also object if I held the door open for her, it's hard to know which way is up some days.

'The profanity we can work on but we need to afford our other clients respect and we refer to them just as drug-users or heroin or cocaine-users if we need to be specific,' says Dee. She's more or less totally alienated me by this time. I reckon she must be pretty new or something; the right-on, lentil-eating cunt. But I keep that thought to myself.

She makes me an appointment to see her again in a week and hands me some leaflets. It's the longest I've spent alone with a woman since my mother died. I'm given a business card and she walks me to the door.

'Well, enjoy the bank holiday,' she says and then unbelievably adds, 'I expect that will involve taking lots of ketamine, but do take care,' and there, bang I'm out on the street again thinking what the fuck? And then; 'yeah, I suppose it will involve lots of ketamine,' and I went from there straight round to the dealers very exasperated. The K would help calm me down I thought.

Drug councillors talk of relapse prevention; drug addicts look for excuses. Someone dying is a great excuse; it buys the addict the emotional leverage to explain their using. Nurse Jean was big on this, no matter which periphery person died she always seemed to be at the forefront of of the arrangements grieving the loss of a great friend with tons of drugs, a friend by the way who may have privately said what a pain in the ass she really was.

Yes, I was disappointed in my first ever visit to the drug treatment unit yes, I was disappointed that they hadn't handcuffed me to a bed and yes, I had turned Dee's weekend farewell into a relapse trigger but the fundamental oversight to my mind was that she hadn't asked if I actually wanted to stop using drugs. Because, and this is where drug services could save an awful lot of money, unless you want to stop, nothing and no-body can actually do that for you.

I couldn't really blame my drug worker for my going and getting more K, she had a shit kind of bedside manner and worse was to come but down the middle of every road in London there are painted big white-lines; there are triggers everywhere. I wasn't actually ready to stop at that point of my life anyhow; I figured my life would surely be over if I quit, what the fuck else was there worth doing anyway?

I did go back for my next appointment; again I was called out on my use of profanity - yet at the same time they'd ask us to be honest with them.

'I'm sorry, it's the way I talk; why would you ask me to censor myself?' I asked.

It was just an Alpha-Female thing, it was so obvious to me; this sort of thing happened to me all the time with guys, particularly in places like builder's merchants. People have to try an assert some kind of authority over me, guys with small cocks probably but was a newish situation to me with a female, it dawned on me I was out of practice of engaging meaningfully with women and tried to explain; 'I was the youngest in a male household of four. I was a mechanic in a garage full of men, then moved to an all-male sales-force. I'm a gay guy, I only really socialise with guys. This is how I talk, I do apologise but if I had a male-counsellor I guarantee it wouldn't be an issue.' Oh shit, it kind of went a bit off the rails at the end but no bloke has ever called me on my diction.

'Well, you don't have a male-advisor, you have me,' she said. We muddle through and I make it through the hour without being too bitchy.

'Let's wind up for today, I'll make a new appointment and you can have time to consider if we are able to help you,' she says. I'm still a bit pissed off but I might have sounded sexist I think - as it slowly it occurs to me; they don't want it to be easy. If it was easy to get off drugs she'd be out of a job. I certainly didn't expect asking for professional help to be quite such an uphill climb though; it was really quite depressing.

Previously on the way out of the door of a regular GP appointment, I'd mentioned that I was addicted to Ketamine. She wrinkled her nose as if I'd said I was eating kitty-litter. 'Why not chocolate?' she asked as she pressed the door button back to the waiting area.

'Oh, I'm addicted to that as well,' I said as she bade me farewell and that was that.

The next week I can't face orange Dee bollocking me for my semantic choices for a third time, so the day before my appointment I email and let her know that I'm doing other shit and can't make it.
Four days later a letter arrives saying she 'is closing my file since I had failed to engage with services,' it was obvious she hadn't read my fucking email.

So I sent proof of the email, a copy of her letter, a complaint about her chastising me for the way I spoke and I pointed out that I was a drug-addict seeking help not a PhD student seeking lab-time. I suggested some re-training and well, I was a bit of a clever-fucker I suppose but really I was glad of the opportunity to highlight some of the failings of the system.

Of course they apologised, confirmed retraining (result) reopened my file and assigned me a new male worker. He was just dull. Tolerant of my potty mouth sure enough but it was like being trapped in a cubicle for an hour with someone talking about kitchen cabinet hinges.

Yes, I'd take the form to complete a drug diary but what was the point if it's the same every day I'd asked. Wake up. Tell myself I knew I was going to score drugs, get up and on with it. Score; which could take up to six hours some days. Go home, consume drugs until they ran out. Eat, (reduced section) sleep, repeat.

I never completed even the first line of the silly fucking diary form – but that's what they did, fill in forms that no-one else would read. And hand out leaflets. It seemed to me that when shit hit the fan, they gave you a leaflet for it. No one ever seemed to think to turn the fan off and get a cloth out.

At Braindeath's place, a dealer with a dingy flat who looked like Charles Manson, there was a bit of excitement one time about an upcoming "K-day". Some university was having an Information Day, exclusively about ketamine. No-one seemed to know much more about it but we were all gonna go, all us regular K-users. Thank fuck, finally we could get some advice about how to wean ourselves off it and maybe even quit. But no one really wanted to quit though did they? No, I didn't think so, we just wanted to find better ways of taking it to be honest or maybe a new way of cooking it.

It was quite busy, a hundred plus user types milling about waiting for shit to begin and there were free tote bags, key-rings and rubber wrist bands; I was kind of surprised there wasn't actual fucking face-painting but it was a relief to get through the doors to be honest. I recognised a few faces from various scoring venues here and there but I was glad I could finally get some sensible advice. There were though no new leaflets, nothing I hadn't seen before and none terribly specific to ketamine. The commonest describer of K being that it was a form of *horse tranquilliser,* that was about the sum of it. It seemed no more relevant to me than that learning Jelly Babies were made from gelatine or mashed up cows eye-lids or whatever; it sure didn't stop me eating them.

It was certainly an information day but not quite what us addicts thought; they weren't giving out information, they were trying to get it in. From us, the users.

'So, if you want to contribute please raise your hand and we'll get a microphone to you and if you'd be good enough to tell us your experiences of using Ketamine and, indeed trying to get off it, that would be great,' someone said as the Town Hall got under way. Groan. After a short, slightly uncomfortable pause this ginger-haired kid with glasses that I vaguely recognised from dealer Sideshow's place was the first to speak. I always kind of fancied him.

'I've been taking K for about six years...,' he says and gives a potted drug history that starts with cigarettes, through weed, E's, acid and ends on six years of K that he now can't get enough of , 'But,' he says dramatically, 'now I quite often have to get in a warm bath to piss 'cos it hurts so much.'

Wow, and I thought I'd had it bad. I had actually had the most painful experience of my life pissing on K once, like passing a piece of barbed wire down the whole length of my knob. But, amazed as I am, not only that this has happened to the red-haired guy as well, but also shocked that I hadn't thought to get into a warm bath to pee to ease the pain. I made a mental note that next time it could be worth trying that. Some one else says similarly the peeing can be painful, like real fucking agony. And there was me thinking my piss experience was a one off with badly cooked ketamine. It had seemed to me that somewhere in my system a small piece of it had crystallised or got stuck in my water works and the actual pain was it passing down and scratching the inner-tube of my willy; I hadn't thought it was commonplace. I knew Tom had had a stoma fitted so he could piss in a bag and that he'd snorted K in the actual recovery room after that operation but come to think of it no-one had really gone into what had actually caused it; I guess we were in denial. Shit, this was sounding serious.

Someone else got the mic and talked of the health-service inflating their bladder with air to stretch it back to capacity or some such scary shit; it sounded horrific. Another said that they were awaiting results on a fucking biopsy; again of the bladder. Others that they pissed little more than a thimble full of wee every time but many many times a day; that could have been me.
And then of course there were tales of the K-cramps; severe abdominal/chest pain. Quite commonplace too; I myself had been fetal on the floor a few times, writhing around in agony. It was like the aftermath of being punched in the stomach but without the initial blow. It arrived like a slow freight-train and there's very little would get it out of the station before it was ready to go. We'd all tried every over the counter digestion and pain remedy going. Nothing worked. More ketamine worked, or at least we'd tell ourselves it did; it probably made it worse.
We all knew about the K-cramps, just not what they actually were, but

that the piss and bladder thing was quite such a wide-hitting issue was a shock for most of us as it's just not the sort of thing you'd mention socially. The last thing you want if you're scoring drugs is some Joy Killington ruining your buzz, so that afternoon we were all looking for answers to previously unspoken questions. I don't recall anyone saying we should actually stop using ketamine, seriously. I think we all doubted it was possible anyway. We defo all felt we needed something to take the fucking edge off and K was cheap, easy and effective.

I left the K-day with another fucking tote-bag and a few more leaflets feeling really really depressed. I felt my life was quite likely to be a downward spiral of urinary decay until I had my own colostomy bag and eventually I would probably get penis, nose or liver cancer and die an excruciatingly painful death. I suspected my peer group of the time would, however, find a way to snort lines of K off my coffin at my funeral only to tender that; *'it's what he would have wanted!'*

Twenty-four.

I remember one evening being sat at my computer with my pants around my ankles having watched some porn; I had a bottle of poppers open, a can of cider on the go, some K lines racked out on a small mirror; a joint lit, the ash from which was littered across my desk and well, you know there was now a ball of soggy tissues too. My head was spinning from the poppers, my heart beating like a bastard and I found myself thinking that that was how I would be found one day, dead, albeit decomposed since it would surely be several weeks or even months before anyone thought to raise the alarm.

If anyone wants an example of unconditional love, my body caring for me and taking everything I threw at it is surely a great example. No matter what happened it just carried on, took me to bed, tried to repair itself as best as it could and accepted whatever else I threw at it with love and without conditions. If I owe anyone an amends then there has to be a pretty big one due to my poor body. For the record dear body, thanks for looking out for me all this time and I'm sorry I treated you so appallingly over the years.

People died. Of course they did, quite a few actually; One-arm-Tim, Sideshow, Douglas, Kev, Pete, Washing-machine-Barry (so called 'cos he danced like a washing machine), Paul E, Sketch, Rod, Maria and scores more on the periphery. Some would obviously deteriorate, others came out of the blue but very often the elephant in the room that squashed them was largely ignored. Cocaine takes tons of people, as many as alcohol in some circles but very often the real reasons are glossed over by family doctors keen to spare the families from difficult truths, as happened quite often with AIDS deaths in the early days.

Lupa was one of the first, the verdict: suicide. I guarantee Lupa did not kill herself as she 'was unable to handle her body dysmorphia and that she was assigned male at birth,' as concluded officially. I was working at the brothel the day of the inquest and couldn't go, not that I was even actually called in spite of my alerting the cops. She loved her new titties and took every opportunity to walk around flashing them off; I'm certain that had she wanted to kill herself she wouldn't have done it wearing Den's t-shirt and boxers, she'd have gone out looking fabulously feminine as she usually did.

She'd stayed at my place a couple of night having come over from New York to detox herself off of heroin, a practice I now know is called, 'doing a geographical.' She'd rung me as a friend of a friend, I didn't know her at all but sure we could meet and soon she would stay a couple of days. She ending up staying with Dennis, another ex of mine. Lupa was good fun, she'd be on the phone claiming our activity as her new role, 'I'm just styling a band out at Wembley darling,' when she was carrying shopping for Shawn and he was the one doing the styling, (Shawn was better at fashion than teaching). But after she'd say, 'shall we all go get snockered,' and we'd head to the pub where we'd do exactly that. The term snockered arrived in my life and left with her but I'll never forget it.

Dennis called me one morning, 'Lupa's in my bed Charlie' he said hesitantly.

I'm like, 'O....k?'

'And she's dead.'

'Don't touch anything, I"ll be right over,' I said. Oh fuck. I needed more drama like a hole in the head.

She'd been dead a while, cold as a stone. There was orange

juice and soggy Weetabix, concrete at the edges, on a tray next to the bed, it had been there a while. Dennis had taken it to her and thought she was asleep and only gone back some hours later. I think he must've known she was brown bread and smoked whatever skag she had left to get over it.

I called the police and ambulance immediately although the latter was pointless and I said as much on the call but I knew my phone history could be analysed. If I left too much time between getting round there and calling them it would leave room for doubt. Dennis had already 'removed' any drugs that could get him arrested – it was his flat after all.

'Have you been through her bag and stuff?' I asked meaning like drug wise, to spare the family too much agony - or us arrest.

'Yeah, she only had a bit of cash left,' says Dennis, he's sad but not overly distraught. I don't quiz him about the time delay, I can hear a siren.

'You took her fucking money?' I asked.

'Well, she ain't gonna need it is she?' I couldn't fucking believe it. Well, I could Dennis was a bit of a wanker at the end of the day, a ponce truth be known. I told my part in the tale to the police and slowly the scene returned to what passed for normal in our worlds.

The front-page local headline would eventually read; *'Transexual Prostitute Takes Own Life to Escape Sexuality'*, so much for trying to spare the family unnecessary pain.

Someone else died on the stairs of the pub and likewise was cold when finally discovered having been there a few hours. Everyone just thought he was sleeping, me included. He had probably been passed about two hundred times before someone thought to check on him, poor soul. It was a close shave for the pub though; had it not regularly hosted the Gay Policing Group it might not have escaped with it's licence. It also hosted one of the areas biggest drug wholesalers in an upstairs flat too so it was very touch and go that particular day; I don't think the gay police new that bit.

Every now and then you'd hear of someone else croaking but it was usually periphery people not that close to home and you'd think they were just idiots really, that you'd never mix drugs like they obviously did, you yourself were much too careful but in truth, occasionally, it got a bit out of hand and mixed up.

The cleaner guy at the club would often give me packets of white powder he'd found, I didn't always know what it was but it never stopped me taking it, cautiously at first. Dealers would occasionally get me to do a test, to take something before they started to sell it, see if it was any good – and didn't blind or kill me I suppose. When I look back and see how moronic that actually was it makes me grimace. At the time I felt a mixture between like a hard core trustee who knew his drug shit and like bingo! at having got a deal for free.

We'd more or less taken over the pub where the guy died on the stairs. It was the nearest gay bar to my house, maybe fifteen minutes walk but when I first looked in midweek there was some twat in a bow-tie playing show-tunes on a keyboard to like seven people. Next time there was a really tiresome pub-quiz with like ten or twelve gay fogies answering questions about nuclear physics and Abba. After a few weeks I asked Robin the licensee if I could run a Saturday club night as he actually had a dance and late night licence. I'd bought a sound-system off some guy who needed money to pay his dealer and had had a couple of parties at home. At one point I thought I'd become a top international DJ until I found you couldn't really mix records on ketamine - and buying records ate money. So yeah, I had the equipment and we put together the first sort of clubby rave night in the pub on Hackney Road. Eventually it took off, in fact the bar became one of the edgiest destination in East London and was soon frequented by celebrities and stars but my interest waned with the popularity. The more people arrived the less space there was to dance and that killed it for me but for two or three years it was golden; I gave my Saturday night slot away in the end.

One night however, Colton, a '*gay for pay*' short-arsed straight guy who preyed on women who went to gay bars handed me a bag of white powder he'd found, 'Here Charlie, I don't know what this is but you and Shawn can have some if you want' he said passing me what looked like cocaine. 'I found it on the floor, I've taken some,' he added, 'but I didn't get much off it,' and so Shawn and I went into one of the bog cubicles; I racked out two grasshopper lines, just in case.

Shawn wasn't impressed, 'fuck off Charlie, that prick's always taking the piss, put more out'.

'But we don't know what it is,' I replied. The taste, smell and constitution gave nothing away, it could have been talcum powder. He grabs the packet and racks two honkers out, snorting his without a moments hesitation. I take a half-line gingerly, 'Nah, fuck it, I'll come back when I know what it is' I say, Shawn leans in and snorted my leftovers.

Within minutes I knew it was heroin, or pseudo-heroin which could be worse, and we've fucking snorted it - not the best decision either of us have made but Shawn's had like triple my dose.

Luckily I'd had nothing else so far that night so I knew that whatever happened in my head or body would be down to that and I undertook to monitor myself. Although we're not heroin virgins neither of us were regular users at this stage and Shawn was perhaps only 80% of my size. Normally he's exuberant, full of energy and like a whirlwind but he started closing down, sat on a stool and barely moved; it's a worry. I'm manageable, but I know what's going on. I explain to friends that we need to keep Shawn awake; he is starting to drift off.

The thing is, too much heroin really affects the respiratory system; if people drift too far away their system can actually just stop breathing for them. Whilst awake they can sort of remind themselves to keep breathing, crazy but sort of accurate. Often you see heroin users in shop doorways 'gouging out' their chins on their chests – but that's where they want to be, it is a euphoric place of utter insouciance; but the distance from there to actual death isn't so very far at all. The users don't actually want rousing to consciousness, it's why they buy the shit in the first place - to escape their reality.

Shawn could be a pain in the arse, a difficult drunk; as we baby sat him we all joked about chipping in together to get him an actual heroin habit just 'cos it shut him the fuck up for a few hours but it was a very close call, he could have died. He'd had adrenaline direct through his breast bone before but that was 'cos people were unfamiliar with ketamine and an ambulance had arrived before he climbed out of his k-hole. He and Poppy-Pete another night were both sat on neighbouring bar stools and fell off them at almost the exact same time as each other; it was hysterical. Robin the landlord panicked and wanted an ambulance again that time but I just put them on the sofa and left them to it. Twenty minutes later they were dancing again.

The landlord Robin, was a bit of an old worry-head, mostly for the sake of his licence but even before I came along he was a piss-head; he sometimes took drugs to calm his anxiety and often got wasted, 'If I have to do six months for this Charlie' he said to me one night while he was dancing his way around the pub, 'it'll be worth it,' he was having the time of his life. It killed him in the end the booze but we all felt *'it's what he would have wanted'*.

The pub got fucking insane for a while, it was hideous fun; I grew a beard there one weekend; I went Friday and was still there Tuesday morning. There were sofas upstairs in another smaller bar where you could catch emergency zeds. It's reputation grew and soon gangsters moved in; hence the drug warehouse upstairs but since I wasn't there to make money, just to dance and have fun, I let them get on with it and I got slid drugs often enough not to care. Occasionally I would tell big guys, big drug-lord type guys to just fuck off, I didn't care how big they were, they were guests in our pub and to behave or they could just fuck off and somehow they sort of listened. Mirrors, smoke-machines, we had it all in that pub.

The bigger the bullshit the more people believe you sometimes. Besides I looked the part and whatever intoxicants I took gave me the bravado to act like a right tosser. Probably more relevant, I had this habit of befriending all the regular nut-jobs, everyone knew I knew people, people who could actually do what I pretended I could; I'd only ever wanted to be a dancer. Colton was a fucking psycho; I kept him close.

One night some big bouncer type was gonna duff Shawn up. I pushed in between them. 'Oh look,' I said into his face, 'the big straight-guy is gonna bash the lil' gay-boys head in! Won't that make you a fucking hero at the Bridge?' The Bridge was a neighbourhood stripper bar, 'Well have a go at me you cunt,' and I pushed my chin towards him with my index finger pointing at where he should punch. He could easily have killed me to be honest but he did back off. The next time I saw him he actually came over and apologised, like literally said he was sorry and bought me a drink. For an ego maniac like me that was some kind of result, but it was all bravado. I was just a big wuss really; someone would soon call my bluff.

Eventually I had my skull fractured in two places and was more or less left for dead in a doorway near the pub. I think there was quite a bit of cumulative anger came out against me that night. Consequences.

Oddly it sort of enhanced my reputation; I'm told whoever instigated it stopped coming to the pub after that, worried that he was marked man. He may well have been but - and no one knew this - I didn't have the foggiest clue who it was no matter how many times they described him to me I just couldn't bring him to mind, but he wasn't a regular. To be fair, I did deserve a duffing up that night. I'd pissed down the staircase in his direction telling him to suck my piss apparently. I might have gone a bit far but as you know, I know I'm a knob too sometimes. We all get the occasional comeuppance.

It's very easy for me to lay out my side of these stories, the way I saw things. The time I put a guy's nose in my mouth and closed my teeth over it I felt he deserved to be frightened, I can't even remember what happened to be honest but I do remember laying out my stall in terms of justification. *He was this, he was that*; indeed, that he was some kind of twat may well be true but usually I didn't ever look back at my part in the creation of these situations. And I never actually bit anyone's nose off, not ever.

Addiction and alcoholism are sticking plasters for what's actually going on inside. That I can even just say *I deserved to get my head kicked* in for weeing down the stairs is kind of ridiculous if you think about it. I deserved to be kicked out of the place and, if I wouldn't leave quietly, then I deserved to perhaps be arrested. Everything else was excessive. It's not as if the staircase was in a graceful hallway or anything, the pub was mostly a shit-hole.

But from the point of view of whomever kicked my head in, I was no doubt a tiresome bore who dogged him off and I deserved a pasting - he'd lost this patience and perhaps spotted an opportunity to vent some resentments.

I didn't know who was behind it, still don't in spite of knowing his name but I never went looking either; my bruises were an occupational hazard of getting wasted and I wasn't going on some dumb vendetta and ending up in jail. I put it about he was barred from the East End but he could sit next to me on the tube tonight and I wouldn't be any the wiser. And the thought I could ever bar anyone from the East End is patently absurd.

And even with bruises the colour of aubergines all over my head, I still didn't think my drinking or using was much of a problem.

Twenty-five.

Back aged twenty-one I'd announced I was going to get baptised. The sky didn't cloud over, no-one put their hand over their mouth as their eyes widened in shock but I did wonder if my mum knew I thought I was dying, 'Why pet?' she asked.

'Because I might not go to heaven if I die.'

'You're not planning on dying anytime soon are you?' she wondered.

'No Mum, course not,' but I have always had a pending sense of mortality. Even now I don't get spots, I get skin cancer, I don't get headaches I get brain haemorrhages so when my brother Seb told me they were expecting their first baby I was sad that I would be dead before it was born, not that I mentioned that. Since I hadn't passed away when the baby arrived I had made appropriate cooing noises and congratulations, saddened again that I wouldn't be there for her Christening.

But I was still around, and by that time I had likewise been both Christened and Confirmed myself. So my own passage to heaven was smoothed out.

I'd had to go to Bible study for a few weeks with some other people, mostly folk who had already been baptised but wanted the promotion of confirmation. I had the water splashed on me and I'd gone to a cathedral some weeks later for some other archaic ceremony with a bishop in a funny hat, candles and incense. It was a bit of an anti-climax if I'm honest though heaven knows what I was expecting but, for a while, I got up and went to the village church every Sunday morning, prayed, ate the biscuit and sipped the chalice wine but while god never spoke to me directly, I felt I might even belong. I didn't mention any gay shit.

The vicar, a nice chap who made no molestation overtones or anything, casually asked after church one Sunday if I wanted to do the apprentice vicar thing myself. If I'd had time to think I might have gone for it; nice easy life, free housing, a lot of days off, not exactly digging holes in the road etc. Hardly a spiritual approach but it's what I thought about on the way home but had replied; 'Oh no, I couldn't. No, thank you. No, that's impossible.'

I knew I was almost certainly irreversibly gay and I knew that that was sinful in the eyes of these fuckers. In that moment I kind of wondered why I was putting myself through all the churchy shit in the first place; why was I going to worship in a place where if they knew the truth about me they might try an exorcism or something?

The next weekend I got so drunk on the Saturday night again that I pissed the bed and didn't make it to Church, being sidetracked by a wet mattress and fan heater. Call it divine intervention or more likely self-sabotage but Sunday lunchtime I went to the pub and the old church warden guy, James, was behind the bar, small village that it was. Pulling me a pint he looks up and says accusingly, 'Where were you today, I didn't see you in church?' and with that my dalliance with Christianity was over; seriously that's all it took - the judgemental, pious prick. I never went back other than for ceremonial stuff; weddings and funerals mostly - organised religion wasn't my tribe either.

Not that I had given up on the idea of a god per se yet, never say never, and there was always the other lot; I was to meet the devil worshipping lot in my clubbing days down the line in London.

When mushrooms were around the witchy-looking goth-types

were the people to know. This one freaky wizard-type old guy at the club always had good drugs and occasionally he would come up with some fucking weird a-la-carte shit; PCP, Opium, DMT, 2CB's all of which I tried but my preference then was always for acid or mushrooms. The problem with acid was that I always had to plan it. If I didn't know where I was gonna be in six hours, I didn't like risking it. There's nothing worse than having to get a fucking packed bus or train when you're tripping off your nut. With mushrooms, you couldn't be sure how intense they might be or even what the fuck you'd actually been given.

One time in Turnmill's, the fucking freaky wizard guy, Patrick, had given a couple of us some alleged magic-mushrooms. Operative word 'given' - we were his metaphoric blind testers it seemed.

Juan said, 'That don't look like any fucking mushroom I've ever had,' but nonetheless we both ate these things that looked a bit like dried daffodil stalks and went to dance.

And I started to go blind.

I was just annoyed really, not even that scared or anything but my vision was tunnelling and it seemed like just a matter of time before I would be entirely blind and I could certainly live without that drama in a club, even on the dance floor.

'Juan,' I said to the man-mountain shaking away in front of me, 'I'm off home, I'm going blind,' and he just waved at me and turned back to his dancing. I may as well have told him I was off for a pee but later in the week he did tell me he'd heard me, it was just he didn't care that much at the time and he got through his trip by mostly dancing with his eyes closed; life was like that. If you were off your face, people bringing you down were to be avoided at all costs.

I went to get my coat from Bez, a petite very good-looking boyish girl who worked the coat check or occasionally the bar, 'You going Charlie?' she asked handing my jacket over, it was fairly early doors, I usually stayed the course, we were friends, she got me guest list if I needed it.

'Yeah Bez,' I said 'I took some mushrooms and I'm going blind; I need to go home for this one.'

'Oh cool,' she said but not in regard to my optical dilemma, 'can you drop me off at mine?'

'Bez, I'm going blind, I've got tunnel vision, it's like looking down a Pringles Tube, I'm not safe,' I said.

'Oh that's okay, I can tell you where to to steer,' she really didn't care. I was concerned for her safety, not mine though funnily enough.

'I would not get in a car with me Bez honest, it's not safe,' I said.

'It'll be fun,' she replied grabbing her own coat and with that we were off. My vision got worse and worse but I got her home. She jumped out without so much as the remotest enquiry about if I would be alright but I was to learn the next week, she was off her face on coke and feeling pretty para herself. In the land of the blind, yada yada.

I went all scaredy-cat driving away alone; squinting, slowing, speeding, squinting but I got home eventually and put on some music when I got indoors to lift my mood. One of those shitty disco light things added colour to my limited vision; at home with the door locked I was better, resigned to just let the mushrooms do their thing but it was a weird fucking trip - but if you've experienced it once, the second time, you just don't really give a shit.

Patrick, Pat, the wizard dealer guy asked me to play the devil in a satanic black mass; I was high on liquid acid when I eventually did, that's like super-strong acid. I'd necked a couple of microdots too, another form of strong acid but I had a high tolerance by then and I took the shit for two reasons. One, I wanted it to be a madly enjoyable experience and two, I was a little bit scared something bonkers, like horror movie bonkers, might actually happen and needed a bit of a diversion from my own worries or I might have pulled out.

Attracted mostly by the lure of free drugs I had started learning black, grey, and kinda questionable magic with Pat; I think he was perving over me but I didn't give a stuff really. Gimme the drugs you old cunt.

I'd been away with him and two other *'neophyte'* apprentice 'magicians' to join a witchy crowd, maybe twenty-five of us, to some farmhouse dormitory affair in Derbyshire one Halloween. Except they didn't call it Halloween, they called it Samhain though it's at exactly the same time. As my 'mentor' Pat told me write actual reports about the trip and design a magical working, like a real spell, following spell writing guidelines, (nah, me neither).

So in the paddock I got a group of about fifteen folk to dance naked in a circle for some health spell I cooked up over a small fire. I didn't get a cold that winter which was the intention of the spell but perhaps more to do with good luck than spiritual intervention though it was good fun and I saw some penises – fannies too but it was dark; no one had even heard of Harry fucking Potter at that time.

Dancing naked, shivering, I'd stirred their written (and chanted) intentions briefly into hot water and strained it to make herbal tea. The thing is, I was as sceptical as they come but I didn't really give a fuck if we did open a door into another dark dimension, that would have been exciting.

In the subsequent *'report'* Pat asked for, I concluded our shit dormitory accommodation was a rip-off, I also observed that a lot of people seemed to use the magical workings as a form of therapy; that there seemed to be some quite damaged members amongst us. Rather than take it too badly he'd said I had just the right attitude for another working he and some other cross-denominational magicians were developing and that I would be perfect for playing The Devil. The Devil in allegedly the first public Black Mass in Britain for over two hundred years. How could I possibly refuse?

We had rehearsed it but these people seemed deadly serious; more so than on the Halloween trip. I think they actually believed they were going to summon the devil. And well, I was gonna be the fucking host. Luckily I found most horror films just daft – the minute they strayed out of the realms of known physics they'd usually lost me; mind you I never watch them on my own, bravado only works with an audience.

By this time I was pretty convinced that there was no god so by default no devil either but none of these black-magic people knew I thought like that. It was the same bravado that had me start my own football team or going on the TV show that got me saying yes, but I was quite intrigued. I wasn't people pleasing so much as testing myself and truth is, no-one else had the balls.

The diabolists had gone to great lengths; I wore bespoke hoof-boots, like with a cleat between the big and next toe, furry tailed-pantaloons, a rubber-vest with six small breasts, long leather gloves, big fine-latex wings with a five-foot wing span which would flap slightly if I pulled a cord as I moved. Topping it all off was a big evil looking leather mask with big fuck-off devil-horns from some real animal or other, a ram-goat probably. The mask had arrived with great ceremony and was sized to my head; it was the first time I'd seen it, the day of the Mass. It was the dog's bollocks with its own black studded flight-case and when it was opened everyone went, 'Ooh!' The invoice for it was six hundred and sixty six pounds, like £*666*! It was just a fucking glorified hat, I wasn't scared trying it on.

I think they had prepared for me wimping out and they probably had a pointed curly dagger ready to stick in my ribs if I went all ectoplasm freak show and started biting people's heads off or whatever. Some of these weirdo's had probably eaten their own shit to prepare but I'd left it a lil' bit late to start asking for resumes, however, like them, I really wanted to know what the fuck would happen too. As I rehearsed folk would huddle up and chant and stuff; fuck it - if next day I was farting fire and being chased by priests with crosses at least I could claim the rights for the video game.

The venue was a nightclub for a straight-fetish crowd in Islington. It's enough said that the biggest queue in that club was to have outfit photographs taken; all types of camera were forbidden for privacy issues ostensibly but really the club made a fucking fortune out of pictures. The punters would lightly slap each other on polished latex bottoms or some woman would occasionally twist some guys nipples for comedic effect but sex per se was discouraged. The busy gay-fetish club of the time was called Fist and you couldn't take cameras in there either; that place lived up to its name. No-one ever had a free hand to hold a camera.

Before I climbed into my costume for the ceremony, Patrick, the pervy puppet-master had decided to do a small 'working' to invite the spirits into the space and he burnt pentagram stars, in liquid paraffin, on a couple of the participant's backs. It burns quite cool and well, like walking on coals, if you're quick it doesn't hurt at all or leave any lasting mark, indeed it's quite pretty and buzzy. A nice light-blue flame, which gets blown out within seconds of lighting it. But the pervy cunt let mine burn a good five seconds longer than everyone else. Five seconds is a fucking eternity when your skin's on fire.

'OW, you fucking cunt!' I screamed, and he was, a cunt I mean.

'Oh give up you baby. Here, take some of this and stop moaning,' and that's when I got the couple of drops of liquid acid. He knew how to shut me up.

Oh yeah, my costume had a foot long rubber dildo incorporated too, I forgot that bit and in a way it was the bit I liked least. Part of the Black Mass is that the the altar is a naked-female and the host is supposed to fuck her - at least in this black mass anyway. They'd assured me they were following the ancient texts but the promoters would not, under any circumstances, allow for a living sacrifice to be made as the texts required. Theatrically they shot a glove-puppet on stage without telling anyone the blood it squirted was from a real chicken they had murdered that afternoon. Not something I was aware of either until afterwards but hey, that they didn't sacrifice me was a result I suppose, I'd seen The Wickerman.

On stage I'm behind a curtain, a smoke-machine poised and out front, all this Latin chanting bollocks is underway like in some Stanley Kubrick movie; people holding skulls with candles in; smoke, incense, summoning. I'm breathing heavily into my £666 mask, sweat running down my latex sheathed back to soak into the waistband of my furry pantaloons, my sweaty hand gripped the wing-flap mechanism, my rubber knob protruding from my groin; I felt like a pantomime horse what with my face in the long mask and my massive big cock but I mustn't miss my cue.

It comes, ominous music thunders throughout the club, the

smoke machine bursts to life behind me, lights flash onto the smoke instantly fucking up my already limited vision and the curtains start to part. I mustn't move too soon on account of my massive wings which I remember to activate. I pause and look up into where my third eye would be and say quietly inside my mask, 'come on then you fucker, where are you?'

The curtain opened, the smoke cleared a bit, I ventured toward the roars of the crowd towards the naked altar who parts her legs theatrically and guided my rubber phallus into place to simulate fucking. The noise from the crowd assured me it was going well, there were a few flashes. The satanists had engaged a pro-photographer for the night; I was subsequently only ever shown the pictures, never allowed to keep a copy and yeah, it looked fucking awesome!

What happened next wasn't something we'd rehearsed though; back stage safely behind the curtain a couple of people helped me off with the mask as some woman stood in front of me with a book chanting in Latin and blew smoke and incense right into my face; like uncomfortably. I was shocked and instantly annoyed, 'What are you fucking doing?' I asked.

'Exorcism squad, trust us,' said the woman.

'I don't need a fucking exorcism,' I screeched, 'I'm okay, fuck off blowing shit in my face!' And, that I think, is where I lost all credibility with the Satan squad. Maybe I've always needed an exorcism but I think they knew enough not to press the issue; so I never had the full exorcism, I may still be possessed to this day. I calmed down a bit, 'I'm all right, thank you', I concluded but felt I'd missed a golden opportunity. Had I known they were planning an exorcism, I could have pretended to actually be possessed and dribble spittle like I was dripping ectoplasm and make out I needed an exorcism, maybe even talking in tongues. But I genuinely didn't know it was scheduled even though they were convinced they would need to do it. Me telling them that I didn't need it, meant, no matter how brilliant it looked on stage and how good the photos were, they had basically failed in summoning Satan. I have no idea what they really thought was gonna happen; like I would fly up to the rafters or something – I'd have loved that too, sadly they just had me.

Not that I needed an excuse to fuck off from the club but I found one in this, in spite of a ton of drugs I basically felt stone cold sober and went home, alone, knowing that my time chasing real demons was probably over. If the devil hadn't shown up to a party like that he was never coming, he didn't exist, and yeah, very probably neither did god either - but it had been fun trying to meet both of them.

When later processing/remembering everything that happened I came to the conclusion that we all had both good and evil inside of us. I wasn't a totally bad person, but I wasn't a saint either – where I was, somewhere in the middle, was a reasonable enough place to be.

There was, however, the increasingly annoying recurring theme that again, these were not my people. I was just an experience seeker, maybe an adrenaline junkie too or at least that's how I saw it. Quite what they thought of me I soon ceased to remotely give a shit about.

Twenty-six.

It had also seemed an entirely reasonable request and, I was in some kind of social arrears with Bill Carter anyway, so when he phoned and asked me to entertain his overseas visitor for an evening I kind of felt I had to do it really.

It was worth keeping in with Carter, he'd told me to call him that, but I did enjoy his eccentric company anyway. He was always formal and only ever called me Mr W and well, he introduced me to some top drawer living in my early days of London life - but it had been on the back of him chatting me up in a then rent boy bar, the Golden Lion in Soho. I swear I had gone there to give a message to an actual rent boy on behalf of another older friend; I didn't do rent, I had a spotty back.

Old before his time Carter, with his boffin-style tortoiseshell specs, had invited me for dinner having phoned after getting my number in exchange for a drink. Whilst I was kinda poor when fairly new in town I'd never done rent, not least because I still had the idea I wasn't attractive, and well, I had this bad acne all over my back so I hated the idea of people seeing me naked - but those spots might well have kept me alive through the AIDS epidemic. I'm pretty sure that otherwise I'd have shagged with anything that came along, for money or not as it happens, but it also meant that people like Carter never really got anywhere either - which kind of enhanced my attraction weirdly enough. I'd refused the dinner invite at first; having given him my number by the way because I just never got chatted up that often. Mostly on account of looking like I'd swallowed a wasp I suspect and might duff folk up if they came onto me and I wasn't actually gay.

'Nah,' I'd said down the phone, 'I appreciate the invite but I have no money and I couldn't come if I couldn't at least buy a round.' True.

'But Mr W, that's the beauty of Miss Sandra's,' he said enthusiastically, 'we neither of us need any money at her place, it's all free. Do come,' he insisted 'I would love you to meet Miss Sandra and it will be no fun on my own.'

I didn't dare ask who Miss Sandra's was, I felt that as a sophisticated young guy around town I should probably know by now but a decent dinner out wasn't to be sniffed at. 'Okay,' I agreed, 'I can come as a friend,' nailing my platonic colours to the mast.

'Great, I'll meet you at the Golden Lion at 8pm,' he said and I agreed not realising that having me meet him there was kudos of sorts. Whilst I might have had spots on my back, I didn't on my face and whilst I felt ugly, people like Carter clearly didn't think so. I would go on to be the face of an international safe-sex campaign and had already been on Blind Date remember, I clearly wasn't the freak show my head told me I was.

Miss Sandra's was a pet name Carter gave to a casino in Mayfair, in the Hilton Hotel and Sandra was a woman who worked there. Carter was a member of all the decent London gambling clubs and would turn up on his top-range BMW motorcycle, bringing a spare helmet for me when I was the arm candy; which went on to be quite often. The food was indeed often free, on account of him, and others he took along, losing so much money. That first night the bottle of wine he ordered cost as much as a shop - assistants wages for a month. I was astonished. He got it comped, for free.

So yeah, when he called that night in a fix of course I could help him out and entertain his German visitor for a night. With him I'd once sat between billionaires Adnan Khasogghi the arms dealer and

Kerry Packer an Australian media tycoon playing blackjack while I had just seven quid in my pocket. Carter had covered my bets but it was such a buzz. He didn't give me any actual money to play on my own account but would let me play and turn the cards over for him; correcting very rarely but we never sat there for hours, we were mostly there for the freebie dinners. That particular night, sat between the high-rollers I was holding in a piss as I didn't want to have to tip the cloakroom guy a quid from my own seven. It was inconceivable I wouldn't tip if I went for a wee so tried to avoid it at all costs. The Australian billionaire had been known to tip waitresses a year's wages just for fetching a fucking ashtray; it was a very surreal situation.

I wasn't really expecting the German guy to be a billionaire but I should have realised in sending him to Brixton where I lived then, that this wasn't one of Carter's high rollers. Carter lived in a basement by the way, not a basement flat but an actual scabby basement; one without a bathroom and he pissed in a saucepan which he emptied down the outside drain. Seriously. His motor-bike was brand new (on finance) and his suits and shoes were immaculate - from the best tailors and shoemakers – he really was what you might call all fur coat and no knickers. He showered at the gym and did own the eight-flats above his basement on a massive mortgage but his gambling debts meant it was all hanging on a knife-edge and he would just gamble the rents he got in and not pay the bank their instalments. But he looked rich and had funds so the casinos gave him plates of overpriced fish and chips to make him part with his cash on the tables. Now and then he would win and it was all going to be all right again. Until the next visit when the casino would get most of it back.

The visitor he assigned to me was my kind of age; tall, slim, quite attractive but he was wearing black riding boots which were a bit out of place in Brixton. Dark pants and top, sort of goth like but in an almost business like way. His dark hair, parted on one side occasionally dropped over one eye and he would push it back into place as he walked with the other arm crossed behind his back. Sort of fucking weird, almost familiar, but in a way I couldn't quickly put my finger on. Oh and heavily accented with a German brusqueness but he spoke good English, 'My name is Mathias,' he said as we walked to leave the station where I'd met him.

We went round the corner to a pub on Coldharbour Lane and having got him a beer I decided we should play pool, not least to avoid having to force conversation. It had all the potential to be a very long night but, well, it was a form of payback. I think Carter might have farmed him out because he was a bit odd looking and 'cos he seemed a bit dull. I figured he was some kind of German rent boy is all and I didn't want to embarrass either party with inane questions.

I bent to take my shot, 'Tell me,' he says loudly as I readied to hit the balls, 'is Mr Carter ze *ho-mo-sex-ual*?' Okay, maybe he wasn't a rent boy after all. I took my shot and took a second to think how I should answer as the balls slowed; nothing went in like it would have done in the movies.

'Well, you should probably ask Mr. Carter about that,' I replied; he prepared for his turn.

'And are you --' he asks as he hit the cue ball '-- are you ze ho-mo-sex-ual?' the balls rattle about the table to little effect. Another pause.

'Yep, I am. Is that an issue?' I ask calmly, lining up and quickly taking my shot. Nothing is going in; in the movies we would re-shoot the scene until they did.

'So tell me?' He asked loudly in this cosmopolitan, mixed, Brixton bar. He clicks the cue and yes, a fucking red ball does go in.

Looking up smugly he flicks his hair back into place before continuing loudly, 'And tell me. Have you ever fucked a *nigger*?'

I often imagine the whole pub went quiet at that point, that there was a rag-time piano player who stopped playing like when the gunslinger comes through the double doors but no one exclaimed or said anything.

'I have had sex with black men if that's what you mean but that's not a term we use in England,' I hoped it was just a language thing but the hair, the boots, the arm behind the back. What the fuck was going on I wondered, was this tool some kind of Nazi?

'Oh, I see,' he tempers and well, whatever I think other people might have heard or seen, Bicycle Tony was in that pub then and he's never really spoken to me since in spite of having been a fuck-buddy. Carter and the wannabe Nazi had met in Munich, he wasn't easily giving much else away so I decided to get him tipsy to see what I could find out - which was mostly that they liked the same music, skinhead music.

The idea of Carter listening to skinhead music was kind of laughable but I wanted to find out what their deal was. Turns out they had both been arrested and released without charge, Carter had stayed that night on his sofa, they were arrested for associating with the band, an illegal skinhead band, outlawed because of their politics and insignia. It was getting clearer that he at least, Mathias with the funny Hitler hair, was some sort of fucking neo-Nazi. But I found it hard to believe about Carter. Mind you he did know that famous skinhead Nev in the West End who manifested as some kind of far-right thug but everyone knew he just was glorified rent.

So yeah, obviously I had a rainbow duty to fuck some sense into him, the neo-Nazi with the funny hair - consensual of course - I'd just started sort of selling him the idea as we played pool, saying he was sexy and didn't he want to try it, and he stayed the night only to disappear embarrassed more or less as soon as we woke up, but not before he asked for my details; the things one has to do in the line of duty!

Carter had phoned to see how we got on, I said, 'fine thanks' ignoring any implication and asked, 'what's the deal with him Carter, he's a fucking Nazi?'

'Come for dinner on Friday night when he's gone and I'll explain.'

A couple of weeks later a letter arrived from the German, 'I never expected I could fall in love with another man' was one of the lines in it. I threw it in the bin. Thank fuck we didn't have Facebook back then so he'd be able to stalk me.

Yes, Carter had been hanging out with a skin-head band in Munich, or 'the orchestra' as he called them; no, he wasn't far right; no, he didn't like their music or their points of view, it was just a fantasy that was all. To be locked up in a police cell with a gang of skinheads was a wank dream come true for him but the Nazi had put him up on his sofa after the arrest and asked if he could visit him in London one day. 'How was I to know he would actually come?' Carter said 'but I'm glad you two got on. Tell me am I going to need a new hat?' he asked presumptuously - for any subsequent gay wedding he meant. Still a legal impossibility at the time but I certainly didn't tell him I'd fucked the Nazi; I still wasn't entirely sure what was going on but I certainly wasn't providing wank material.

'That's for me to know and you to wonder about,' I said.
Carter thought he was onto something, 'Aha; I thought as much, he was quite flustered when he came back in the ahem...morning,' I neither confirmed nor denied his speculation, just smiled and he would get the benefit of the doubt for now. I wanted to believe he wasn't a

secret Nazi, though he did get referred to as Nazi Carter in conversations with my friends from then on; were it not for the occasional glamour his company offered I might have been more exacting in my friendship with him but fuck it.

I was decorating one of his rentals for him when I found a video in his basement about Holocaust-denier David Irving which I watched. I have to be honest here; I found a lot of what was said on the video quite convincing but I never even mentioned I'd seen it to Carter mostly on account I was supposed to have been painting - but we never talked much about politics or shit. On the video I learnt that to even question the holocaust in Germany was illegal – I didn't like that bit at all. If you couldn't ask questions how could you get answers I thought but it was a rabbit hole I only briefly grazed around, I never went down it very far and went back to the decorating.

Before I left the countryside for the big city I used to follow the hunt. You know, toffs in red-jackets on horses with packs of dogs who would chase foxes to keep their numbers down. It was only as I matured and developed as a human that I was able to see how fucked up that was. I never even saw a fox on the hunts, just lots of horses, humans and dogs. We followed in cars and heard if they had got one of course but I'd never stopped to consider what that actually meant. I mean, I already knew I didn't fit in to country life; I could barely tell the difference between a field of daffodils and a field of fucking cabbages to be honest but I knew both usually stunk of cow shit. I liked shooting air-rifles but not at living things, just bottles and targets, not seagulls and birds like my school mate Clem did. He shot and grazed my hand once, it swelled up like a tangerine.

Like hunting, I'd never really been educated much about Nazi's, only that we won the wars. There was probably lots of stuff on TV but I didn't get to see much of it as dad only really had the telly on for the news. At mum's we watched the Muppets, Black Beauty and Antiques Roadshow. And did I really care enough about what happened in the war or who Carter really hung out with? I was too busy getting wasted to care about anything but myself to be honest, who gave a shit if he occasionally wanked off a skinhead?

Multiple-channel TV later plugged a lot of my educational gaps as did the internet when it came along. The school I went to was crap and also entirely white and many of the pupils were perhaps related in ways they never knew. My brother's wife was in my class at school, his first girlfriend had slept with all three of us brothers, well sort of, I couldn't get it up with her but I was able to blame that on the brewer.

Chasing foxes was never touted as anything other than as pest control and, shooting game birds was providing food, albeit for the posh fuckers and, as a kid, I was recruited as a bush-beater to shoo the birds towards the guns. I gotta be honest, the money was good and I kind of enjoyed it; in our dull countryside surroundings, the possibility of being accidentally shot was quite an adrenaline buzz and there was a camaraderie between the beaters, similarly between the shooters. Except they had their lunch in a big fuck off mansion and we sat on crates in the sheds.

Dogs would retrieve the birds but one day some wounded bird with a long-beak fell flapping around near me. No dog came to get it. My school mate Clem said, 'pick it up Charlie, kill it!' I'd kind of hoped I could just ignore it but there was no escape. He was the other side of some mild undergrowth and we were supposed to maintain a sort of marching line.

'How?' I asked nervously; I didn't even want to touch the fucking thing to be honest, it was flapping around like a lit firework and well, I thought it might even bite me, it had a long beak.

'Grab it and wring its neck,' he shouted, 'like this' and made a twisting motion like you might wring out a towel.

'Why?' I said 'it hasn't done anything to me,' a phrase that would go on to be repeated in ridicule for the rest of my school career - but only in banter!

'Oh for fucks sake!' to be fair, him coming and doing the deed for me was a favour to the bird as much as anything, it's not like anyone would take it to the fucking vet or anything, it was just a number for the tally, food and stock. To them it was never an innocent bird; they just didn't think like that.

I never went back bush-beating after that, I was asked but turned it down in spite of the money at which point the teasing about the bird started. I eventually realised that the fox-hunting thing was pretty fucked up too but I can't pretend I suddenly went vegan or anything, but the less my food looks like an animal the happier I am.

Yes, I was largely ignorant about a lot of things and had the internet and multi-channel TV not come along, that may have remained the case. In a house of limited TV viewing and my attending perhaps the shittiest school in the whole of the east-coast I hope I can be forgiven for my ignorance. I mean, yes I questioned the holocaust at one time, but I was gay too, and also pretty fucking homophobic as I didn't want to be gay in a stupid straight world. But yeah eventually I came around, I mean how many people can say they once re-educated an actual Nazi right up the fundament?

Twenty-seven.

The first time I took heroin was an informed, conscious, experimental decision. It was in the early days of my drug-using career after we had all gone to Juan's flat to chill out after a night clubbing. There was Miles, a rotund petty fraudster, Nicky his boyfriend with the dreads, Juan the best-night-of-your-life dance guy, and Bez the bar/coat check-girl from the club. Juan had asked bright-eyed if anyone had ever done heroin before and no, no one admitted to it so he said, *'we should try some,'* and we all said it was a stupid idea but before we knew it, Juan, Bez and I were heading from Hackney to Hammersmith in Bez's pink VW Beetle while we left Miles and Nick to get on with their gay stuff alone for a while.

Bez was half pissed pretty much but we didn't care, it was Monday morning, we doubted a random stop but, at the address, Bez caught her leg in the seatbelt and fell out of the car. At the time it was really funny; it's not that I'm trying to make light of it all but peer-pressure, drug-addiction and alcohol make people do stupid things. Things that at the time seem to make sound and perfect sense. I apologise looking back for the danger we put other roads users in sometimes but yeah, once we had decided to buy heroin it just became another drug scoring mission to complete.

I suspect Nicky, Juan and Bez had all actually tried it before; I certainly hadn't and I didn't think Miles had either. It was Bez's contact we were buying it from so I felt she must have had insider knowledge and Juan wasn't shy in saying he'd tried it a few times; I often wonder what eventually happened to him.

We needed to prepare ourselves to learn how to 'chase the

dragon' which was inhaling smoke off of tin-foil. We were to heat the underside of the foil on which small amounts of the brown-drug were placed. It's so called as the smoke allegedly resembles a dragon; as it burns you have to chase, or follow, the smoke with a home-made pipe, manufactured usually by wrapping some more tin foil around a pencil to make a straw. It sounded a right faff to be honest and Juan had even said, we also ought to know it tasted pretty dire and, if you'd never had it before, you might well be actually physically sick. Why would anyone bother with all that shit, I thought, besides it was sort of expensive compared to acid. Never one to shy away from a new experience, however, I lined up for my turn. Miles had defo never tried it before, I could tell by his wrinkled face and spluttering reaction, he sure wasn't expecting that taste and didn't know how to follow the smoke, most of it was wasted. But yeah, Bez, Nicky and Juan all seemed to know what they were doing.

It tasted quite unlike anything I'd ever experienced before, like burnt chip fat in baby powder; something the grim-reaper himself might use as a stick deodorant; it was pretty fucking repugnant. Within two minutes I was puking my guts up over the toilet bowl but oddly, I was glad about that; I'd been told it might happen so I sort of felt at least I had smoked it correctly, that it must be good stuff and that the euphoria Juan had promised us was in the post.

For someone keen on hallucinogenics and dancing though, what the opiate postman delivered was quite unlike anything else I had had before. It was like I was a chocolate-lover being fed the distilled essence of a thousand Easter eggs in a thimble. Like so much chocolaty niceness that I seemed to fuse with the sofa and into the softness of the room. But not in the style of a hallucination; the main sensation wasn't visual and wasn't chocolaty at all; it tasted more like actual shit; it was just an enveloping feeling; a feeling of calm, of relaxation, of a seeping-euphoria that consumed my being. Until I felt the bile rising in my throat again and I tired to rise up on glue legs, walk with Velcro feet over a Velcro floor to make it through the sticky-toffee hall into the self-adhesive bathroom. I knew I couldn't touch this shit again ever; this was a feeling similar to like when I'd taken my first tab of acid; dangerous stuff. I didn't need to do this again; oh sure, I could see the attraction but this shit had a bad reputation and I wasn't stupid. I didn't want to become an actual drug addict, *'nice Juan'* but, *'no way Jose'*.

Fast forward twenty years, I'm a fucking heroin addict.

Twenty-eight.

We used to think it was a big conspiracy that drugs were illegal, sometimes it's still hard not to think that. The very name Heroin was designed to make it sound heroic and promote sales – it was even used to soothe infants through teething at one point and a quick web search will reveal that cocaine and heroin used to be available on the high street. It was obvious to us users when we were off our nuts that the global elite had made drugs illegal so they could milk the cash cow at both ends; selling them and fighting them. We all knew that stuff the filth seized in raids would be back on the streets again within weeks.

When I didn't hear back properly from the the government about my generic batteries for electric cars idea I started to have a look around the internet to see what else was out there. Maybe someone else had tried it and it proved impractical, maybe the batteries would be too big or perhaps there weren't enough raw materials in the world. I was still convinced it was a good idea; I asked about on message boards, I made a short animated film about it. No one came up with anything other than praise for the idea. But then I came across a documentary film called, *'Who Killed the Electric Car?'* and it totally blew me away; it was like a real fucking conspiracy.

Some of the first horseless-carriages had been battery-powered and even over a hundred years ago had a range of over 40 miles and could do 20 mph but eventually the internal combustion engine took off and created a massive demand for oil. Some of the biggest fortunes in history were made on the back of oil.

As any bright kid with a magnifying glass could tell you, the sun is capable of providing all of our energy needs - if only we were more pro-active in harnessing it. Solar farms have recently started springing up worldwide but fashionable, modern electric cars were again rolling off productions lines in the late 1990's. They were widely lauded by the press and celebrities everywhere but suddenly the manufacturers; General Motors, Toyota, Honda and the like recalled ALL of their electric vehicles and crushed them, literally crushed them. There was, in the opinions of myself and almost anyone who ever sees that film 'Who Killed the Electric Car' a genuine conspiracy. Maybe there was a conspiracy to silence my idea as well; it was a bummer if I'd have to wait for my Knighthood.

    I decided to write to the then Prince Charles about the film, I felt he would want alerting to this movie and eventually an aide did write back thanking me warmly for the information saying he had passed it on and that the prince also sent me his warmest good wishes. I felt that warm guff meant he might have actually seen my letter; previous curt replies about other stuff often suggested he hadn't, (couldn't 'Defender of *The* Faith' be changed to just 'Defender of Faith' for example).

    The e-Type Jag Prince Harry drove on his wedding day had been converted to electric power if you recall, so I'm sure at some point, someone in The Palace had had the electric car conversation. The Aston Martin, Prince William drove on his wedding day had been converted to mostly run on surplus wine, this being about four years after I wrote in about the film. Publicly it was revealed that Prince Charles had insisted Aston Martin engineers find a way to run it on other than fossil fuels or, it is said, he would simply never drive it again; a potentially large commercial blow to the carmakers. I'm not claiming anything here, just saying what I did, Charles has always had his finger on the environmental pulse let's face it but maybe I was a small step closer to the knighthood.

A year before Prince William wed I was outraged when I saw news of the Deep-Water Horizon disaster where a fucked up oil-rig was puking pure crude oil into the Gulf of Mexico in a horror story of pollution. They were so stumped they actually asked on the news channels if anyone had an idea how to stop it leaking. I did.

To me it didn't seem that complicated, it was basic physics. If they dumped enough weight on it, like gravel, rubble, and rocks and then sealed it with concrete it would surely stop the leak. I was taking lots of ketamine at this stage, and deep into my conspiracy research so the normal mechanisms to contact people seemed inadequate. I wrote to the then President Barack Obama; the US Ambassador at Winfield House and at the Embassy; the boss of BP, the people on the news and anyone else who I thought might listen. Oh, and I telephoned the White House too but my call never went anywhere directly. The President and Ambassador failed to reply, (they could all learn a lot about manners from the British Royal Family) but, and I swear this is the truth, two nights after I posted my letters to the Ambassador, there was a car parked openly outside my house with two guys sat in it all-fucking-night. And I know it was all night 'cos I couldn't sleep knowing they were out there and kept peeking; I was certain they were CIA. I went out early in the morning about six and looked closely through the windscreen at the papers on their dash, they nearly shat themselves having not seen me come out as I was deliberately doing terrorist evasion tactics. (Something you sometimes do when you're a paranoid drug user.) They drove away about ten minutes later but it was very freaky. I mean having been there for nearly eight hours and then just driving off. What the fuck else were they doing? I ran their registration plate through Google but got no results, I didn't expect any really but if my browser was being monitored I wanted them to know I was on to them.

If dealer Kev had not been in the car with me when BP themselves actually called from fucking Texas I might have been tempted to leave it out of this account for it is pretty unbelievable that it happened. I pulled over outside the Ambulance station in Homerton High street and explained to the woman on the phone what my idea was to stop the oil gush; drop a ship load of aggregate, literally a ship load of heavy bricks and shit directly on top of the leak, top it off with concrete and physics itself would help make and reinforce the seal. I'd also by this time left my idea all over the internet and, whilst it was more or less the temporary solution that was actually used, I didn't even get a free tank of gas. In a way I didn't care, at the time I was just happy the fucking thing had stopped puking out its nearly five million barrels of oil into the pristine waters of the Gulf of Mexico. I was starting to hate oil and everything it stood for.

My ideas had been ripped off before though; I once came up with the idea for a disposable cat food bowl; an early smart TV (like a videophone but through the TV) and even, three years before it happened, I'd publicly envisioned You-Tube itself.

The first two ideas I submitted to major firms, one even run by an aristo, but they put out shitty bastardised versions, and they flopped (ha ha!). Both endeavours must have cost each company seven-figure investments; they were both massively advertised, I first saw the cat-food bowl idea emblazoned on the side of a bus. Had they paid me a few quid and wanked my ego off a bit they could both have made fortunes by sticking to each basic premise. I did get some free cat food though and a clock with a black cat on it; *'great minds think alike'* they had said. cunts.

I can't mention either firm by name as they have much bigger pockets than me; the cat-food people in the end basically just said, 'so, sue us'. I'd had to choose between buying cat food and fucking stamps at one point so you can guess how that went. You-Tube I never submitted as an idea commercially but I envisioned it very publicly online three-years earlier as I was making short films and wanted somewhere to show them online – besides one can't copy-write ideas anyway, only the execution of them. In a largely dial-up internet world, I was told that technology would never allow for the streaming of more than a few video feeds at a time. If I hadn't listened I might be a zillionaire by now - but the world is a better place in that it exists at all.

Oh yeah, I also wrote to the city mayor Boris, and suggested they elevate bike lanes. Although millions have since been spent since doing something similar (too-low) I didn't even get a reply. There's a time-stamped video I made about it somewhere online, posted way before they started raising them and also before a famous architecture company claimed to have come up with the idea over train lines too. I put together a letter showing how they had plagiarised my idea as I thought I could get them to collaborate on something about tidal-reach power generation but I lost the impetus deciding they were already untrustworthy. (By the way you'd need four tons of tide-water rising seven meters just to make two cups of hot coffee in case you wondered; impractical but not impossible.)

I say all this not to come across as some frustrated know-it-all knob but because it happened, all proofs on file as they say and well, though it was frustrating it's quite another thing being paranoid but, if major companies and even local government were already bastardising my ideas, it was perhaps natural to feel a little bit conspired against. I fully expected some other twat to be claiming my generic battery idea and seeing streets named after them would be a step too far.

In the same news reports about the oil spill where they were asking the public for ideas to solve the leak, they were also calling for the same public to, *"send in offcuts of hair"*! As much hair as people could spare because it was apparently terribly efficient at mopping up oil if they filled booms with it. I recall thinking that sounded a bit odd. Big fuck-off vacuum-cleaners mounted on the deck of empty oil tankers would be much better in my view but hey, what did I know. I mention it here because later when I went deeper down my own little conspiracy theory rabbit hole, the hair would take on a sinister dimension that kind of blew my mind for a while. It still does every now and then.

Twenty-nine.

When I eventually started to get some help with my head (on account of my going actual bonkers and telling the doctor I might be a serial-killer to speed up my treatment) I had no point of reference about psychology beyond popular culture and well, to be honest, I figured they would take one look at me, say how they had been waiting for me and immediately wire my brain direct the National fucking Grid to power the nearest super-computer.

However, far from catch my therapists vigorously disputing my diagnosis or, claiming I was the most remarkably complex case they had ever encountered, they were much more interested in online shopping and learning how to clinch bid eBay auctions. Whereas Hollywood might give the audience a doctor determined to unearth some repressed childhood trauma, reality sent mine massive caseloads and intellectual indifference - but we could help ourselves to free coffee and toast in the mornings though.

At the Mental Health Unit, they did sit in circles for, 'Group Therapy' or just *Group* but as one of twelve, my polite upbringing left little room to jump in and talk. One day when I wanted to talk about being so angry I'd considered running over a random stranger most of our group time had been spent on some whining girl having a breakdown because she had run out of frigging dog food.

I was paying a fair amount of income tax at the time from e-Baying and that the talk in the tearoom was mostly about how to rinse as much from the benefits system as possible, well, that used to really piss me off. Dog food girl was actually her boyfriend's carer for example and he was hers. So they each got their own benefits then some extra on top for pretending to cook each other's dinner and wipe each other's arses. Literally. It was really quite nauseating. I had a crap phone at the time but others on benefits would often arrive with the latest expensive tech.

We went on a group outing to the Science Museum one day. To avoid parking issues I took about a seventy minute walk and I was cool with it until one of the other patients arrived alone in black cab. He had been given a cab account by the benefit people because he claimed public transport stressed him out. Apparently, on average, he could use one free cab a week. But even though he claimed he couldn't use the tube, he did also have a free travel pass he would readily 'use when it wasn't too busy'. By claiming he couldn't go in a supermarket or be around crowds he was able to access another tier of financial support and well, he did sound like he was in a bit of a state, poor lamb. Two arms and two legs though but hey, not all disabilities are visible and I wasn't there to judge. He could easily have offered me a lift though; two isn't a crowd after all.

But one day in group he comes out with being excited about the upcoming Notting Hill Carnival but he's a bit annoyed because his boss has asked him to work another Saturday night *in the pub*. I'm like WTF! - this was so fucking annoying to listen to. The thing is, you have to sign a confidentiality contract to get to stay on these programs; you aren't allowed to even acknowledge where you know each other from if you meet the other nutters on the street and everything you hear inside must stay in the building. Like patient-doctor confidentiality but extended to each other as patients too.

'Er, excuse me! You're claiming cab fares because you don't like crowds and then you announce you're going to the fucking Notting Hill Carnival?' I asked, and I did swear, as you know I do that a lot and at least they never tried to censor me in the looney-bin. I mean, I know some people do actually fiddle their claims while working and stuff but c'mon; rubbing everyone's nose in it? Twat.

'How can that be right?' I continued 'and now you're telling us that while you're claiming every fucking benefit going you actually work in a pub?' The guy is going red but I doubt he's going as red as me, 'Excuse me while I just go outside and puke' and I storm out and try to slam the door but it having one of those hydraulic closer things my rage get absorbed silently by the compressed oil.

'So Charles, how do you feel?' It seemed like this was the only question I ever got asked by the therapists in that place; lanky Lee had followed me after a minute or so to the kitchen area where I was busying myself angrily washing a few mugs and plates from breakfast.

'I feel like shit' I said 'what I really wanna know is, when do we get to do something about that?'

There were never any solutions in that place; they never said I should take a walk around the garden, shadow-box, have a wank, go and listen to some classical music, paint my anger out in my own pulsating blood, even fucking meditate or something; just endless seemingly stupid question after stupid question about how I felt.

'And why do you think you feel that way?' Lee asked. Therapist Lee's entire existence was about the Edinburgh Festival, either recounting a previous year or planning to go to the next one. I never got to the bottom of what he did there, probably playing a lute strung with his own mother's fanny hair, but I suspect he was a frustrated performer paying for his hobbies by doing this therapist shit - which his heart didn't seem in at all.

'Are you telling me you're okay with that phoney twat working in a pub yet claiming he can't shop for food or travel on a bus?!' I asked him.

'I can see how that might be frustrating for you Charles,' he says placatingly.

'And what about you, don't you get frustrated Lee?' I paused briefly, 'what pissed me off the most is not that he took a taxi to the museum but that he didn't think to offer anyone else a lift in it. Piss taking prick!'

Even in the *looney-bin*; and I know it's wrong to call it that but I was crazy mad and I was in it so I'm kind of allowed to; it had fucking twenty-foot high fences and double security-gates and other sections that people never came out of, it was the real deal a bin, or warehouse for the mentally challenged but yeah, even in there I managed to alienate myself to the point of being the outsider again.

For the first four Mondays there this young, effervescent large woman would come into group and tell the same story; she'd taken an overdose, an ambulance had taken her to hospital, her folks were distraught. She didn't know why she was such a fuck-up. Four Mondays straight. She would use a lot of the group time every fucking week. I was bored of her after week two but when it happened again on week five I'd had enough.

'Erm, what is it you OD on?' I asked and she mentioned a familiar anxiety medication and when asked further that she had taken four of them. I made some appropriately soothing noises and filed the name of the medication in my memory until I was able to research it at home.

Week six, the woman turns up and sure enough she's overdosed again and been to hospital again. But I've had enough of not getting time to air my own shit, 'Er, I researched the toxic dose of those pills,' I began, I had everyone's attention, 'but it would actually take three-hundred and sixty of them to kill you-', there was a hush around the room, she was clearly a little embarrassed by this so the punchline made her colour up even more, '-*if you were a mouse*', and I quickly continued, 'There is no real toxic dose on those pills for humans, the worst thing that might happen is you could end up sleeping for a day and half and wake up with a bad headache', the room was stunned, as I'd hoped.

'Oh wow. Thanks Charlie,' she says, 'thanks for looking that up for me,' but I suspect she already knew to be honest, it was all fucking theatre for her but I wasn't finished.

'You know what you should do?' I said, she looked at me quizzically, 'You should get a job in the circus as a trapeze-artist,' I hadn't actually planned this bit of my feedback, 'it would suit you down to the ground,' I added, 'it'd keep you fit and there would be a sense of real danger but meantime you'd be the focal point of everyone's attention and your parents could be looking on terrified. But there would always be the net there to keep you safe.' Oh, now I instantly felt a bit mean, but it's what I said. Dog food girl barely stifled a snigger but no one else in the room said fuck all, not a word for what seems like five minutes but was perhaps only a few seconds or so and then the therapists facilitating asked who else would like to speak and the group moved on.

The next week was different, she hadn't taken an overdose but if I'm honest I didn't care a bit; I kind of hoped she'd either found some proper poison or would leave the group; she was another fucking fake in my less than humble opinion. There's no doubt that in that group a lot of people labelled sadness as depression; but then there wasn't a benefit available for just being sad.

The following week we were told as a group that she was fine but she wasn't coming back and would join the next intake but did we want to all sign a card for her? I didn't, that'd make me a phoney cunt too, I just felt sorry for her mum and dad but I didn't ask if I could send them a card. Eventually I heard she'd actually taken a course in circus performance at the famous Circus Space near Old Street and was doing great. I kid you not but I can't say that's a fact, it was just hearsay; but I do hope she does well on the trapeze if it's true. As patients we never even knew each other's last names - if so I could look her up and see if she's jumping motorbikes through flaming hoops and ask for some free tickets. Perhaps I sound brutal but I guess you had to be there - luckily for them though my own comeuppance was in the post.

Over the next few weeks as I got more comfortable I felt I started to understand the methodology of group. The biggest point being the interaction with the other patients; we would say to each other what the therapists couldn't say to us in a month of fucking Sundays. Like that me calling the prize-prick out on his free taxis and benefit-charade was potentially a good thing and something that had frustrated many of the staff because they were bound by confidentially too. They may well have wanted to call trapeze girl out on her lame overdoses but it was more than their jobs were worth.

'*I fell into the pub on the way home,*' said this other young masculine woman one day.

'What the does that even mean?' I asked, 'no one falls into the pub, at some point you know you are going there and just keep going, don't bullshit us, we aren't your parents,' and the therapists would just watch us as they might a pet budgerigar pecking at a dead spider, then at lunch we'd see them in the staff-room shopping online for toilet roll-holders or something.

It was voluntary that I was there, three days a week and I was supposed to be going for eighteen-months solid. They held classes like on giving a bit of thought to what others had to deal with and how that might effect their dealings with us. Other people go through shit too, give them a break sort of thing. It wasn't rocket science but they sure tried to make it as complicated sounding as they possibly could.

    I left the program after six months, the constant negativity and talk of benefits really pissed me off. All I was learning was how to function around flakes and mental patients and I actually worried that it was making me worse mentally than when I went in. To be fair, I was entertaining myself by snorting K in the toilets as the whole experience was just giving me more stuff to be angry at. I did feel that with one or two carefully aimed letters I could get the fucking place closed down and sincerely thought about it but there were people there who actually needed and benefited from the messed up support, toast and therapy they got there. What kind of person would I be if I fucked it up for them I wondered.

    What is crazy though in retrospect is how little thought was ever given to what some of us patients were actually using to self-medicate and how that might influence our sanity. Neither there nor at my GP surgery would anyone give me any calming medications at all, mostly on account on me being a self-confessed drug-addict by that time. I kept what demons I could away with street drugs but I think if they'd had a class showing that many demons were probably born of those very street drugs it could have been a revelation. Not that I would have listened I don't suppose.

Thirty.

Leaving the looney bin didn't mean my mental health got better though. I used to walk into the west end of London three or four times most weeks, usually to get stock from the wholesaler's for my eBay business or just to meet someone for coffee or something but I always enjoyed the walk into town. One of the things I like most about London is the constant state of flux; that it will never be finished. Every now and then I'd walk down a street that I'd been along scores of times previously and they would have knocked something down and I could spend ages trying to work out what it was they had demolished. Often I got the feeling that whoever lived in some of the swanky places I passed had lives I could only dream about; that they had swan's egg breakfasts but then I would see people at night simply watching TV – and whereas I'd fully expected them to be having costume parties in cavernous ballrooms, they were just staring at screens.

Walking into town I used to regularly pass this woman's hairstylists. I went past so often that I started to think they must wonder who I was and why I passed so regularly. This in a city with a population of nearly nine-million but such was the nature of my self-obsession. By this point on the inside of my flat-door there was a small note the size of a business card I had printed, *'How many more near death experiences do you need Charlie?'* it read. I would see it on the way out to score drugs and tell myself, 'Well, just one more!' smile and go score.

Inside the hairstylists one day I noticed one of the workers, bubbly, mid-twenties, cheerful, washing the hair of a client as another woman, perhaps her mother/boss, was chatting to them both. It made such perfect sense that I introduce myself and I went into the salon; they were probably just chatting about me anyway, 'oh look, there's that lovely guy walking past again,' sort of thing perhaps. I felt the least I should do is introduce myself!

'Er, hello, can we help you?' asked the mother type. Daughter pretty much ignored me and added some liquid stuff to the client's head, backed into the sink.

'Oh yeah,' I said, 'I come past your shop quite often, I just thought I should introduce myself as you probably wonder what I'm up to,' upwards inflection of the last syllable to create the question. Nothing, 'I'm Charlie', I added. Pause.

'Oh yeah, erm, hello,' says mum and I see the client trying to open her eyes only to clamp them shut again as chemicals stung her. The daughter type said nothing, she seemed less bubbly and cheerful once I was inside the shop, tense even. It dawned on me that I may have misjudged this one and that I had all the hallmarks of a fucking psycho. I was only still at the door but I felt it was time to go. If they had a hidden emergency button I'm pretty sure they would be pressing it furiously by now. I half suspected shampoo-eyes was actually shitting herself.

'Okay, well I just wanted to say hello. Have a great day,' and with that I was gone and spent the next hour wondering if they might actually have called the police. I still walk past the salon regularly, but I now stay on the opposite pavement, and I look very much more healthy and different from the time I called in; I often cringe thinking about my visit as I pass.

Oddly enough though that's not the craziest walk into town I ever had; that happened when I was deep into my conspiracy theorising; so much so I even changed my appearance twice on route to throw off any tail I had. I wore one baseball hat and took two others with me, calling in at Ironmonger's Row public baths to change my jacket and I developed a fictitious limp on leaving to throw off the CCTV operators who would be scanning monitors for my tell-tale gait. I chucked the first hat into a bin heading to the post office in Rathbone Place where I felt I could post my small parcels fairly anonymously; I did an outer garment swap again as I got nearer. Since I had already scoped out all the municipally operated CCTV I felt almost certain I had swerved imminent detention. However, outside the cafe-bar opposite, enjoying a coffee when I came out of the post office was the very same researcher who had got me onto the Blind Date show many years before! Weird. Weird as fuck.

'Aren't you...?' He had asked in an almost carbon copy approach of the day he had seen me on the Gay Pride march years before.

'Oh hi,' I said by way of confirmation. Maybe I looked rough, I did look rough. But he wasn't entirely sure it was me I didn't think, 'Yeah it's me, Blind Date guy,' I said, I was pretty unforgettable on account of the police investigation after the TV show I figured.

'And what have you been up to lately?' he asked, perhaps he meant had I put my penis through any toilet walls recently but I don't think he ever knew the juicy details.

'Oh nothing much,' I said *'just saving the world'* and to me, at that moment, at that time, it was absolutely, totally true.

I realised too late I had said too much; I'd fucked up already. He was probably one of them and had been rushed out to try and find out what I was actually putting in the mail. He told me he now worked for a big media company run by, to my thinking, obvious aliens.

'Sorry I have to go!' and I got away sharpish annoyed that after all my careful planning to avoid CCTV I had made such a fundamental error. If he reported back what I had actually said that about saving the world I could be dead by the weekend. It could just be coincidence I thought, it was media central around there after all, I just had to deal with any consequences when they arrived. Besides it was public knowledge I was on a mission to save the world; the advert I'd placed in Private Eye was hardly subtle. If I was going to develop any of my ideas, the one thing I needed was money or credit and I had fast been running out of both.

'Unsung genius needs financial help to save the world; seriously,' said the magazine ad along with an account number and sort code. I'd always wondered if those begging adverts worked and felt certain whoever was monitoring me from afar to ensure I was carrying out my planet saving mission would see it and send funds. It seemed like a logical approach at the time.

Not long after the Private Eye ad appeared I got a weird sounding recorded message on my voicemail; at the time it was unlike anything I had heard before; it sounded like whoever had left it was using a robotic voice-changing machine, *'I have many numbers for you'* it said *'let us know if you get this'*. To my brilliant mind this was clearly a coded-message and hidden in it was the winning numbers for the lottery.

For two days I tried to dissemble the code; the number of letters, the number of consonants, vowels, words, the time it arrived the length and so on. When the first four lottery-tickets I bought on the back of my workings didn't win, I chastised myself for deciphering the code wrongly. When I eventually realised it was just one of the new text-to-speech messages and it just meant someone didn't know which number to call me on, I felt like quite a knob. I mean, my ad hadn't even had a phone number in it after all, just bank account info. No-one added a single penny piece to the account by the way; it was looking increasingly like I was gonna have to save the world all on my own.

The post office trip had been to send some mail-outs to alert some of the world's most relevant parties to just what was going on. Or at least to people who I thought, in my wisdom, might want to thwart the nefarious activities of some of the world's most powerful and troublesome secret societies. By this time I had worked out 9-11, lo-energy light bulbs, fluoride in the water and was busy investigating secret-societies, but if they could kill JFK what chance did I have? It even said there on the Georgia Guide-stones that they were going to kill us all for fuck's sake.

It seemed obvious to me spending most evenings off my nut and on the internet; yes, clearly we were being fattened up like cows and in the meantime we spent all this time and effort mining fucking gold, which had no great practical purpose at all. It just sat there in a bank vault. Allegedly.

Clearly humans had been programmed by aliens to mine the gold for them so they could particulate it and blow it into their own atmosphere to reflect the sun and reduce their own global warming. It was obvious the gold in the world's vaults had been substituted for gold-plated brass or something. And oh look, the Vatican has a room shaped like a serpent, so they are in on the deal too and meanwhile this young kid from Nepal invents a solar panel that can be made for peanuts the main constituent of which is human fucking hair? Whoa, what??? A solar panel made with human hair! That revelation defo needed it's own line of ketamine to process. Obviously they were going to harvest us for our fucking hair; I knew it! Humans had collected the hair of others for millennia and of course it explained all the religious encouragement to grow it out. I told some people I really liked that if the UFO's arrived they should shave their heads immediately, Shawn thought it was hysterical, Chacks said I was taking too many drugs and should spend less time on the internet.

I went deeper; of course there were no written records of how the pyramids were built; it was done using i-Phones and i-Pad type devices. I even went to the British Museum to physically compare the size of engraved clay tablets with modern phones and was vindicated to find them almost identical. The fact the monarch themselves carried a pointless orb at ceremonial occasions showed how we had mimicked our alien overlords for centuries. It was simply a representation of a drone, with a ruby for a laser and the cross represented a rotor blade. Used by alien visitors to measure who knew what, well, pyramids and Stonehenge stuff obviously.

My bias was soon confirmed by the algorithms again when I came across the Cargo Cults of the Pacific islanders who had created effigies in the shape of the light aircraft which visited them in the war. Delivering god like astronauts with the command of fire at their fingertips (cigarette lighters) and food in magical tins, (corned beef) they longed for their alien overlords to return with goodies. So they made palm frond altars in the shapes of planes and helmets out of driftwood. That kind of explained to me why Stoke Newington church looked like Thunderbird Three and religious images of deities all had aura hats; I was a fucking genius working all this shit out - wasn't everyone seeing these things?

And didn't one of the Greeks from mythology so fear his creation that he had torn it in two so it would spend entirety looking for its other half ? Yeah, I kind of got it. We were defo self-farming animals designed to fatten ourselves up, grow our hair long and dig for gold. And when the Mayan calender ran out we were going to be harvested. I didn't have much time.

So I had put together a file containing all my biggest fears and considerations, what was happening, and why, and I'd burnt a load of copies onto discs. Self-farming animals, genetic engineering, distant planet needing gold to bounce the sun's rays away; foodstuffs to encourage obesity, nefarious groups profiting off of weaponry sales, lo-energy light-bulb to facilitate mind-control. The curious observation that so many world leaders had very narrow upper lips and well, that the solar panels made from human hair was the ultimate destiny of all human locks.

And that day, when the Blind Date researcher had asked me what I had been up to and I had said 'saving the world,' I had literally just posted about fifty DVD's discs out with it all on. A recording even of JFK's secret society speech, some video connections to cargo-cults. Some information on a weather weapon, Haarp, which I felt was causing earthquakes and other related stuff. Oh and a Word document joining it all together; with a proper paper letter complete with links in case they didn't trust the disc. There wasn't a finger print on any of them, I was forensically aware after all; but I could also be as thick as a brick.

I got home and looked the TV Blind Date researcher up on the internet and compared him to some world leaders and other people I thought were probably aliens. Yeah, thought so, same narrow upper lip and large chin. He was totally one of them too and was obviously rushed there at that time to question me. Well, maybe I was getting a bit carried away; but oh look, yeah just as I thought, now he does works for that Machiavellian tycoon figure so defo he's a fucking alien.

I put one of the spare discs I had produced into my computer, I felt sure by now that someone would have intercepted some or all of the packages anyway so I needed to just remind myself what I'd written to see if I really would have to be eliminated. Well, it might be mostly bollocks I thought, but if just 5% of it were true then society had a fair bit to worry about. I then found something I personally needed to worry about more; the Blind Date guy wasn't my biggest mistake. My biggest mistake was sending out fifty discs with my very own name and details hidden in the meta data of each Word file! Oh shit, I was brown fucking bread!

I had sent out fifty of my own death warrants and accidentally signed every one of them myself. Oh fuck!

It's crazy, oddly, but when you're in the thick of this kind of stuff it does seem very real, I can see a lot of it is bonkers now but remember, the same mathematics that might help any regular middle-aged man shop more easily for a greenhouse can also help irregular guys like me believe they have a special purpose on earth. I'm not the first person to have thought they were special and different after all. Or even Jesus.

That night I actually considered setting fire to the post office; had it been a nearby regular post box and I probably would have done but I concluded that the wheels were already in motion. They parcels would all be in transit by that time so I was really fucked. Time for a line of K - talk about ever decreasing circles. The same evening as the posting business I updated my social media status to read *'If a plane crashes into my house in the next few days it is NOT an accident.'* It got no likes or comments.

Thirty-one.

A great example of confirmation bias in recent times, exacerbated by pesky algorithms, was the whole 'flat earth' movement where a host of people started claiming the earth was actually flat and the globe idea a sinister hoax though quite why anyone would hoax that I'm not even sure. And of course there was something to it but even I'm not *that* gullible, that one was all about advertising revenue. People would queue up on the original clips to type lengthy explanations as to why they, the flat-earthers, were idiots. Or visa-versa. The longer the rebuttal the more ads they were served so the original post would generate further income for the originator, the host and the web-browser. This is often why it's difficult to get controversial content pulled, because it generates such a lot of money. Meantime, however, the confirmation bubbles grew as the birds-of-a-feather stuck together.

The racists, terrorists, wife-beaters and fascists can now all get together in their own groups as easily as innocent collectors of Teddy Bears can and cultivate confirmation bias all of their own. Whereas the teddy bear folk might well be sharing pictures of a cuddly bunny, hare-coursers might be sharing videos of a real one getting torn to pieces by dogs.

This may go some way to explaining how, with the aid of hallucinogenic drugs, I was able to go from having a sound idea about electric car power systems to being the son of an alien put on the earth to help prevent its destruction. My job as I saw it, was to save the self-farming human race from being harvested for its meat and hair; oh and the gold, clearly the aliens also wanted the gold, *We Buy Your Gold* was one of the most popular TV ads at the time.

Even stone cold sober with a few years clean under my belt, when the world went into Covid lockdown in 2020 and people got stuck indoors feasting on junk-food, unable to exercise and they were unable to get haircuts a little part of me quite seriously wondered if I was about to be proved right and UFO's would suddenly land on the lawns of Buckingham Palace and the White House to negotiate collecting all the human meat, hair and gold.

Conspiracies do happen; that cigarettes caused cancer was known by tobacco producers for over forty years before it was finally acknowledged that the information had been suppressed by a huge conspiracy. In the UK the Post Office Horizon scandal saw hundreds of innocent people imprisoned on false evidence. And the movie 'Who Killed the Electric Car' had showed me that big players of industry didn't really want electric cars running around. I felt certain I was being watched and listened to. Remember the CIA did seem to have been parked outside my house before and the FTAC cops had been asking my doctor about me and maybe poking around my computer; it's not paranoia if they are actually watching you.

As the pressure inside my head intensified over the disc-mailing bungle and I thought I might actually explode – which would have saved them the actual job of killing me - and as the evening wore into the next day and I took more drugs I felt a lump in my mouth on my inner lip. I couldn't be sure it wasn't a RFID tracking chip, but in actual fact I was pretty sure they were littered through bits of my clothing so I could be tracked at all times anyway; another reason for dumping the baseball cap on the way into the post office. I'd stopped wearing other fancy gear movie Tom had given me, he was clearly undercover and giving me t-shirts, caps and jackets with movie logos on was probably an efficient way of tracking me.

I'd given other items away too just to confuse any trackers but I was still occasionally concerned about one of the root-canal filings in my teeth, mostly when it hurt; I thought the recurring issues that sent me back time and time to the dentist just gave them an opportunity to charge the battery in the RFID chip. I did think about ripping the whole fucking tooth out myself more than once but I concluded whilst not impossible, it was improbable.

So, the lump in my mouth, okay rationally it probably wasn't an RFID chip because well really they could follow me most easily of all with my actual fucking phone, hence why I often left it at home. Which meant then that the lump on my lip was definitely cancer.

Somehow I had ingested something sinister that had brought this on, it was obviously the most aggressive type of oral cancerous cyst and what was now little more than full stop sized would soon be the size of a pea, then a table-tennis ball and then an orange before it would no doubt consume my entire face; I'd become the new fucking Elephant Man and Channel 4 would produce a documentary called something like 'The Man With Two Heads!' Unless I was murdered in the conventional sense by the global elites first; I really couldn't cope; head cancer or a knife in the night. It was very, very real to me wasted on K.

It all sounds crazy just revisiting these thoughts but I actually had them, sometimes only fleetingly, but the cumulative effects of them always added to the feeling, something weird was happening – if only I could just get to the heart of what it was. More drugs would help.

I looked at the cyst in the bathroom mirror as I heard a car door closing outside. There wasn't yet much to see in my mouth but it was easy to feel, I mean, I was playing with it constantly with my tongue behind my lip.

Oh fuck, what had I done? They were defo coming for me. Tonight or tomorrow. Those fucking discs!

I grabbed some water, my phone and coat and jumped into the car. A plan was starting to formulate in my mind and well, it wasn't entirely bonkers, if I could get admitted to hospital I might be safe; surely they wouldn't kidnap me from a public hospital?

But again, it's not like the movies. In the movies they don't have triage nurses and two-hour waits. Two hours by the way in which much of the effects of my narcotics wore off but the sense of paranoia was still quite real, as was the lump in my mouth.

'I need to see a psychiatrist,' I'd told the triage desk; half-way through their night shift by now.

'What's wrong sir, what's the issue at the moment?' a nurse asked, un-phased.

'I fear for my life, I need to be in a place of safety to avoid harm,' I replied; I must have looked a bit of a mess to be honest but it's not like I was covered in blood or anything and I had just quoted their own text book back at them, they had to let me in. I needed a break, I *really* needed a break.

'Are you or anyone else in immediate danger or pain; is there an external situation we should be aware of?' or something like that she asks me.

'No, not at this exact moment,' I replied thinking that none of the DVD packets would probably have been delivered yet, but I'd need to be somewhere secure when they were.

'Take a seat over there sir, someone will be with you as soon as possible but we are quite busy tonight, you may be a while.' I'm gutted, I haven't been triaged into the right stream obviously but I have little choice but to wait. At least I can see the door and if anyone is coming to kidnap me I should stand a chance of escaping through the hospital kitchens or overhead air vents like they do in the movies. Actually, not the vents there, they were barely big enough for a large rabbit but I supposed I should work out where I might find a knife? I scanned the signpost poster for a kitchen; it didn't even look like they had any to be honest and the shutters were down on the Costa. Life is rarely like the movies when the shit actually hits the fan.

I did seriously think about going home as I slowly started to realise that the drugs may have been more responsible for my scary thinking than actual events - but the mistake I made posting the discs with my ID on was very real. If I could get sectioned for a few days I would be able to work out a plan. Eventually I got called in front of a young Australian-sounding male doctor and a female nurse; he enquires as to what is the trouble.

'Some men are trying to kill me and I have a lump in my mouth!' I blurt out.

'And why are they trying to kill you do you think?' he asks. I suspect that he and the nurse are rolling their eyes at each other out of my eyeline.

'Erm, I can't really tell you I'm afraid. It's to do with the government.' Inexplicably I burst into tears; embarrassed I tried to muffle my sobbing, 'I found all this stuff on the internet about earthquakes and devil worship and stuff and I wrote about it and now they have my name and address and are coming to kill me,' I stuttered.

'And have you taken anything tonight, any drugs or alcohol?' he asks with that Aussie upward inflection I also use when I'm a bit incredulous.

'Well, I had some cider and spliff and a bit of K,' I admit, 'but, it doesn't really touch the sides these days,' I meant it didn't affect my thinking or anything any more, my being so hardcore and used to it by now, but, and I never seem to learn the right way with this, sometimes when dealing with health-professionals you have to sound like a minimal-user, other times a committed hard-core junkie. When you have other medical stuff going on you see, they have a really nasty habit of writing everything off as drug-related when it so patently isn't.

'I'm worried that I might hurt myself or even someone else,' I said in a last roll of the dice before they go onto the next patient in line. This is the language they use, I just want a bed for a few days for fuck's sake, so I can work out how the land lies with the fucking Illuminati types.

'So, shall I call the police for you? They can take you to a place of safety,' he says like the pure clever cunt he is. Checkmate.

I can't afford to take the risk that I might be killed in police custody like had happened to Pete of my Daily Drug Delivery time. Fucking clever antipodean cunt. He knew he'd called my bluff.

I had no choice but to go home, in actual fact not an entirely bad thing since I hadn't thought through leaving the fucking car and if I was locked up it would totally have been towed. Walking along I toyed with the lump in my mouth when it occurred to me they hadn't even bothered to look at it.

You might think that not having a plane crash through my bedroom ceiling and not having been murdered by the global elite in the next three or four weeks that I could have put the whole DVD thing aside and gotten on with my life. However, like the government not hiring me to oversea the great electric car revolution, it just didn't make sense. Clearly I was being kept around and alive for some other reason, it didn't really bear thinking about but as time progressed it did start to seem clearer; more and more obvious. If I was supposed to manifest as the Second Coming well, clearly I was going to have to be crucified; but I thought I'd need a good PR first.

If I was going to save the human race from being harvested then surely I was going to have to do it? To kill myself live on the internet and in the meantime convince the planet, well, as much as possible, that I was actually some kind of Jesus 2.0. I kinda knew it was aliens though rather than an actual god although the public might go for the god angle with a good press officer. I just had to stop the fucking New World Order doing a deal with the aliens for our meat, hair and gold. Fuck, life could be quite complicated sometimes; and really me being a bona fide coward and all? Although many times I would have been happy to go to sleep and not wake up I actually didn't want to have to fucking crucify myself.

This is how Jesus himself must have felt I thought; the man who sold the world – on freaking religion. Now it was my job to do what, sell them off religion and onto aliens or further onto religion? I didn't know; a part of me wished I'd just stayed as a fucking petrol pump attendant; this deity status was looking like a tough gig.

Thirty-two.

They say if you want to know why you took drugs, stop taking them; mostly being gay and letting my mother down were *my* reasons. Not excuses, mitigations. Having subsequently lost any sense of control over the narrative of my upbringing, I may have been clutching at flimsy conspiracy straws - but they were my straws and largely I could control what I drank through them.

I have guilt around my mother in the idea that occasionally I was crueller than I might have been to her - since she had left us - and I might have disguised that as comedy *'just having a laugh,'* but it still bothers me a lot. I bought her a silver photo-album once and the cover had slots for six or eight pictures and I went through what pictures I had of her and put in the least flattering ones I could find. Rationally, I could contest that I wanted to hang on to the best pictures of her for myself and that it was her album/frame and she'd be putting her own choices in but the truth is I didn't need to put any pictures in it at all - and I did take a perverse kind of delight in her adverse reaction to the pictures. Truth is, I just don't know, on a conscious level, I don't think I do know what my motivations were at the time; it broke my heart to discover that I could have loved her more.

I'd also told her about much of my early drug taking, she would die herself before it got totally out of hand but I used tell others it was, 'in case she was ever tasked with having to identify my body with a toe tag on it'. I didn't want it all to come out of the blue if it ever happened and I felt disclosure gave us an adult relationship. There is a truth in that but in retrospect it was unnecessary and cruel of me; intimating in part perhaps, 'look what you did to me.' My father had died before I regularly touched drugs but I would never have said that to him. Learning after they both passed that he was the real dickhead also meant my passive aggression towards mum was doubly cuntish.

These dynamics were probably in play when I called her up one day and asked her to set her video recorder since a drug documentary coming on and I was going to be in it.

The documentary crew had followed Shawn and I around all day, it was a sunny Gay Pride in Soho and although filmed months previously, mum would of course want to see it and hear me explaining why drugs were okay when used sensibly; some drugs.

I had given her the day, channel and time and was quite excited. I'd had like ten minutes of fame with Blind Date so here perhaps was the other five I was due.

'Just so you know it's about drugs on Pride weekend Mum, and they will probably show me using some but don't worry, it's all cool and legal,' I'd said. Ouch! It hurts even thinking back about this.

I remember on the day telling the camera crew that ketamine wasn't illegal to possess, that offering it to others could technically be illegal - so if I just *left it there* and people stole it well, that should be okay. I had quite serious discussions with them about drugs legislation and of course fully expected to come across as a modern philosopher of the drug scene.

The documentary had other non-gay drug users in it, unconnected with us or Gay Pride but they all seemed quite sad, smack-heads jabbing-up and the like. Then it was our section, the gays; dancing, rainbows, music, then oh look, me, getting a blow-back from a spliff with Shawn. Then me snorting a big white line, then gurning, then appearing to almost feint, then dancing around. Then getting my actual cock out and helicoptering it in the crowd. Hmmn,

I'd forgotten about that bit; I wonder if my mum had told Aunty Betty to tune in too? Oh fuck!

They had edited a huge chunk of tape down to basically make me look like a prick. I mean, I am one, I know that - and I did do those things - but the gurning was mocked for the camera crew as was the feinting. I supposed them editing it to make me look like the Aristotle of the gay drug-taking world would have been a bit much of an ask.

I wouldn't have wanted my mum to have to process that had I known what was coming and I do grimace at the things I occasionally put her through. It's not the sort of thing Jesus would do I don't suppose.

Thirty-three.

It's fair to say that I was half-hearted in my initial approaches to giving up drugs, although I probably needed to I certainly didn't want to. In the cold light of day, I really didn't want to have to kill myself either, if the drugs snuffed me out no big deal and, it was only at my most wasted that I actually thought I could be part-alien or Jesus anyway. There was periphery talk of rehab and clinics now and then but none of us took those ideas seriously since we didn't really want to ever stop partying. The idea of stopping all drugs was kind of ridiculous really and since I thought I might be contractually obliged to try that at rehab, it meant I never did anything about getting into one. And although chaotic, the idea that I was *special and different*, maybe even 'outta-this-world' was actually exciting and comforting. The acceptance that I was just some drug addict twat would, in some ways, be harder. Surely the only reasonable explanation for my shit upbringing was it was beyond anyone's control? And now, if my only real recreation was diversion and intoxication, why stop?

Occasionally I would learn of multi-millionaire celebs celebrating their many years clean and sober and I would proclaim them pointless and sad. Quite what the point of success was if one couldn't celebrate it with a debauched, drunken or drug-fuelled party was beyond my comprehension. Seriously, I honestly thought the lives of such people were dull, over and pointless. Why would you even want a swimming pool if people didn't allow themselves to get so uninhibited that they would rip all their clothes off and jump in it at parties? Well, apart from actually swimming in it I mean?

I was eventually reduced to going through the bins for bread, not scabby left over sandwiches obviously but posh artisan bread with walnuts and fruit in it; finding half a loaf in the baker's dumpster was a real result. It genuinely was. The only other occasional treat was a Sunday roast at the pub with a pint built into the price since I did need to occasionally eat something sensible. This from the guy who could often drink champagne ten-hours straight at the Conrad Hilton brunch on Sundays. The idea of stopping drinking and not having the free Sunday pint and getting a cola instead and losing actual money was just nuts! It was never going to happen so when at a Narcotics Anonymous meeting I first heard talk of 'total abstinence' from all drugs, and alcohol is a drug they said, I knew I was in the wrong place. If I was looking for reasons for it to fail, and I was, that was a good one. They'd handed me a pocket booklet/directory thing listing all the meetings in the country. It was perfectly sized such that over time, edgy-rebel me ripped lots of the pages out and used them as wraps for sharing heroin! We'd use anything to wrap up our drugs; lottery entry slips were always good ones; opening them felt like a little lottery win all of its own.

By this time I had sworn on my poor dead mother's life that I would never touch drugs again (and picked up the same night); gone on a world-cruise to get clean and detox; married a Muslim guy who didn't smoke, drink or use drugs; bought a boat to blackmail myself off of them; threatened dealers to stop serving me; thrown away loads of drugs; deleted every dealer's number I had; been to the drug-unit to ask for help; mentioned it to my doctor; tried psychotherapy at the looney bin; been to the K-Day; tried substituting one drug for another and even fucking prayed, yet none of it, nothing, nothing at all, would work. I'd get some drugs think, well, *when that's gone, that's it*, I'm done and I would go a day, maybe a couple but at some point what felt like a giant invisible hand would drag me back to the dealers. Maybe I could have empathised more with that girl at the looney bin who *'fell into the pub'* that day; karma can be a difficult mistress.

The pages I started ripping out of the meeting directory for drug wraps were used in a logical order. I'd flicked through the book, vaguely interested to learn there were LGBT meetings, my first reaction being to think a clean and sober boyfriend might work but then I figured they must be dull in bed; full of inhibitions and shit. I used the Scottish, Welsh and provincial pages of the directory first and kept the London ones for last. I could see there was indeed a meeting on Monday nights, literally six or seven hundred metres from my flat. I had known about it for ages by this point anyway. The discharge letter I'd been given from the mental health people when I left had urged me to go, no appointment was needed blah blah.

All I knew about Narcotics Anonymous was from the media and I vaguely recalled that the step-programs were based around religion and god. Given that I had done religion to the nth degree, what with the christening thing, the devil worship and actually living with that quasi church in California for a while I knew that I would stand out like a sore thumb. The whole idea that god would take a personal interest in my life just because I went to recovery meetings was farcical and even then only if I didn't take drugs or booze - it seemed simplistic; just the acceptable face of drug addiction as far as I could tell.

At my first meeting, one where I had actually been on heroin, I had heard people saying that it worked for them, that their lives were better. I didn't believe them at all, but yeah, I'd got my little directory and they gave me a sweet little key ring to say 'Welcome' I'd gone there with my sexy but straight younger friend Jamie. His family had previously sent him away, unsuccessfully, to rehab and it had come up in conversation one night that he knew where the NA meeting was and *yeah, fuck it come on then, let's go*; I felt he needed some support to quit drugs so dutifully escorted him. It was mostly down to his presence in my life that I had even ended up stuck on heroin but a few things had all happened at once to create a perfect storm.

  The ketamine dealer's girlfriend, Maria croaked after a massive cocktail of all types of drug shit went into her body; as a result Sketch, the K dealer went into a tailspin of his own and started drinking himself to death caring little for his customer's needs; he was also sadly dead within a year. Then fairly quickly a couple of other big London K dealers were raided at the same time as an exporter in Spain and well, the river of ketamine that had flowed into our circles for years totally fucking dried up. It was a very difficult time; coincidentally big riots kicked off in London and whilst not the cause, the fact that a lot of the borderline nutters could no longer anaesthetise themselves probably didn't help very much. Well, I factually know it didn't actually help but I was much too much of a wuss to get involved myself.

  There were other drugs about, new synthetic-highs were coming out every week but some of them were fucking bonkers, like madness drugs. No one had a clue what they were taking, they had no-idea about safe-limits, preparation, tolerances or toxic-doses. Without knowing people were inhaling cement-dust, plaster and even in one newspaper report, ground-up fluorescent light tubing. There would always be some kind of psychoactive ingredient added but with big money flowing around and no product, people were ruthless in filling the void. The security services probably thought their big busts kept lots of drugs off the streets. True, but what filled those gaps - anger, the new legal highs and the other spurious compounds probably killed and maimed far more folk than the real drugs would have done.

Bravado stopped younger users admitting that what they were taking didn't agree with them, that it invoked massive anxiety and paranoia and established users would long for the familiarity of something they knew and understood.

When I took my first ever drag of a *Spice* spliff (synthetic weed) I had been smoking marijuana for over twenty-years; my second drag a minute later would be my very last. Instantly I had thoughts and voices I couldn't account for or control. I'd had voices run wild in my head once before but after building up a cocktail of substances over a few hours; spice had the voices chatting in seconds. Instead of like getting drunk slowly on lager-shandy over an evening, this was like mainlining absinthe straight into your main artery. I might have been longing for K but I knew I'd never ever touch that spice shit again.

This guy Jamie and I had become friends after hanging around at the dealer Sketch's house, we both took plenty of K; very much an adult he was a bit younger than me but it's not unusual for drug-users to have age gap friendships. He was sexy though so when, previously, he had messaged me to go the pub on his birthday as he was lonely I'd been more than happy to tag along. We'd been hanging out and in a manner that was all too familiar to me he'd started asking about gay life, discreetly, but there was a real curiosity within him. Often these things come about as a result of having little or no success with the opposite sex, guys can start to wonder if they are, or should try, being gay. That they don't masturbate to male imagery doesn't seem to negate their doubt but to clarify, I don't think all straight guys have gay potential in them. I have no interest in shagging women, they just don't make my bits go rigid, (no-offence) so it's entirely natural that most heterosexual men would feel that way about not being into guy's bits and bumholes.

But not long after we started being around each other Jamie changed his *'interested in'* on social media to 'men and women' - I know 'cos I was kind of stalking him but mostly on account of him having taking to messaging me very regularly when he was clearly a bit wasted at home. I swear it wasn't the other way round. Being a bit of a narcissist means I'd make for a shit rapist; sorry, I know how that sounds, but if guys have no interest in being with me then my plumbing fails. Perhaps my wetting the bed alongside other straight guys had been a passive aggressive way of letting them know I actually had a penis.

Anyhow, long story short we effectively agree to meet one sunny weekday on our own, away from everyone else, 'Is it a date?' I ask on messenger.

'Yeah, it's a date,' he replies.

'Is it a *real* date?' I ask. Pause. I mean sticky stuff obviously.

'Yeah, it's a real date,' he replies. Wow. It's really happening I think, what the actual?

Well, the actual was that he was a heroin addict. I think first and foremost everything else that was to happen is clouded by that. I might as well tell you now that no sex ever happened, I think it could have and it came close but really, I'm too much of a gentleman.

Within about a half-hour of us grabbing some cider on our 'date', sitting by the canal, it came up that he was feeling sick, 'Dope sick'.

The K-drought had clearly got him back on the heroin. Since that time back when Bez had fallen out of her pink VW to score I had

had it a few other times. Nadine occasionally came round to smoke hers in my place and every now and then I'd have a bit with her. The thing about heroin users is they like other people to use it with them so they don't feel quite so shitty about doing it themselves but if you haven't chipped in with money they only give out grasshopper amounts so I was never worried about getting a real feel for it.

Since the K-drought I had chipped in with her a couple of times but there had been a lot of water under the bridge between my first and second dragon pursuits.

When Jamie mentioned it, I did actually think *oh what the fuck get some, he ain't gonna put out without it*; I didn't actually think he was gonna put out anyway, I hoped he would but I did get the feeling I was being played from the off. Sometimes I like to pretend I don't know what's going on just to see what will; we're all human right. Besides, better to spend a little cash now to find out he's a tool than a lot later and find out I am. When he was messaging me I had wondered if he was sat with his sister who would tell him what to write and they would laugh about how gullible a gay twat I was.

Our legs over the wall of the canal bridge I asked, 'And so you need heroin to stop you being sick is that it?' our torsos hunched forward over the rail so we could see our feet over the water; it was sort of romantic.

'Yeah,' he says.

'And what's the least amount of money we would need to make it better?' I ask. I mean, I'm in then aren't I, there's no then saying I won't do it after that obviously.

'Well it depends if you want some?' says Jamie.

'Of course I fucking want some!' I said, sounding hardcore, like I did it everyday.

And with that we're on our way. We have to walk to Stoke

Newington to pick it up and then back to mine which takes like a good couple of hours but I'm enjoying his company. His dad had died when he was just in his teens, angry at school, got into graffiti, stuff like that. At one point I noticed he had two small blackheads just under his ear. Normally something like that would gross me out but I find them endearing on him; I realised that I liked everything about him.

We smoked the heroin, his mood lightened, his sickness dodged for the day; I was calmed by it, chilled right out, nothing really mattered. Jamie had had the lion's share, he was sick after all, and I suppose any rational observer might say I was grooming him but nothing happened, we smoked the shit and within another couple of hours he'd gone homeward saying we should meet up the next day. Believe it or not he was always the lead; I could actually argue he was grooming me but yeah, I was technically old enough to be his dad.

As long as I didn't do heroin more than three days in a row he'd said the next afternoon, then I wouldn't get addicted to it. I didn't really think I'd get addicted anyway as I was taking such small amounts, besides ketamine was my buzz, when it was around. Funnily enough with ketamine once *I couldn't actually get any,* it was no big deal – as a psychological addiction it had all been in my head, if there was no ketamine to actually get, apart from being sad, or a bit depressed, there was no physical turmoil in the withdrawal. We tried all these other fucking things and a lot of them were shit but there was always cider and weed to take the edge off - that fucking edge huh.

In the same week as the disappointing Jamie first-date, Green-Andy, as in recycling Andy, lives in a squat, had brought round some scotch and got me to score him a new legal-high one afternoon. Kevin had called it 'OMG!' and it was supposed to be a ketamine substitute but no-one really had a fucking clue what it was, just that it was *'a bit mash up'* - hence the name OMG! I'm not a whiskey fan, spirits make me nasty, but I had a small dash of that just to show willing, Andy swigged it like it was pop and also put out two big lines of this new white powder. I'd had it before, it was okay, just a bit weird but as there was fuck all else about 'cos of the K-drought; I wasn't about to say no to free drugs. He snorted his, I snorted mine, he swigged more whiskey and I settled in to explore the buzz.

'Whoa,' he goes soon after, panic starting to form in his eyes, 'Oh Charlie, I feel really weird!' *Oh here we fucking go* I think to myself; I hate it when folk forget they have taken drugs and start bringing everyone else down with their drama.

'Yeah Andy, that's why we take fucking drugs,' I say slowly, like to tourists asking for directions, 'to feel a bit weird,' I'm still smiling.

'NO! No! This is really weird Charlie,' he goes then, miraculously, 'OH MY GOD!' exactly what it says on the fucking tin! Bingo! I'm quite amused by this though he is kind of weird looking and he had been glugging scotch like it was Vimto.

'I think I'm dying!' he says. This pisses me right off to be honest - the times I've had to try and sober myself up to deal with lightweights like this prick came round all too often.

'So do you want a fucking ambulance Andy?' I ask, but my voice has turned a bit. I'm like the Aussie guy in the A&E unit who'd asked if he should call the police for me. Trying to shock him into being less of a wanker I suppose.

'Yeah, quick!' goes Green-Andy, who oddly enough is going a bit green; my own vision could hardly be relied upon though, I was twatted too. I didn't expect him to say yes to the ambulance though, what a fucking clown. Everyone knows you don't summon blue-lights when there's drugs about. The best explanation may be that he is actually ill.

'Are you fucking *serious* Andy?' I ask.

'Yes, quick!' What a complete and utter cunt I'm thinking as I start to panic. It's the last thing I need, the ambulance are bound to call the cops. Oh fuck.

'It all changes things if I pick up that phone Andy, are you totally, totally sure?' I ask. I probably sound like a cunt myself but this whole incident is less than a minute old and he is on drugs, I hope he hasn't forgotten that, 'Andy, you're on drugs, it'll pass man!' I am pissed but also a little concerned for him now, he is fairly hardcore and this is out of character.

But then he goes all fucking foetal and starts imitating like a cross between a dying fly, a Labrador trying to catch it's own tail and that kiddie in the fucking Exorcist movie – all at once! I dial 999 sharpish and put it on speaker as I try to calm him down but he's sort of spasming like in a fit while possessed by the devil; and I don't even like horror movies but this is nothing like anything I have ever seen on TV before.

'Is the patient breathing?' asks a tinny voice through the loudspeaker.

'Yeah, he must be, but he's moving his arms and legs like crazy,' I said as he goes into a new move like a fly riding two bicycles 'Andy, can you breathe?' I shout over to him.

'Charlie, what have you done to me?' He says out loud. WTF?!!

'ME you cunt!? I haven't done anything to you!' I'm instantly furious. These calls are recorded, why would he say something like that?! 'You did it to yourself!' I shout back whereupon he actually fucking dies, right there on my living room floor with the ambulance people on the phone.

I panic. 'Oh my god!' I shout into the speaker-phone, it was a very accurate drug name after all huh, 'He's fucking dead!' I add. My life too is soon to be over, I'm going to jail.

He totally stopped moving, his legs and arms locked outstretched up into the air like a dead lobster and now Green-Andy is very definitely going green. Well, his lips certainly seem to be, a greeny blue. This is a fucking disaster and thoughts of prison time assault me, however, first and foremost he is my friend and I need to pull it together and do whatever I can to save him. Albeit I'm on fricking 'OMG' too!

'Listen to me caller' says the tinny voice and slowly and calmly she talks me into blowing air into his lungs, mouth to mouth (it's what he would have wanted)! Then she had me pushing his chest up and down; something I had actually done at first aid class but on a dummy with no limbs getting in the way; this fucker's scabby finger-nails could have my eye out.

Miraculously he started breathing again thank fuck but he didn't speak and he couldn't actually move. His back was part arched and his limbs were stuck out in front like this lobster thing - I'd had to push them aside to get to his chest. His eyes were full of terror but luckily when I heard a siren approaching, he was breathing unaided albeit sort of raspingly. Shortly I looked out of the window to see what was taking so long, they knew this was near death. What the fuck? They were sat in their vehicle talking casually to each other.

I was shitting myself so, having checked Andy was fairly OK, albeit sort of paraplegic, I shouted down from the bedroom window, 'Press the bell mate, I'll let you in!'

'We can't come up sorry,' he shouted out of the ambulance window, 'orders from HQ, we have to wait for the police.' For fuck's sake I thought, don't they know there's a dying lobster-human hybrid

230

in here needing rapid attention. I ran downstairs to tell them, I didn't want to shout out the window, no sense the neighbours hearing everything. I don't think he's gonna die right away but if he did from that point it'd be the paramedics fault not mine.

'Ah, we've got a flag man...' says the ambulance guy, 'a history of violence towards police at this address.'

'Oh come on, that's not fair!' I say bewildered. 'Mate, they have a history of violence towards me; oh God! Seriously?' I know I needed this man's help; I pleaded with him, 'Honestly, I have a clean criminal record mate,' I say, 'I swear there will be no trouble from me but my friend really needs your help upstairs,' I add.

He looks me in the eye, 'You promise?' he asks, meaning no trouble promise.

'I swear mate! He could even be dead already!' I say which galvanises him into action. He grabs his day-glo bag and follows me up the stairs.

Luckily Andy was still breathing but he hadn't moved much otherwise. He looked like a voodoo doll where the limbs had been pulled forward prior to pulling them off. The paramedic checked whatever it is they do and he radios down to his mate to get a stretcher; 'He needs to go to hospital, I have no idea what this is,' the bloke says and I'm like really relieved they'll take Andy away, I mean this was weird for all of us but if we could all get out of my flat before the filth arrived I might be able to work out a plan.

Within five or so minutes they have a pouch of clear liquid stuff going into his arm and have somehow folded him onto the stretcher but he still looked like he'd had a stroke and been put through a centrifuge. As they are taking him out he's unable to move or speak. I concluded it would be better if he were to actually croak than remain prawn like. I thought he was fairly well estranged from his family and he did live in a squat for fuck's sake. I doubted anyone there would feed him, much less wipe his chin or crusty arse for him. It was a fucking disaster, first and foremost for him - but for me too. From my perspective the shit was *really* gonna hit the fan as soon as the filth arrived. He shot me a look from the back of the ambulance like I have personally fed him a smoothie made from dead babies or something; paralysed with fear his eyes accusingly say this is all Charlie's fault. They screeched away on blue lights as soon as the doors shut. I reckoned I needed to get away pretty fucking smartish too, at least for a couple of hours until my head cleared; kicking off with the Old Bill wouldn't help my outcome either; I need to calm down and sober up.

The first problem was supply. They were his drugs but I had organised them for him and he had said, *'Charlie, what have you done to me?'* while I was on the landline phone to 999, which would be recorded. I was probably going to prison at the end of the day, even if he was only paralysed I had then called him a *cunt*, also on the recording; what would a jury decide if he did croak; murder or manslaughter? I could just imagine them in the Jury Room saying that the last thing he probably heard was me calling him a cunt.

Eight-years minimum I reckoned so there was no room for fucking about, I split my two phones from their batteries and sim-cards and threw all six bits into the canal as I walked along, I couldn't afford any mistakes or to even reboot the numbers. All the drugs that were left had already gone down the toilet when the paramedics were attending to him. At best I could 'No Comment' my way through the police interview and hope they struggled to build a case.

The second problem was what to do about Andy. This took some serious thought and I walked for a while along the canal and around the park playing out the scenarios. Did I own up to him having been at mine and taken drugs before he died? What if he were a vegetable, did I leave the folk at the squat and his family to find out when the police traced them or did I tell them what had happened so they could say goodbye before he died or went into a greenhouse to be fed through a tube in the soil like a carrot - but would that implicate me? Did I go to the hospital myself? If he was on life-support did I turn it off? If he was stuck limbs up like a fucking lobster he'd need tons of special equipment and care; no-one was gonna step up to cut his toenails, they were gross when he could reach them himself. It would perhaps be better (for him) if he died. I'd have to just risk pulling the plug and eat the jail time; it's what he would have wanted.

All of these played out in my drug addled head.

Worst case scenario as I saw it was he survived as a vegetable and could only communicate with his left bollock or something and the first thing he would spell out on his alphabet board would be 'C.H.A.R.L.I.E. - G.U.I.L.T.Y.' because that's what his eyes had already said from the ambulance. In fact the Old Bill were probably sat by his bed trying to get him to sign a statement implicating me by sticking a pen in his mouth and moving like a his head like a puppet to sign his name. They did still want me after all. Even the paramedic was aware I had duffed a copper up once, allegedly. Yeah, my life was over regardless. It was either manslaughter or GBH and/or possibly administering a noxious substance. I had to just take what ever happened on the chin; I could mitigate by getting rid of the phones and shit but the writing was on the wall. I could easily be locked up by nightfall – even if I was eventually cleared I could spend six months on remand waiting for my case to come up. Better get on with it, get a book and toothbrush and shove some drugs up my arse.

I decided to go to Andy's squat on the way home. He was their friend they would want to be with him, even if only to nick his laptop and phone and stuff if he did croak. He wasn't gonna need 'em if he was gonna be drinking through a straw. What a cunt! Why did he have to OD on me of all people? Fucking scotch. Who'd he think he was, James fucking Bond?

I wasn't entirely sure what I was going to say when I knocked at the door of the squat, a few folk lived there, it largely depended who answered I guess, *'Andy's in hospital, he's in a bad way, someone should go'*, would be my best opener I reckoned. Freddo opened the door, a vaguely sexy Spanish straight guy who smoked spliff almost every waking moment. My mouth opened to speak but Freddo jumped in first; 'You want Andy?' he asks in his accented English. He turns his head and shouts up the stairs,'Andy! It's Charlie!' He must have thought Andy was still in bed or something.

'No,' I say, 'it's Andy I've come about-' but with that Andy bounds into view coming down the stairs smiling - fucking *smiling*! Very much fucking alive. Very much not in hospital. Very much not paralysed. Thank fuck yes but, I am actually instantly angry! Livid, relieved, speechless and confused all at the same time.

'W- wh- w-hat happened?' I manage to utter.

'Oh they gave me adrenaline and oxygen in the ambulance and I was right as rain by the time they got to Cambridge Heath Road so I asked them to drop me off here. And they did.'

'B-b-but?' I had a lot of buts, like but, why didn't he fucking call me? But, I thought he was dead? But, I thought he was paralysed? But, I thought you knew you only ever called the blue lights in a real emergency? Forgetting all too soon that he was demonically possessed for a while and did actually die. But, don't you know the Old Bill will probably be still sat outside my house waiting to arrest me? But, don't forget Charlie he couldn't phone you as you no longer have a fucking phone. Oh twat of twats!

But none of these actual 'buts' came out of my actual mouth. I was full of emotions, glad he was okay, furious he was there in front of me and not actually in hospital oddly enough. But happy he wasn't because there would be less of a case for the filth, but anxious as fuck as they almost certainly had a search warrant by now. I couldn't speak, not anything of note. And I'd chucked two phones in the canal for fuck's sake - with credit, photos and messages on them.

'I have to go Andy, I really can't handle this right now,' I managed.

'Okay, sorry Charlie,' he said, sensing danger perhaps.

'Yeah. Later,' I could cheerfully strangle the guy to be honest. That's why I had to leave. Fancy putting a friend though all that shit. Prize cunt. I'm down two fucking phones on the back of his amateur dramatics. I go home slowly - cautiously, scanning the roads around my place. When I don't spot the police I expect them to be inside waiting but oddly there's no sign of them having been and they don't show up. I can't phone Andy and ask him what he told the paramedics as his number is swimming with the fishes. It was a prize fuck up; there weren't even any drugs left.

He did come and apologise eventually and gave me some multi-tool thing as a thank you for saving his life. I hadn't said I'd done that so he must have had some recollection of the fucked up events around it and probably got off on my having to kiss him - by proxy. I forgave him obviously but I haven't hung out with him since. Once bitten, twice shy. It was traumatic, fucking traumatic; like even a bit PTSD'y. It's one thing having to babysit someone whose taken a lil' bit too many drugs when they think demons are coming out of the walls but it's quite another when you actually see the possession as a spectator. It makes you real cagey about who you do drugs with to be honest.

So yeah, the whole new alphabet of 'legal' fucking highs were pretty much a no-go area after that and the Spice. The thing was, Andy got away with it, if the chemist that put together the OMG! had moved one molecule left or right Andy could be eating via a straw and shitting in a nappy even today. Clearly it was some kind of synthesised fake ketamine, since it had similar cerebral effects as a K-hole and it seems to have lasted about as long but, the physical stuff, the dying-fly and demonic effects, were a new one and a step too far. Word got round fairly quick and we all avoided OMG! pretty much after that - but we later heard dealer Kev himself had been arrested for running naked down his high street. Probably more off-putting than the Exorcist effect.

Thirty-four.

Jamie didn't ever try stop me taking heroin, but why would he, in his head it was probably a good move if I got hooked since it might ensure he always had access, at least while I still had money. I do actually remember the thought process I had with myself, *'Oh fuck off Charlie, you barely take enough to get a grasshopper stoned, how bad can it be?'*

But the biggest turn on to heroin at this time was that there was nothing else familiar around. Not that you wanted to take indoors on your own; not after the OMG! and crazy lobster drama. Cocaine was an expensive party drug I needed lots of and I didn't really want MDMA to sit in and watch Coronation Street and I would end up humping the sofa. Acid just went on way too long but had actually got hard to find anyway, after K had arrived.

Cheap pro-rata and easy to score, Heroin offered pure relaxation and it's main effects wore off after a couple of hours. I couldn't imagine it posed that much off a problem. Day five I was still just doing grasshopper shitty sized hits, three bags between the two of us and only ever smoking it. Jamie hadn't ever jabbed up and we both agreed that was a step too far. If we were in the park we would snort it but really *'Chasing the Dragon'* as it was called, following the smoke with a small pipe to inhale it, was kind of romantic since I would often solicit his help to hold the foil - and I was kind of falling for Jamie. When he suggested the next day we should get some crack as well I was in straight away and my daily outgoings doubled on the spot. Three and three we would ask of the dealer on the phone. Or three brown and three white, like the code would fool a jury that we were ordering fucking finger paints for our kid nieces or something.

Kev was most disapproving. Not so much of the crack but the heroin he hated - or rather he hated heroin users. I played down whatever I was taking, even though there was no K around he was always trying to flog something or other. 'Crack will steal you life,' he would say, 'but heroin will steal your soul,' like I was gonna take life advice off of someone who let his dog shit in the hallway.

'Crack's great if you've got problems,' he laughed another time, 'if you have problems and smoke crack, all your other problems disappear and all you'll worry about is how to get some more crack'. True that.

The first time we took heroin and crack in the same session I asked Jamie to kiss me. And he did, briefly on the lips, without hesitation. We sat holding hands on the sofa, nothing else happened but I knew I would buy more crack the next day. In a way taking crack with heroin is like drinking an energy drink and then sipping a hot chocolate, they make little sense theoretically but really, what you're doing is looking for the mysterious Utopia of Bliss. Just buzzing enough off the crack so as not to have heart failure and just chilled enough by the heroin that you couldn't be bothered to murder anyone. Throw in a few cans of cider and well, I suppose it could be an advantage takers delight.

Jamie actually said one time; *'you need to get me really pissed,'* - he meant to fuck with him but that was so never my style, I'd been raised with fairly good manners. I'd get pissed with someone to have fun *with* them, not to have fun *on* them - actually I did wee on a few straight guys in my time as you know but not to take the piss as it were. But in him going in for the kiss and holding my hand I felt this would all work out; I felt a little bit guilty that he might be acting out on some kind of daddy issue thing but I wasn't about to hurt him. That much I knew for sure.

Two nights later he asked if he could sleep with me. Like literally sleep in my bed. He'd stayed before on the sofa after which he'd said that I should get him pissed, presumably to rape him. Of course he could sleep with me.

I lay there like a frightened lamb in a fucking slaughterhouse.

I'm not backward in coming forward about sex but usually guys that came round and got into my bed, got in it to fuck, not to sleep, they weren't coming round to make macramé doilies. This was a whole new ball game.

On the sofa we'd briefly kissed again, no tongues, before turning in to bed, it was looking good! I figured he was just nervous it being new and all; maybe being in an actual big-bed in a bed room was the permission he needed to give himself. After a few minutes when we'd settled down I nervously moved my hand over his crown-jewels. And the cunt pushed it away!

'Don't, I'll cum!' he said and quickly he turned his back on me. And then pulled my arm over his shoulder to sort of cuddle him. This was way too much to bear. It was the most exquisite sort of torture I'd ever experienced. I tired to prevent my semi rubbing up his behind. We slept.

Well, *he* slept. I sort of tormented myself for a few hours wondering what else to do and worrying that I might wake him up and break whatever weird kind of spell this was. It was like going to sleep with an adorable pedigree cat on your bed only to wake up and find it was a dirty pillow case that had been stuffed with old spunk-covered socks.

'So what was last night about James?' I asked in the morning, deliberately using his full name to give him a bit of distance.

'Nothing,' he said, clearly a little bit embarrassed. I figured I may as well make it easy for him.

'You're not gay at all are you,' I asked but as more of a statement than a question.

'Hmm, dunno. Maybe not,' he could barely look in my direction; it wasn't revulsion though, I felt he didn't want to disappoint or upset me.

'Look do me a favour bud, take that off your status where you say you're into guys and girls will you?' I said pragmatically adding, 'Let's just put this behind us and move on as friends huh?'

'Yeah sorry,' he says, all genuine like.

He still asked to sleep with me a couple of times in the next week or so and we did, on our own sides of the bed but I found it all emotionally torturous really. He was round most days, or I'd go to his where he still lived with his mum, only ten or twelve years older than me as it happens. But she was always super polite and kind to me.

Crack, heroin and unrequited love *eat* fucking money. I was haemorrhaging funds fast and we'd soon tripled our first day order. If Jamie had money he would chip in and he did work two or three days a week at a carpentry workshop near the Oval. When Jamie fucked off for the night some nights I started to score some more skag on my own that I didn't have to share with him. He'd found a dealer on my actual road just by standing waiting for another one to show up. On one occasion I got a delivery less than a minute after calling. It was drug users dream; while there was money about.

Drugs often make silly ideas seem really brilliantly sensible. Like handing letters to the fucking Prime Minister sensible - so one night when the subject of sexuality came up again Jamie said he still wasn't sure he wasn't bisexual. If he wanked to vaginas and tits he was straight I'd said, if he wanked to cock and hairy arseholes he was gay. If he wanked to both then maybe he was bi; why the big mystery? Cash was getting short and I was rinsing my way through various credit lines, I didn't care about the money, it would all come good when I could be bothered.

'Maybe we should get married,' he says after I'd mentioned the acid sexuality test. He knew I had been married to Chacks, well civilly-partnered.

Jamie suggested this, not me, 100%.

'Seriously? That's a shit idea!' I said but to him it wasn't, not then at that drugged up time. To him right then, it seemed to make as much sense as me going to to see the Prime Minister had to me.

'No seriously, if we got married then it would all be respectable and I'd be able to do it!' he said. Quite what Freud would make of this was not something I stopped to think about, I was wasted too. Maybe it was a good idea after all.

'So what, you wanna get married, to me?' I asked.

'That's no proposal. Ask properly!' he said. What a cunt, he did actually say that. It hurts to re-live it, I mean it *really* hurts to tell the truth. I do literally go down on one knee.

'Jamie, will you marry me?' I ask half-expecting some kind of punch line.

'Yes! Yes I will!' he says and gives me a non-kiss hug, 'but we can't do it 'til after we're married,' he adds, 'and I'm the man,' and I'm so deliriously happy with the idea of it, wasted though we both are, that I don't really care about the plumbing implications of it all; it's a simplistic notion about what gays do in bed anyway.

Later we simultaneously update our social media profiles to

'*Engaged*' though agree not to append each others names as he needed to speak to his mum first. Fair enough.

He was due at work next day, but to cement our happiness we agreed I would meet him for lunch. And I have to admit I was very happy as he left that morning - hubby leaving for work and all that shit - I didn't think there was anything we couldn't work out.

Clearly the gay shit had all been on Jamie's mind for a while and if this was his solution then, fuck it, I was in. Mind you, I hadn't even seen his dick by that stage; if I tell you I still never have you might guess what happened next.

We met at the Oval station at lunchtime and his body language right away was cold, guarded and suspicious. I have to say, I wasn't expecting it but also I'm not there to do a sales job. I LOVED the idea of him wanting to marry me. I'd often wanted some of the straight guys I'd hung with to fall for me so I was delirious it had finally happened and I'd thought this was unsolicited and genuine. Fucking mug.

As I have said, I'd be a crap rapist, I need people to exude some kind of genuine enthusiasm, and what could be more enthusiastic than wanting to marry me? I'd even got the Nazi practically begging for it otherwise that wouldn't have happened so I know what I'm looking for and I also know right away when I haven't got it. This was a busted flush.

Yet when he had left my place earlier he'd seemed perfectly happy so I just hadn't got around to thoughts of being blown out for a second time. Genuinely, I had not. I had had the most delirious evening and morning ever on account of both the intoxicants and the romance and now they were both gone. There was no fighting it. I had to check though, 'Oh no! Are you fucking serious, have you been yanking my chain again?' I asked before we'd even gone ten yards.

'If you liked it you should have put a ring on it,' he said, like from the song. You evil cunt I think. He raises his finger almost giving me the finger. I'm fucking furious and heartbroken at the same time. My world was over once more but really what was I thinking? He's just a fucking smack-head; almost young enough to be my own son at that. If there were any cunts in this equation Charlie it's you I'm telling myself, silently in my head. A mantra earworm starts up to remind me I'm a cunt.

'Fuck this. I'm going home!' I say, walking off, 'I'll speak to you later,' I was very dejected but drugs make crazy things happen; I had let myself get dragged down again. Surely this was my rock bottom I thought as at the tube station. I wondered if the windscreen wipers on tube trains would get bits of my brain off if I jumped in front of it at high speed. I wasn't really about to jump but I might push that cruel cunt Jamie in front of it were he stood there. What a cunt, he's a cunt, I'm a cunt, the world is full of cunts. And for a gay man that's no version of heaven.

I mention all this simply because it happened; there's no doubt I've repeatedly had a tendency to fall for straight guys. There was an internalised homophobia that came with growing up around the most homophobic town in the country where they burnt the only gay bar down and any sense of difference was weaponised. There was one black family in the whole town and everyone knew their names; that I still remember their name all these years later shows how it must somehow have been banded about. I honestly don't recall bad things being said but for sure they must have been; I probably stared when I saw them in the street I suppose.

Whatever feelings I had about being attracted to my own sex I had largely kept to myself; I didn't want to be the subject of bad utterances. Had I grown up in the great metropolis I might have found affinity with groups of gay people but by and large, when it came to hanging out I wanted it to be with 'real' men. My own internal shame about being gay really meant I felt uncomfortable being seen out and about with obvious gay folk, you know campsters and the like. As some kind of back-handed compliment people used to say to me, *'I'd never have guessed you were gay Charlie,'* and I'd take it as praise when really they're saying all gays are poofs; I'd challenge it nowadays, quite theatrically, actually but I can still be cautious, particularly outside of London.

So the idea of dating someone who might identify with my own struggle was a big draw. The problem is, many times I had mistaken a bromance for romance. There was Philster from school, who had once made noises about wanting to try gay stuff – but he blew me out when I asked him to wank me off. I realise I should probably have offered to wank him off but we live and learn. Nothing happened. Then there was Newman at college; he looked a bit like my brother's mate Carl who had threatened to kill me. I pretended to like a band, The Stranglers 'cos he liked them and we both drove to London and slept in my car to go to a concert and see them. He talked dirty and hardly ever mentioned vaginas and stuff, mostly cocks and spunk, I fell for him. Nothing happened.

Aiden was skinny, blonde and wore these tight drainpipe jeans; he had a convertible Triumph TR7. I managed to share his bed one night, as friends after we got drunk together. Nothing happened. Well, I pissed the bed and he woke up covered in my wee but there was no sexual element to it. So a kind of 'nothing happened'.

An almost identical guy, Gary, an American GI stationed in Germany when I worked there, also woke up covered in my piss, in a hotel we had booked on some away-day. Apart from that nothing happened. I always wanted stuff to happen, like sex shit but this inherent need for reciprocal desire always got me holding back – that and, of course, the biggest fear of all, rejection.

There were others but those and Jamie were all heartbreakers really; and Jamie was the biggest heartbreaker of them all because well, he offered that brief glimpse of it all being possible. When I think about it and do the maths, I probably spent about twelve to fifteen years of my life pining for guys who enjoyed my company but probably wouldn't go for my plumbing; most of them not even knowing I was gay - so the reverse could also be true. That's not to say they were wasted years; I had some great times and liked being around them but I was probably in love with an idea as much as anything else.

So the biggest catalysts for my drug taking to excess had certainly stacked up; I had an inherent shame about my sexuality and an associated inner homophobia. I had my mother abandonment issues and the parental deceits I had learned about. Now I had this fucking Jamie, failed romance, head-fuck shit to contend with; my car had recently been stolen; my actual gay marriage had long since collapsed; I was surfing along on a credit line that was soon to run out, my eBay business was boring and pretty much over and, before long, I would eventually sell and smoke almost everything decent I owned, oh and the cat had died. That was a dreadful time. The cat dying was one of the worst days of my life. I don't even want to talk about that if you don't mind. I think he loved me.

But the truth is, even with wedding bullshit ringing in my ears I still didn't want to dump Jamie as a friend, it would perhaps have been the easiest, most sensible thing to do but at this point I didn't have many friends left to be honest and well, I had actually become a heroin addict by now. So I had the, *'let's just put this behind us and move on,'* conversation with him again and did, pretty much get my head around the fact that the sticky stuff was never going to happen. I still wanted it to but once bitten, twice shy. In fact I was very shy about it now: I wasn't going to get rejected emotionally a third fucking time. He would still rattle around my brain several times an hour though. If it was my rock bottom, I stayed coasting along the barnacled-arse of it for another couple of years and remained friends with Jamie, at least when I had money.

To be fair Jamie had started to beg for us; I would look out for him security wise, I was just still a bit too hung up to actually beg myself but I did do it a couple of times - though he had a hound dog expression he used that would get us money quicker. I did feel a bit like Fagin from Oliver Twist and I have to say, in my fucked up head, it was all still a bit romantic - when it worked at least.

What he made out of begging had no rhyme or reason to it; we could get enough to score a two and two in half-an-hour some days, others he would barely make enough to buy a newspaper all afternoon. When it didn't work it was fucking excruciating, it was no kind of life.

Thirty-five.

There followed an unremarkable couple of years or so where really my only motivation was to find ways and means to get more heroin. I was physically addicted by this point and without it I would now get dope-sick. Yeah, I lost that one.

First you think you're going down with a cold, you start to ache and shiver - I never thought it was going to happen to me, the big I Am. I was so shocked when it didn't turn into an actual cold, it just went deeper; next your actual bones start to itch and hurt. So, if you have the money, you just spend it to feel normal again. I sold my stuff; cameras, jewellery, chains, a five-grand Rolex I'd vowed I'd never sell; I got just over two grand for it, I smoked it within three weeks. I had some diamond earrings, should have bought me ten bags of heroin. I got two bags.

Heroin steals your soul Kevin had said. I sold my late mother's jewellery. I didn't even pawn it, I knew it was never coming back when I went into the shop. The three bedroom house I'd bought up north when my dad had died? I'd snorted that long since. The boat? Snorted and smoked. My car, via an insurance payout? Snorted and smoked. Oh and my third of my mothers estate, enough to have bought another modest terraced house up north, that went too. Every penny I had earned and saved was gone. And at one point in the good times I had been paying eBay more than twice a shop-worker's annual salary just in listing fees and commission – so it was a healthy income but without a partner around I had no motivation to answer dumb customer emails along the lines of, 'These two quid earrings are they real diamonds?'

Eventually I even sold my computer.

The thing is I didn't really seem to care for myself too much; certainly not when I was on my own. Having Chacks around had given me a motivation to be semi-businesslike. But with him learning how to run his own online business, when I went a bit bonkers, he was very well placed to strike out on his own; he still trades today and is now quite rich with three houses. We're still friends.

But eventually I had nothing much left to sell and no credit left and I ran out of money; I think I knew it would happen sometime and as I was 100% never gonna risk my liberty to get funds, mugging people or dumb shit like that, I think it was probably an engineered real rock bottom.

Every two weeks the government would send me enough to pay the bills I absolutely had to pay; electric, water, gas, phone and with whatever was left I could get high for a few hours. The money would go into my account at about half-past midnight; if the dealer was still around I would have smoked seven-days budget in about three hours. The money I put aside for the next two weeks food would be spent by the very next afternoon. In those days if you'd asked me what my favourite food was I would have answered *'reduced'*. I soon got to learn what time to go to the supermarkets to get the grub that had just been lowered in price. This from the guy who had once consumed the finest food and wines at some of the finest restaurants of the world. Reduced, out-of-date lasagne and tofu; whatever the fuck that was. And then there came that point of going through the bins for bread.

Food isn't that important when you get dope sick. Which is one of the reasons why heroin users can often look so scrawny. It's not that they don't want to eat, but if you're clucking, you sometimes can't eat anyway. It hurts too much to even swallow so until you get your fix, food isn't even on the agenda – and the idea of cooking food or somehow arranging for something to eat all becomes a bit alien. Users will feed each other though, go to a squat and when they cook, they'll offer you food. They also have lines into the supermarkets security staff and charity food donations; there are soup-drops and sandwich hand-outs a plenty in London so the truth is you don't need to go hungry. But heroin users will - because their primary concern is a desire not to feel sick and that takes money not a packet of yesterday's sandwiches.

But then something odd did happen for me; fairly unremarkable in the scheme of things but Shawn, the ex, had years before bought me a crystal-ball, something I'd asked for. You know the sort of thing fortune tellers look in to tell the future; obviously it didn't work for me or I might have looked in and seen the nut-case I was to become. But this one day a pal, Tom the truck driver, best described as a functioning user, had come round to smoke some hash at my place – like grasshopper strength spliffs but hey, beggar's can't be choosy. He spots the crystal ball, wants it for a present for someone and within minutes I'm packing it up for him for the price of a bag of heroin and I can't wait for him to fuck off.

Very few people ever knew I was taking heroin, he was one; skag had always had the stigma of shame about it, that very idea Kevin articulated about it stealing your soul. Tom eventually fucked off, I got the heroin delivered soon as and settled in for a bit of bliss.

Well, if my first experience was like that essence of a thousand Easter eggs this was like an out-of-date Milky Bar had been left on a radiator but there was a feint buzz of sorts. Sure enough the pain had soon left my legs, it was always worst in my legs, my calves in particular and the big bones under them but that's it. In next to no time I'm out of gear, out of friends, out of money and I've just sold something special. Whatever else I had sold prior to this I felt I could one day replace, even the jewellery, but this was different, it had been a present from Shawn.

My inner dialogue started calling me a fucking loser; *why would you do that you fucking cunt?* I asked myself. Shawn must never find out he probably wouldn't notice or I doubt even mind that much but he would think you're a loser Charlie, if he knew and he was an actual loser; he'd lost his teaching job to ketamine. He was worse I thought as I acknowledged my trusty old competitive nature shining through, even in my darkest hour.

This was my rock bottom, I knew it there and then, that this had gone too far and I needed to do something about it. Which was a lot easier said than done.

Thirty-six.

I was aware of a synthetic opioid called Subutex (Buprenorphine) that Jamie had talked about and I had tried a tiny amount once; it allegedly kept the heroin withdrawal sickness away. Technically if you took it and then took heroin, there should be no effect from the heroin and if you didn't take heroin it was meant to keep the sickness at bay, making buying any a bit pointless.

I made an appointment with my GP prepared to fully turn on the waterworks and confess to being a heroin and crack addict; the ultimate patient shame; they already did know of my ketamine problem not least from the looney-bin discharge report.

'How can I hep you today?' she asked; old-school, no messing.

'I need to get some Subutex to get off of heroin please doctor?' I said wistfully; I felt little actual shame.

'OK, you'll need to just have your urine tested by the nurse. I'll write you a script for two weeks to start, come back and see me then and we'll put your dosage up,' she said very matter of factly. And that was that. Mostly this kind of drug was a supervised in that you had to actually take it in front of the chemist but she'd given me a regular take-away prescription to consume at home. It was a real result.

I peed in the cup and tested positive for alcohol, marijuana, heroin and crack. There was no test for ketamine but it was off of my radar anyway, my having become a regular crack and smack head. Apparently the Buprenorphine in me would show up in my pee too, so they could check I had taken it when I next come back. My manipulative head made a mental note of this, being pretty sure I could sell some of the tablets to buy crack.

The dose prescribed was the lowest one going. I took just one as prescribed but later called the surgery to complain, and tried to get more. The message came back that that's all I was getting but the procedure would be to increase the dose slowly so as not to poison the system. This made no sense to me at all, but no matter how much I argued they refused to put me through to the actual doctor or change my appointment – unless it was a genuine emergency and why didn't I just give it a try as this was not the first case the doctor had dealt with, she was quite experienced with local service users. Touché.

Over the next few hours I scrabbled enough money together to score some brown as I couldn't risk being sick; somehow I decided not to eat more of the pills on the first day but in spite of not feeling too bad did get some heroin just in case. Skag in hand I settled down to smoke it and was looking forward to at least gouging out for a while but it was such shit gear that it barely touched the sides. I wasn't even sure it was even heroin as I felt quite put off by the taste and smell of it - it was probably synthetic I thought. Slowly it dawned on me that this was the desired effects of the medicine so I was actually quite impressed. If I took the pills then the heroin wouldn't even work – that totally registered with me. These pills make heroin obsolete and it does seem they might well keep a lot of the withdrawal sickness at bay. They work. Who knew.

Once I took one of these pills in the morning, to then buy heroin would seemingly be an utterly pointless exercise. I'm suspicious the wheels would come off somewhere, I mean people are on methadone for decades, but then of course they might *need* to stop opiates, but did they really *want* to? But although I had the tools available to me to stop being dependent on heroin I could still fuck it up, I'd have to be diligent.

That was, I think, the second last heroin I ever bought; the next one didn't work either and money was way too precious to keep losing it on maybes. Seriously. I didn't see any point if it wouldn't work. I wasn't stupid. And the medicine did stop me getting dope sick. Getting off the Subutex itself was quite fucking hard though but there was also, another slightly harder nut to crack in the meantime, the actual crack.

At the point of first seeing the doctor I had pretty much given my life to the acquisition and use of heroin for maybe four or so years; the crack too but at least I wasn't injecting. Nor did I think I ever really would; same as mugging folk, a step too far. So far.

The doctor though had started me at 2mg of the magic potion and when I went back they wanted to double the dose. I made all the right noises but this made no fucking sense to me at all, not if it was *already working*. I could get good money for the spares from a couple of people I knew who couldn't or wouldn't line up at the chemists, they had proper jobs. As long as I didn't screw up the pee tests at the doctors I could actually close the door on the heroin chapter of my life and whilst I was a little bit sad about it, I was ready to do just it. The piss test would only show I had taken some not how many so I could do my own detox program. It was though essential I didn't get a supervised script that I would have to swallow in the pharmacy.

'Oh thanks Doctor. I really appreciate your help,' I'd already said how pleased I was that the tablets were having a positive effect straight away, I still tested super positive for booze, crack and marijuana but I'd told them I would; I got my next script for double-dose for another month.

I sold the extra ones about an hour after I got them and bought some crack. There is no magic bullet for crack unfortunately. I kept on taking enough heroin medication to keep its demons at bay and pass the piss test again. And they doubled my dose again. Seriously. I couldn't fucking believe it. Now they were giving me 8mg per day and I'm using 2mg. And the next month they doubled it again to 16mg. I couldn't believe how retarded the system was. I hadn't gone in saying I was climbing the walls or anything, I'd gone in enthusiastic, that I had seen potential light at the end of the tunnel and had they suggested they leave me at 2mg I wouldn't have objected because I simply had no idea they would so willingly hand out more.

This seemed, as far as I could find out online, to be the accepted practice. I didn't do a lot of research before first going to the doctor to be honest because I was fairly serious about getting off of heroin. I wanted my soul back and too much information with me can be a dangerous thing. I didn't want to read what people could do with it, abusing it and all. That's why I was swallowing it as suggested and not snorting, smoking or injecting it. As people sometimes do.

But in the same way I didn't want to be on heroin forever, I didn't want to be on replacements for ever, I was increasingly aware of the growing opioid crisis in the USA since I did see bits about that on the news so I decided to do my own harm reduction detox. If I had done what they prescribed and gone up to 16mg I daresay I could easily have been stuck on it today but instead by month four I was down to just 1mg so 15mg was practically profit. Everything else I sold apart from a few I always gave to Jamie, he though just didn't want to stop the heroin as much as me. I think he liked the lifestyle rather more than I did, the begging and shit, but all the money I got in I spent on crack. It's not like I'd become some living fucking saint. Yeah, I was ready to get off the smack but in a way the crack was a bigger problem and yet another health risk you don't get physically dependant but the psychological addiction is a like a super-magnet.

People do take crack intravenously but we had always smoked it. I was a bit annoyed because I hadn't gone into the crack thing with any kind of aforethought it was just suddenly, pow, fuck *another* addiction. To smoke it you fill the bowl of a pipe with a bit of wire-wool; easily accessed as pan scourers. Adding the crack you hold the whole pipe vertically and inhale the smoke through the tube. Crack gets its name from the crackle noise it gives off when your burn it this way. Heroin users can often have black faces from the soot of the foil, crack user have tiny burns on their cheeks and in their upper garments where bits of the pan-scourer have burned; all will have burnt and blackened fingers. The wire-wool deteriorates each time it is heated and for sure, ever time you smoke it some micro-sized bits of metal shit can end up in your lungs.

I did inject once, speed. It was just such a tiresome long-winded way of getting drugs in me, and since I did it with some weird guy, I was left wondering if he'd secretly infected my needle with HIV as these were urban tales bandied about; so it wasn't a great first time. I favoured snorting or smoking drugs as being faster to mechanically consume and that I was a lot less likely to end up with a whole alphabet of diseases from needles. He'd brought drugs which helped when he wasn't quite the guy in the profile, older and well, less Photoshopped lets say. He did however, have drugs so I wasn't about to throw him out. As he'd prepared the needles and injected me, I'd told him of my fantasy to have sex with a motorcycle courier and would he wear my biker jacket and do a bit of role-play? Oh and tell you what, I have crash helmet too. Would he humour me and put it on, just for a laugh? Ha ha.

I'm surprised the poor fucker didn't inject me with a massive air bubble, give me heart failure and burn my flat down but maybe he was used to getting guys bung various paper bag-like substitutes on his head. If an Olympic swimmer had come round clutching needles that day, I might very well be dead from drugs already.

With another fella who also had a face for radio I had pretended he was a washing machine engineer in a bit of creative role play, 'If you put your head through the porthole door into the drum cavity you might be able to see the loose change causing the rattle,' I'd suggested and was so relieved when he did. It's the only time I've ever bummed anyone who was wearing a washing machine as a hat. He had drugs; quid pro quo huh.

But crack we all just smoked. Tom, who was already pissing into his colostomy bag on account of his kidneys giving up, once cancelled a scheduled MRI scan 'cos he was worried about the bits of metal he'd sucked into his lungs. The scan was for his kidneys but he was so sure the super magnets would suck all these lil' metal wire worms out his lungs and his chest would look like a Play-Doh Medusa that he persuaded them to go for an ultrasound instead. Quite apart from the wire though, the tar was repugnant, you could see it forming on the glass-pipes from the very first use. Eventually though we would all scrape the tar out and smoke that as well before turning our minds as to how to get more.

Jamie turned up one night with some money, unusual but not unheard of, enough to keep our respective wolves from the door for an evening anyway; we scored, brown for him, white for me but soon he started blubbering, like crying - which was a bit weird.

'I mugged someone!' he says and, asked to elaborate through what were probably crocodile tears, he told me how he'd held this guy up with a knife. Taken a good days wages off of the guy and given him a bit back, 'to get home,' he said and, 'because I wanted him to know I was desperate and not a total bastard,' and, 'the guy said, *no problem mate, I know how it is,*' allegedly. Jamie's making out he's one step away from friending this poor fucker on Facebook, like he was doing him some big altruistic favour giving him his own money back.

I'd like to be able to say that I was big enough to call the Old Bill or even to give Jamie a thump or even a proper bollocking but the truth is I still cared/had hots for him - and his own mental state wasn't exactly built of a firm foundation. I wasn't impressed though.

Homeless Mick had once turned up at Braindeath's gaff trying to sell a bag of workman's tools and I had kicked him out the house saying he was a prize cunt for nicking someone's living. But I was never burning a candle for Mick and in a way this was much worse. In my further defence I was high on crack so a fairly big part of me didn't give a shit. But I did know what happened next could be influential on Jamie; although I hadn't discouraged him from begging for us, quite the reverse, this was just fucking nuts. If he was gonna go down it should at least be for a bank job and a decent pay-off, not pocket change. I remembered what my father had said to me about drink driving that time, *'if you ever drive home in that state again I shall call the police,'* and how it mostly had the desired effect.

'Well, Jamie,' I said, 'it's happened, we can't go back in time and undo it, you have to live with it and move forward, but it is a pretty shitty thing to do. Just don't do it again!' I doubt those were the right words but they were what came out, besides I didn't know what I'd do if he did it again; spank his naughty pert-bottom most like.

'Yeah okay,' he goes, 'I'm not gonna do it again,' and to be fair I have never heard that he did. Not that I supposed he'd tell me again anyway; I'm not even sure why he did in the first place to tell you the truth; well apart from the drugs I mean, drugs - which I'd help consume. That made me a cunt too really if I thought about it, and I did.

The next morning after the mugging confession I felt sadder than usual; he'd fucked off home anyway and there was no food in the house worth speaking of but the familiar opiate aromas hung around the place like a cheap scent for camels. I genuinely never wanted this actual junkie life, I just ended up in it by a sort of default. I hadn't aided and abetted the mugging but I'd benefited from it, albeit after the fact; this changed things for me with Jamie really. I didn't want muppets turning up at my place with the filth in tow; it was just stupid and cuntish. I'm not a saint but any shenanigans I had perpetuated to facilitate my drug use had never put another person in fear of their life.

I had practically concluded that having no money would help me get clean eventually; I could earn money, I wasn't stupid, it's just having much was a bit too dangerous at that stage. I also knew I was never the type to mug anyone; I hated even visiting prison, being the other side of the wall would be the death of me.

Coughing my guts up again over a bitter mug of tea without milk, since I didn't have any, I figured it was probably time to go back to an Narcotics Anonymous meeting.

In what I had left of my torn NA directory I found an LGBT meeting in town which I had decided upon. I kind of hoped I would meet some amazing rich guy who would either help me kick drugs or at least buy me some in the meantime.

I had to walk into the West End and eventually found the meeting in some basement, easing my way past two guys at the door who I assumed must be going too, I didn't speak to them and them not to me. I followed some others to the line for some tea and biscuits; I took two Club chocolate biscuits and six cookie types, no one seemed to watch or remotely give a shit as there were plenty and I found a seat at the back and tried to hide.

Everyone seemed to know everyone else's name and they

hugged each other in this phoney fake way that I knew I would never be a part of but I thought I may as well stay for the tea and biscuits and listen at least. What the fuck else was I gonna do without any frigging money?

And then the cunts start passing around this girl's purse thing with sequins on it for a collection. I put in fifty pence as it went past me, a fairly large percentage of my total net worth at that point. So much for free biscuits, it was so depressing. Then they read all these fucking rules out; we do this, we do that, we pray to god this way, we ask forgiveness and shit. Bear in mind when I first ever went with Jamie we were wasted on heroin, in the cold light of a comedown day and without him to distract me, this was tiresome. And I didn't believe in any god anyway so quite what these bible bashing fuckers would make of my satanic black-mass and mushrooms with witches was anyone's guess.

Having read out all the rules and explanation cards, this guy starts to tell his life story over about twenty minutes. Well, what a cunt. What a total cunt.

He's got new this, new that, new cat, new dog, (one or the other or even both possibly) new boyfriend, his health is brilliant, he's been on holiday, he is surrounded by love, he sleeps well, he's got money, new teeth, his mum loves him, his dad too, oh yeah new job. Did he mention his new boyfriend, giggle giggle? Everyone giggles along with him and their mop haired heads are bobbing up and down like fannies on a spring. And I hate everyone; I have never felt so alienated in my entire life. And oh yeah, he hasn't done drugs for four years and everyone's like 'well done!' in this bizarre Pavlovian response they do every time someone mentions their *'clean time'* - a phrase I hate as by default it makes me feel dirty. I mean, I kind of am physically and drug wise, but that misses my point.

Then there's this weird section, like in an old TV show, where people put up their hand to speak back and say he's, *'such an inspiration,'* or, *'just what I need to hear,'* shit like that, and that they love both him and his awesome message; real vomit inducing stuff.

But then they start playing some sort of emotional Top Trumps; whereas the main guy had said he had a shit childhood and life before everything turned to gold, everyone who put their hand up now seemed to do competitive feedback; like his life wasn't nearly as shit as theirs. I almost expected someone to say they lived in the leaky coal shed and a lucky day was if they got to lick the frying pan for their dinner. It was kind of indulgently crass but no-one interrupted whoever might be speaking which was odd; someone should have done, it was painful. After three-minutes they were signalled to shut the fuck up; most did but there were some total cunts who carried on for five minutes or more. No one objected or shut them up - it was a narcissist's dream in many respects.

Now and then someone would speak with no relation to what the guy had spoken about at all. Like they had lost their gym bag or some such irrelevant shit and I sort of lost track of what their point was but it was clear these were all damaged people. I mean, this one guy was saying how he had nearly had to have his leg cut off because of injecting and people actually laughed at that; they seemed more concerned about the lost gym bag really.

Towards the end after time had run out for talking, there's some more praying and shit and then an announcement that some of them are going for pizza and everyone is welcome. *Hell will fucking freeze over before I'm seen dead with these sad fucks* I think. Imagine my real/using friends seeing me out with them I think, all one step away from singing cum-by-ah. All I definitely knew was it wasn't for me all that cult shit, I was on my own again, I just didn't fit in.

But before it's all over they literally join hands like in ring-a-roses and do this weird chant prayer thing and I'm roped in and obliged it seems to just go along with it. Then the guy on my right hugs me, without even asking, and before he's released me the guy on my left is waiting to do the same. These people are fucking weird; I head for the door and get out as fast as I possibly can. I have never needed the oblivion of some crack more in my entire life.

I managed to talk the dealer into some tick on the way home and with every step I took all I could think was that I was one step nearer blowing all that phoney bullshit out of my brain with some crack. I was never going to know these people, I was never going to have all the new shit, the new boyfriend, the new job or new life and I certainly didn't want those self-indulgent types as friends, and I was probably never going to be able to shake off drugs. I needed to get back onto ketamine I decided, at least I knew where I was with that. I got some crack though, smoked it and lay in bed that night probably the most depressed I had ever been without something really bad happening. I didn't sleep well at all. Discovering that there is no real solution to your drug addiction problems is depressing.

Thirty-seven.

Poverty did get me in the end; running out of money and having to go through the bins, dumpster-diving again, it all just got insanely boring; like, not having *anything*; food, drugs or even cigarettes. I was reduced to picking discarded butts up off the floor and rolling them into something smokable. You can see questionable folks doing the exact same thing most any day in London but it's no way to live. I found a whole chocolate bar in the road that had been run over by a car and the filling was all seeping out of the edges. For a minute or so I felt like a lottery winner genuinely happy as I feasted on it and then, later, I just felt terribly sad when I reflected on what I had actually done.

The next Monday with fuck nothing to do, nothing left to eat, nothing to smoke and nothing other than water to drink, I knew the NA people would be having their dumb meeting at the hospital annex place near my house. I knew they would have biscuits; hopefully chocolate biscuits. So I went for them, ostensibly. I wasn't literally starving but I could sure use the sugar rush.

After the last meeting it wasn't as excruciating on this occasion and, being smaller and straight, it wasn't so fricking *gay*; they'd asked me to read some inane shit out off of a card so I did. But I had to introduce myself to do so, because that's what everyone else did. I thought I may as well not kick up a fuss about their rules just yet and I didn't want to look like a novice so I just said it, *'My name's Charlie and I'm an addict.'*

'Hi Charlie,' they all said in reply like parrots and I read their inane reading, *'we are under no surveillance at any time,'* it said in the text – that was so fucking simplistic; I mean come on are y'all that gullible?

After the meeting finished they did the final chant and huggy hug bullshit thing again and through gritted teeth I pretended I was cool with it whereupon someone invited me for pizza. 'Nah, I'm okay,' I said, 'I gotta get home.'

'What you rushing home to?' this builder guy asked with a wide smile. I smiled back, 'Come for *fucking* pizza,' he said, 'I'll get it don't worry', and suddenly I felt like crying. I didn't sob but it was touch and go and I swallowed a lump in my throat. The way he'd said, '*fucking* pizza,' reassured me somehow, and if I'm honest, it was the first time anyone had invited me to eat in years. I went for pizza with him and a handful of other folk from the meeting.

I was very cynical, they didn't seem to want anything or really care whether I'd listened or taken their message on board or not. When, at the earliest opportunity, I got up to go they just sort of echoed this phrase; *'keep coming back',* that was some kind of novelty when you're used to "and don't come back!"

They hand out keyrings at those meetings to mark the achievements of a month, two or even years clean and sober. I thought it was a fucking moronic exercise, I was thinking like, Awh bless 'em. Sad cunts. Like how many keyrings does one person even need and also why, if they have years clean, do they still turn up to these painfully dull meetings?

I walked away from the pizza kinda glad that I wasn't barred already. And this one phrase someone had read out about actual drugs, *'one is too many, a thousand never enough,'* stayed in my brain - so simple an idea really but bang on the money. I thought about that a lot; it's pretty much all I could remember of the details next day.

A fitful week later I did go back again and one or two of them even recognised me and remembered my name and some guy suggested I could make myself useful at the end by washing the coffee cups. And to help myself to biscuits; exchange is no robbery I thought and agreed to do the dishes. And we went for pizza again and some other guy gave me half of his, since I'd insisted I didn't really want one. I just didn't want to look like a charity case to be honest.

Over the next few weeks I went to occasional meetings in other venues and whilst no-one really talked to me at them, I did get tea and biscuits but I kept a low profile, not doing any readings or saying I'm an addict out loud again or anything, just watching and listening really; some of it wasn't total bollocks. But at the Monday meeting, the one near my house, they always made me quite welcome and I got slices of pizza here and there. I was slightly worried that they might have kicked my head in when they found out I was gay as they were a bit geezerish so I outed myself one night just in case, *'nah, I'm gay,'* sort of thing, in answer to a football question.

Barely an eyelid was batted but before I went home from the pizza place this bruiser type has a chat with me, all innocent and that. Tells me his kid is gay and he's brought out his own make-up range and he, bruiser guy, is, *'proud as fuck'.*

For the first time in a long time, I felt like there may be a light at the end of some weird long tunnel. Although I was still using crack if I had any money, the long periods without cash were cushioned a bit with the recovery meetings, tea and biscuits. Would I have gone if I had had enough money for drugs? I doubt it to be honest, not at that stage but I was finding myself at their meetings more and more often; no one gave a shit if I didn't put money in the collection. I soon went from, 'what will they think of me,' to, 'I don't care what the think of me,' to, 'oh nobodies is really thinking about me anyway'.

After a few months, this teacher type guy I didn't really like asked me my 'clean-time'.

'About thirty-eight days,' I said.

'Well done, your first key ring. It's a big deal!' he replied and goes to hug me like I've won Eurovision.

'Oh they're not joined together,' I said, dodging the hug. My clean days weren't consecutive but even getting one day off was a big deal to me; I wasn't even counting the days that joined together. That might work for them but I wasn't there to quit forever anyway. Their first key-ring is to mark thirty-days solid, clean and sober. I wasn't there to give up drugs I was there to get through not having any money and reboot my system.

At the end when they do the key-ring malarkey they would finish up by handing white-ones out to the newcomers, people who were at their first meeting or to people back from a relapse. Folk who had fucked up and fallen off the wagon would get up walk forward and everyone else would applaud - I hadn't understood that bit at all. Like, why would they clap people for taking more drugs? It made no sense to me. I wasn't ever doing that, the walk-of-shame, besides if they knew how often I still actually took drugs surely they would bar me, but I clapped for the other losers.

It was just crack for me at this stage as money and circumstances meant there was hardly an option for anything else. But the gaps between using it got longer and longer; up to nearly a week quite often but I could have picked up maybe forty of their daft white key-rings; hardly the best white to pick up in the neighbourhood when crack was on tap.

At one point I found myself looking for a thirty-day keyring on eBay as I thought it would be funny to wave one at my using friends. That was a bit fucked up I suppose but I never bought one, money was tight and oddly enough, lying to get given one at a meeting just didn't seem right either.

I saw it all as a kind of reboot, like you do with computers, turn it off and turn it on again and any glitches will solve themselves. Give my body a bit of a holiday; my bladder was recovering slowly since I'd stopped the ketamine but I was still coughing up dark shit regularly and my short term memory was shot to fuck, I could barely remember anyone's name even being told it four or five times, much less read a book.

Look for the similarities not the differences they would say, probably because there were so fucking many of the latter; they would talk in riddles of things like *fellowship, abstinence* and *sponsorship* but the crazy thing is, slowly it seemed like they were my kind of people after all. You know, party people; I wasn't the only person to have started on drugs slowly only to have eventually sold all their shit, taken heroin in spite of vowing never to; occasionally someone would admit to also having pissed the bed. But the god shit was a big no-go to me and I was glad it was so full of it to be honest. That meant I need never take it seriously or do their daft 12-steps, seven of which included or alluded to a *'higher power'* - besides their readings all said *'God', 'he'* and *'him'* so it sure seemed like religion by stealth. I wondered what they'd think if I told them about my stint as the devil but although a simplistic system, I actually didn't want to get barred; it was fulfilling a need for human contact I hadn't even been aware I needed.

They encourage everyone to speak but it's by no means compulsory; one day the meeting near me was sparsely attended and everyone had 'shared' except me and the pressure was on and I felt I had to speak or look like a nerd. So I piped up with the, '*My name's Charlie and I'm an addict,*' opener and like I'd heard others do thanked them for being there, you know, polite stuff and as I'm doing so I inadvertently mentioned I'd had crack over the weekend. Not like it was a big deal, no-one really cared besides lots of people said similar shit. Later though by applauding me into submission the cunts made me get up and get a white key-ring and I had to walk up while they clapped! I didn't understand why I deserved a round of applause for saying I smoked crack and flicked my palms out in a what-the-fuck kind of way as I sat back down. Someone leaned over and said 'they're clapping your surrender not your relapse' - and there in that moment one of their big differences became a similarity. Oh, that was *surrender* was it, was it that simple?

They recommended newcomers do ninety meetings in ninety days - what kind of loser would do that I wondered? I supposed I'd been to the pub as often, definitely dealers; three-times a day sometimes but I did notice something odd; if I went to a meeting then generally, not always, I wouldn't use drugs that day. Even, and this was incredible, even if I did have money.

One day they asked if I would cover for an absent *Greeter* a week hence; you know point people to the right door, the shitter that kind of thing. I agreed but thought little more of it until the day arrived and I was due there that evening but mid-afternoon I got the urge to get some drugs and had enough actual money to do so. I was all set to go and remembered my agreement to cover the greeting thing. I was gutted, I couldn't exactly greet people at a fucking recovery meeting off my nut on crack and I'd agreed I'd do it. So I did, clean of drugs. I was kind of both happy and sad. But oddly I didn't score that night after doing my stint greeting either, I felt it would be bad manners somehow.

I dipped in and out but I would go most Mondays to the local group and a couple of other meetings; I still wasn't looking to stop everything. Although an, *'abstinence based program,'* that was for other people, I couldn't imagine giving up the free pint with Sunday lunch. Yeah, even that was off limits; like I would ever say no to a spliff if one was going round. A year or so passed; life was a little more manageable but money was still tight.

One night some woman from the fucking meetings saw me and pal pissed at a squat party. I was mortified. When I saw her at a meeting a week or so later she just smiled, she didn't say anything but we both knew. From there every time I 'used' the meetings would intrude on my thoughts in a sort of blanket of guilt, it was weird.

Bored one Saturday morning I went to a 10am meeting at a freaking church in Shoreditch; yeah, a church! I kind of knew some of the NA people whom I didn't already hate would be there. It was okay as meetings went, no big deal but, and this is a big but, I didn't buy or even go searching for drugs, or even a can of beer later that day. My first ever adult Saturday night sober, and it wasn't actually that hard. And I had cash, not tons but enough. I was bewildered; it couldn't be that simple could it?

Next day, Sunday, I went to the same church for a meeting at lunchtime and handing out the keyrings this guy got to the orange ones and says, 'anyone for thirty-days and a thousand-nights?' and something clicked inside my head. I still hadn't ever got to thirty-days, I hadn't even been bothered to be honest, but it was many hundreds of nights, over a year, since I'd started going to their meetings. I found myself asking myself why didn't I just try it; why didn't I go for thirty fucking days, how hard could it be? I didn't use drugs that Sunday either. Fuck it, go for it Charlie, show them you could do it too, whenever you actually wanted. Show yourself. No one said this, I just thought it.

At twenty days without using my phone went and it was Jamie, I hadn't heard from him for a while and he asked, seductively I felt, if I wanted to 'hang out'? I'd said no, that I was fine and I was twenty days clean. I felt that was the point of my *actual* surrender, when I finally knew I'd had enough of that life.

I went to a meeting every day for over a month and got my thirty days; yippee! I went up for my keyring on the actual day but they'd run out and didn't have any; I was confusingly gutted! The useless cunts. Could you imagine, having ridiculed their silly fucking rituals I was annoyed that I was unable to wave my little plastic flag? I did get one the following day whereupon I'd decided to try their suggestion and do ninety meetings in ninety days. I wanted a sixty day keyring badly. I actually liked the applause to be honest with you – it was a long time since I'd done anything I felt was worth applauding.

I'm not ashamed to admit that the ninety day process I thought was only for losers totally changed my life. I haven't used illegal drugs or alcohol since; it simply put a good habit where previously I'd only had bad ones. If normal life is a roller-coaster ride than the ninety day thing is like that clicky-click bit at the start of the ride that you have to go up before your fun train sets off, and each daily meeting was another click up the mountain.

Getting off the last dregs of the doctors pills had been agonising. Like a heroin cluck, even worse maybe; the inside of my bones itching but I made it through a long challenging week by going to the meetings. I had a bit of clean time from street drugs now after all. Prescribed medication when not abused didn't count against that; and taking but a fraction of the prescribed dose probably deserved some kind of medal; but eventually I was off everything. It was just me and the world.

At nine months clean I was asked to tell my story, to sit at the front and explain in fifteen minutes how it had all worked for me. I explained how I'd gone from poppers to spliff to crack and everything in between and how I'd gotten around the god shit by making NA and the meetings themselves my Higher Power; that I didn't need to pray, I could just text another member and unlike god they would usually text back. That god didn't get me to meetings, I just used Google maps. I mentioned selling all my shit and that getting rid of my crystal ball had been my rock bottom.

It went down well, I got a few laughs and people said my honesty was refreshing. They didn't know I'd been selling my withdrawal prescription for money, but what they didn't know wouldn't hurt 'em. When I'd mentioned it to one of my new friends, Garf, and said how I got round the proof of medication pee test he said it *wasn't very spiritual*. So soon enough I even stopped doing that and told the GP I didn't need it any more and wanted to taper off. Something I'd already done for myself anyway but I still sold the pills to get money in. I'd consoled myself that indirectly I was helping other people get off heroin; people who couldn't or wouldn't stand in line at the pharmacy but I supposed I had become a dealer of sorts.

Crazily, when I stopped them all and still passed all the piss tests my GP fetched in one of the practice partners (or some such person) to meet me and shake my hand. They had never had anyone get off them totally before; I find that quite telling - about the addictive nature of pharmaceuticals rather than me I mean.

The next summer, still clean, I volunteered at a boat-club, crewing for a while and they soon suggested I take my Skipper's ticket, to be able to take passengers on the London canal system which

I did. After showing I wasn't a total fuck-up, one day they asked me to take a narrow-boat to Little Venice, a five hour trip, with just one woman crew member up front. I'd been before, it was a nice jolly on a sunny day.

Entering the near mile-long tunnel under Islington the dark made me blind for a minute or two but I didn't crash into anything; my respectable crew member was up front keeping watch as we tootled along. Twenty minutes later, coming out into the literal blinding light at the end of the dark tunnel, this voice from the bank screamed out as I slowly came into view, 'HERE!' he shouted, it was a street drinker, can in hand on the canal bank with his chums adding, 'I KNOW YOU!' my helper looked around as he shouted 'NARCOTICS!' I pushed at the throttle and we sped up to maybe 5mph, still painfully slow, 'you still clean?' he shouted and I longed for a turbo-boost or maybe the tunnel to swallow me back up.

'Ha ha, great to see you,' I answer, embarrassed, 'keep coming back!' and as we pootled slowly past he raised a can to his lips and waved; I knew then that I was the lucky one; that not long previously I would have been the twat on the bank with a can of beer shouting at passing boats. My crew member didn't mention a word, she was right at the front so that might actually be the case but that precise moment cemented a desire in me not to use drugs or drink again, it was a real eye-opener, like looking in a old flaky mirror.

Cutting down had always been hard; it never occurred to me before going to meetings that stopping altogether, *abstinence*, could be easier. There was a cigarette analogy to help me. Imagine, they'd said, just limiting yourself to one cigarette at night at 6pm. Well, at 2pm, 3pm, 4pm, 5pm and 5.30pm they'd said I would just torture myself thinking, 'well, not long now,' whereas if there was no 6pm ciggie, those thoughts never need materialise. And it was true; the ideas in the

12 steps and the, *'one is too many, a thousand never enough'*, mantra got me off of cigarettes as well as drugs.

At a year clean, Garf whose chastisement had got me off selling the Subutex, took me out for dinner, fairly posh - I was touched. As we finished he reached into his bag and brought out a wrapped parcel, a gift for me. Fuck, I hated shit like that. Now in due course I'd have to buy him something; I prepared to pull the right face that he'd expect to see for whatever this was.

I opened it and instantly choked up; my voice faltered, I felt a tear in the corner of my eye. The bastard! For three whole months he'd sat on that information, gone from that other meeting and without a word to me or anyone, ordered, signed for, wrapped and presented me with my gift; there in front of me, just like the one I'd sold, was a fucking crystal ball! Finally, in NA, I felt as if I might possibly be somewhere I could feel comfortable.

Quite a few years have passed since I got that gift and nothing drug or alcohol wise, not even a can of weak lager or a tiny grasshopper line, has punctured my sobriety and my life is golden, fucking golden; I have a TV licence and use fabric conditioner for fucks sake. At one point I even got a buzz out of changing my broadband-supplier; that was pretty weird, enjoying normally dumb, boring shit like that. Beyond all the usual dreams of cars and boats and travel lay this land of contentment I never knew existed and to find out it was actually okay, being sober and gay. Well, who knew?!

Waking up without worrying the police were gonna put the door in was a novelty; my short term memory more or less came back in full. I can now actually read books where before reading anything was like trying to fill a bathtub with the plug pulled out and I now pee not that much more often than everyone else.

That there was a very real connection between how many drugs I took and my shitty mental health was a revelation too; there no doubt that all of the substances I took to 'self-medicate', just made things worse. The very stuff I took to *'take the edge off'*, was what mostly created the stress to begin with; finding that there was no real edge, that life is generally okay and bearable all on its own was living a life way beyond what I thought was possible.

The thing is, I'd never given my adult self a chance to know what it was like to function without some kind of intoxicant. Yeah drink and drugs might have helped lubricate a challenging adolescence; I just never thought to stop when I was supposed to have grown up.

Whilst doing my ninety meetings in ninety days the NA convention happened in London at a big venue in Euston; it was dreadful but mostly because back then I hardly knew anybody in an ocean of hugging strangers. It was like being trapped at a trade union conference on a fucking cross-channel ferry. But at the end they'd collated all the *'clean time'* they'd had coming through the doors. It was 9638 years! I'll never forget it, 9638 YEARS! There's been times in my life when I couldn't go half a day without drugs; I often couldn't go even ten minutes without thinking about them. I could no longer argue with their maths. For some people this shit worked and if I wanted it to work for me I just had to get into the middle of the bed; I didn't have to believe in god, just that there was more power, a higher power in people working together than in me trying anything on my own. I made a choice to just fucking go for it.

If you want to know why you use drugs stop taking them they'd said; internalised homophobia, was big big player on my field; I had to be pissed or wasted to have sex with guys. Finding out that not only could I do it sober but that it was actually better was ground-breaking. I did get crabs from my first ever sober fumble but hey shit happens. I found it hysterical that in NA they said it was a Higher Power moment; yeah, I even 'fessed up to getting crabs. Shame dies in the light.

By doing their 'step-work' something I thought I would never do in NA, I was able to interrogate the very real pain I'd felt over my poor mother, to see that all the adults charged with my care had probably been flawed in their own ways but that they had seemed to want good outcomes for me and had simply tried their best with the fucked up circumstances they'd found their own selves in.

I've also come to realise that, whilst not impossible, it is quite improbable that I was actually part alien or the second coming of Christ. That my finding a narrative I could control in my conspiracies gave me licence beyond circumstances I never could. Even if I was offered one I do though reserve the right to refuse any DNA test that could finally disprove my alien parentage. A little part of me still harbours the notion it could be true and it would be terribly dull to find out I am just like everyone else in thought, word and DNA.

I can't honestly say I like everything about 12-step recovery; I think a lot of the language they use is sexist, archaic bullshit, but I've come around to some of it. I didn't like the idea that they called addiction a disease at first but I realised in many ways it's actually worse; people will at least feel sorry for you if you have cancer - and you wouldn't end up raiding the kid's piggy bank for chemo. I still don't believe in god but I do believe there is more power in my talking to one or more people at meetings than sitting at home on my own. Addiction isolates, recovery connects. I don't like everyone that attends; just 'cos people stop using doesn't make them saints; some of the folk who go to meetings are total arseholes and some of what is said is real cringe. But I can never get away from the fact that it works. I started out cherry-picking the bits that I liked but I keep going back to the cherry tree. I do all of their suggestions some of time, some of their suggestions all of the time, but I certainly don't do all of their suggestions all of the time. I'm not praying to a god I don't believe in but I will hold hands in their huggy-hug thing at the end and say the serenity prayer. I just drop the word god and think of it as a well formed intention.

My friend Michael laughingly says he doesn't understand why I can't just use the god word since I say 'cunt' often enough. He's also said that he didn't like me when he first met me, but he thinks I'm a decent guy and a good laugh nowadays. They let you believe what you want to believe; Michael does believe in god, we've been going for Sunday breakfast with a couple of other pals for a few years now but what's said at the meeting stays in the meeting though we still rip the piss out of each other. My kind of people.

The 12-step program offers me three things as I see it; real strength in a clear-conscience; sincere wealth in good friends and true power through self-control but I am, and probably always will be, a work in progress. I've hosted loads of meetings as secretary and even told my story a few times at the LGBT ones. It's one of the few places in the world one can go and say, 'I hated your meeting and everyone in them,' and they'll all still clap and thank you for coming; that's madly powerful if you think about it.

There's no ifs and buts about it; if I still thought it would be more fun out there still using drugs or I'd have better sex if I was wasted or drugs would actually make people more sexy or interesting, I'd be out there drinking and using. The really great thing about recovery is that they are my kind of people, the piss-heads, the junkies, the party-people; that's what I was, it's just that now we don't use drugs or drink any more. And on the way home from pizza none of them have ever suggested we get some fucking crack. I really feel like I found my tribe and I belong, finally.

There's two other things worth mentioning; I haven't been arrested once since I started going to meetings and I've haven't pissed the bed either. That really is a life *beyond my wildest dreams*.

The End.

Author's note.

The 'c-word' appears over 70 times in this book, suffice to say it was personally produced as finding a conventional publisher was challenging – but if you got this far you'll understand why it features so.

If you've enjoyed reading, a (good) review would be great. Just posting a photo of the cover with a thumbs up emoji to your socials would make you a legend in my world.

There are people out there who really need to hear that it's possible to leave drugs and alcohol behind; my feeling was this was the best way I had to tell them. I hope you can help me spread the message.

Finally, I apologise to the world at large, I could sometimes have been a better individual and will henceforth try to be one.

Charlie W, London, 2024

Printed in Great Britain
by Amazon